WE LOOK LIKE THE ENEMY

WE LOOK LIKE THE ENEMY

THE ENEMY

*The Hidden Story of Israel's Jews
from Arab Lands*

Rachel Shabi

Walker & Company
New York

For Sami "Onu" Daniel
May his memory be a blessing

Published by Walker Publishing Company, Inc., New York

All papers used by Walker & Company are natural, recyclable products made
from wood grown in well-managed forests. The manufacturing processes
conform to the environmental regulations of the country of origin.

LIBRARY OF CONGRESS CATALOGING-IN-PUBLICATION DATA

Shabi, Rachel.
We look like the enemy : the hidden story of Israel's Jews from Arab lands /
Rachel Shabi.
p.   cm.
Includes bibliographical references and index.
ISBN-13: 978-0-8027-1572-2
ISBN-10: 0-8027-1572-9
1. Jews, Oriental—Israel—Social conditions. 2. Jews, Oriental—Israel—
History. 3. Israel—Ethnic relations.   I. Title.
DS113.8.S4S53 2008
305.892'40174927—dc22
2008022107

Visit Walker & Company's Web site at www.walkerbooks.com

First U.S. edition 2008

1 3 5 7 9 10 8 6 4 2

Typeset by Westchester Book Group
Printed in the United States of America by Quebecor World Fairfield

CONTENTS

Prologue   I

Chapter 1: Veiling Its Face   7

Chapter 2: Meet the Family   25

Chapter 3: Development Towns   51

Chapter 4: Babylon Calling   76

Chapter 5: Talk This Way   106

Chapter 6: Everyone Deserves Music   135

Chapter 7: Made to Fail   157

Chapter 8: The Ethnic Demon   185

Chapter 9: We Are Not Arabs!   217

Notes   243

Index   253

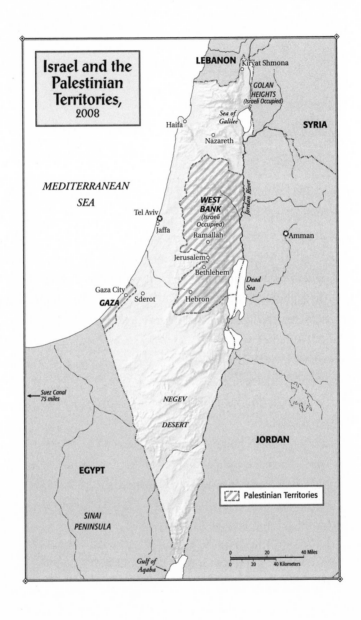

Israel and the
Palestinian
Territories,
2008

LEBANON
Kiryat Shmona

GOLAN
HEIGHTS
(Israeli Occupied)

SYRIA

Haifa

Sea of
Galilee

Nazareth

MEDITERRANEAN

SEA

Tel Aviv
Jaffa

WEST
BANK
(Israeli
Occupied)
Ramallah

Jordan River

Amman

Jerusalem
Bethlehem

Dead
Sea

Gaza City
GAZA   Sderot

Hebron

Suez Canal
75 miles

NEGEV

DESERT

JORDAN

EGYPT

SINAI
PENINSULA

Gulf of
Aqaba

0   20   40 Miles
0   20   40 Kilometers

Palestinian Territories

PROLOGUE

I T'S THE DATES that really clinch their Iraqi origins. A habit
that clung to them as thickly as the Arabic language, music,
and customs. My parents migrated twice, first to Israel and then
to England—but maintained their Iraq-inspired date consump-
tion throughout. They bore children during the Israeli phase but
raised us for the greater part in England, their longest home,
where my father would occasionally make breakfasts of fried
eggs drizzled with date syrup. The jar of brown, thickly sweet
syrup was from Basra, southern Iraq, as the black lettering and
the palm tree on the label—absurdly exotic in our English
kitchen—testified.

Basra: my father's home city and a primary source of pride. The
city whose rivers he paddled, on the banks of which he hung out
with his first friends—Muslim, Jewish; who cared?—eating flamed,
spicy fish together. He lived in Basra for twenty-years, spent
twenty-three more as a citizen of Israel, and finally ended up—as
did my Baghdad-born mother, who'd lived in Kirkuk, in northern
Iraq—with just one passport: British. It's a prized nationality for
someone who once lived under a British Mandate in Iraq, who attended an English-modeled government school there and listened

daily to BBC World Service broadcasts on Basra shortwave—as my mother recalls doing on the Kirkuk frequency. But ask my father now to which country he most belongs? "Iraq!" he pronounces, in the sort of loaded voice that might more often be heard reading human-rights declarations. "Of course, I am an Iraqi! That's what I am!" My mother is not so categorical: "Israel, probably. I don't know." But they both, happy Londoners, dismiss the subject as irrelevant. "Why split your hairs over it?" they'll say, with a migrant knack for putting a very slight bump in the flow of English expressions. "We are here now, *halas*. It's finished."

Iraqis seem to have a particularly devoted relationship to the palm fruit. In the early half of the twentieth century, Iraq had near-legendary status internationally for its succulent, sweet dates—more so than its oilfields—which it would trade across the Middle East. Those dates were a national treasure. A thriving export industry dispatched this Iraqi bounty in myriad forms: plain; stuffed with walnuts, dried apricots, or pistachio nuts; infused with rosewater. They also had mythical powers. My aunt (two to four dates daily) describes Iraqi laborers at her former home in Basra flying up three flights of stairs with hulking furniture strapped to their backs, turbo-powered, she insists, by the date sandwiches they ate for breakfast. In Iraq, lower-grade dates, known as Zahdi, would be sold to neighboring Iran. Thereafter, Iranians would be referred to as *Abu al* [father of the] *Zahdi*, a sneery joke at the consumers of inferior dried palm fruit. Very low down, but still a feature of the list of things that grieve my parents about the current misery piled onto decades of suffering in Iraq, is that it has been surpassed by Iran—that nation of former date heathens—in date export and reputation. Also present on the bottom of this list is an infuriation over the current

British media mangling of Iraqi place names: "Four years in Basra and they still can't pronounce it right," they'll lament over radio reports.

In the late 1930s, or so the story goes, Jewish settlers in Palestine smuggled date palms out of Iraq, out of the fertile valleys of the Euphrates and Tigris rivers and into the soils of the soon-to-be Israeli state. But, my parents say, the stolen shoots never bore fruit as delicious as the original, magnificent Iraqi dates. How could they, having been transplanted into a foreign land? A short time later, 125,000 Jews, my parents included, pulled up roots and left Iraq, migrated en masse to Israel. Prior to that, Babylonian Jews had been living in Iraq for 2,600 years. They trace a lineage back to the Jewish fighters and nobles who were exiled, following the destruction of the First Temple in Jerusalem, to the banks of the river Babylon in 600 B.C.E. In total, around 800,000 Jews migrated to Israel from their native Arab and Muslim countries: Egypt, Syria, Sudan, Yemen, Iran, Iraq, Morocco, Algeria, Tunisia, Libya, and Turkey. They'd been a part of the Middle East forever. They'd borne all kinds of fruit—cultural, linguistic, artistic, religious, and professional—living alongside Arab and Muslim peoples, for the most part in peace, as good neighbors. Now they, just like the smuggled palms, were sowed into the new soils of Israel. And this land, they say, seemed unaccountably hostile to Middle Eastern and North African Jews—so they didn't grow right, either.

Globally, Jews who come from Arab countries are a minority: 90 percent of the Jewish population outside Israel is of European descent—German, Polish, Russian, Hungarian, or Eastern European. They're defined as "Ashkenazi," from the old Hebrew word for German. The Western worldwide presence of European

Jewry is why the idea of "Jewish" usually conjures up images of Ashkenazi culture: Yiddish words, klezmer music, gefilte fish, and the shtetl-life-depicting film musical, *Fiddler on the Roof*. But in Israel, Jews from Middle Eastern and North African countries (also called "Oriental" or "Mizrahi") comprise at least 40 percent of the Jewish population and at one stage were a clear majority. Jewish culture in their context is Arabic words, Oriental music, Middle Eastern food, and the high melodrama of classic Egyptian cinema. Identities developed to the rhythms and patterns of the Middle East so that, for a large proportion of arrivals to the new Israel, Arab was a way of being Jewish.

Israel was created in 1948, although there had been Jewish migration to it, with state-building motivations, since the late nineteenth century. Most of that was from Europe, because the idea of founding a Jewish state had a European birth. Zionist ideology clashed with the concurrent development of self-determination aspirations in the Middle East. Arab nationalism was rising up against European rule, which not only had colonized countries such as Iraq, Morocco, and Egypt but was evidently about to introduce a new colonial player—Israel—into the heart of the Arab world. These opposite national forces created seismic shifts in the Middle Eastern soils that had nourished and raised Oriental Jews for thousands of years. Multi-weave identities rapidly unraveled as both sides—Arab and Jewish—pulled, hard. Terminology rapidly conflated as "Jewish" became synonymous with "Zionist," which became synonymous with "colonizer" and "enemy." The very idea, much less the actual reality, of a Jewish presence within Arab countries seemed fraught with contradiction. Over a tiny slice of time, Jews left long-term homes in Arab lands—not all of them and not all to Israel; but a robust Judeo-Arabic tradition, once a valued and integral part of the region, came to a sudden full stop.

There should, after such a long-standing relationship, have been a bounty chest of legacies, keepsakes, and memories for the departing Jews to take with them. It ought to have traveled across seas and deserts to Israel. But the laden chest was quickly discarded. It felt cumbersome and was a source of shame. In the Jewish state, its contents were appraised as backward and belonging to the enemy. Trudging the treasure chest around seemed to foreclose doors leading into society because, in so many ways, that Judeo-Arabic way of life failed to cross cultural checkpoints operating in Israel. The one item that did survive the journey was the experience of animosity under the rule of Islam, magnified, reexamined, and respun into central significance. In place of multiple narratives that describe full lives steeped in the Oriental, stamped with templates of Arab-Jewish coexistence, there is just one story: the Arabs hate the Jews.

For a Western, Jewish nation building itself in an Arab region, surrounded by Arab countries, the "Arab-Jewish" population presented an awkward problem: What to do with these migrants who, while part of the Jewish family, resembled—and behaved in so many ways just like—the "uncivilized" enemy surrounding the new home state? They had to be absorbed, turned into Israeli citizens like all the other Jewish migrants coming from all corners of the world. One of the central tenets of this state-building enterprise was to create a "new Israeli" who would be an amalgam of all the positive attributes of the multinational migrants, through a process defined as the "melting pot."

That was the theory, but then the attributes of the Middle Eastern Jews weren't exactly viewed as positive—not back then and, many would say, not now either. Official documents, ministerial pronouncements, and media articles from those initial years show how serious the issue was perceived to be. A real fear was that the high influx of immigrants from the Middle East might actually thwart the project of building a Jewish homeland. Israel perceived the Arab world, now the enemy of the Jews, to be an inferior, barbaric world which, if not kept at bay, would drag Israel down to its low level. Jews from Arab countries were emblematic of many of Israel's fears about the region that it was a part of, but wanted no part of. And so a series of assumptions and appraisals merged into a single path, one fateful conclusion. It was never stated as such, and it went absolutely against the Jewish integration ideals of the new country: but it was as though the new Israelis from the Middle East had somehow to be whitewashed, in order to banish the marks of the Arab within the Jew.

Chapter 1

VEILING ITS FACE

Having left—or, in common Hebrew parlance, "de-scended from"—Israel to live in the U.K., my family wasn't party to any Diaspora discourse that contained a long-ing for the Holy Land, the ancient homeland of the Jewish people. Such a narrative, entwining the people with the place, is the propeller fuel of Jewish migration—or "ascent"—to Is-rael. It is what inspires Jews from all over the world, setting foot in the country for perhaps the first time, to pronounce: "I've come home." When my family uttered the wishful words, "Next year in Jerusalem," traditionally repeated at Dias-pora Passover tables the world over, it was not without a trace of irony: we'd left; we weren't going back, not next year or any year. In England, my birthplace was instead fixed as a memory card of fragmented toddler flashes: bubble-gum-scented washing powder; water hoses on a flat white roof; smil-ing brown uncles bearing bright mangoes pulled off backyard trees; a grandmother's soothing lullabies, in Arabic. During my early childhood, Israel was an extended summer getaway: breaking out of an England-acquired, migrant kid persona,

cutting loose in the motherland, running amok with a rowdy
gang of protective cousins. Hundreds of relatives always delighted to see us, and then tears at the chaotic airport; reluctant
were we to lose them again, or to resume our buttoned-up
guises.

Nearly two decades later, I visit Israel again as an adult in the
late nineties—rare trips for weddings and births. Inevitably
distanced from all but a handful of those relatives, by then I
knew all about the bad Israel, the bully nation, the land thief
and oppressor of Palestinians—no smiling and no mangoes in
this version. A British journalist, I wrote about "campaigning
and social-justice issues," but the Israel–Palestine conflict was
never one of them. There was a background worry that, once
I started with it, this subject, so visceral and so personal, might
not let me go. But it wouldn't just shut up, either. I go back
to Israel to research this book—but also, I just go back there
after all.

Israelis seem to embrace the idea of a "returning minor," the
bureaucracy's categorization for someone who left the country
in childhood and then came back to live in it as an adult. It
somehow serves as proof of the state's superiority over the Diaspora, standard vanilla nationalism rippled with a personalization
of the demographic war, the perceived existential necessity of
there being more Jews than Arabs within Israeli borders. Israelis,
some of whom dream of leaving the country, think the English-
bred, late returnee a bit crazy, but in any case nod their approval.
And in the Palestinian territories, too, a comeback is readily understood. "Everyone wants to return to their homeland" is an
evaluation often given in the West Bank, and then sometimes

the conversation's texture thickens with those urgent, unspoken words: "You can; we can't."*

I live in Tel Aviv, the city in whose suburbs I was born, the coastal capital that aspires to be a sort of Jewish Barcelona: hip, happening, and beachy to boot. Tel Aviv happily embraces the recent description of it by *Time* magazine as "the Mediterranean's most unlikely capital of cool."[1] In pious, stone-citied Jerusalem, the beach capital is more often appraised as, frankly, godless. Deliberately divorced from its political reality—after stark years of suicide bomb attacks, in 2001–2003, that turned its buzzy streets graveyard-quiet—Tel Aviv is a cocoon of secularism, hedonism, and ambivalence. A standard response to most things in this city is "*Sababa*"—variously, "All good," "Cool," or "No problem." Initially irritating for its disconnected oblivion, Tel Aviv turns into a refuge for me for exactly the same reason after spending some time in the region. I get an Israeli ID card, bank account, and healthcare card, more and more proof of a loaded identity. I am not so "*Halas*, it's finished" over issues of nationality. I spend too much time weighing the implications of a passport inscription: "Birthplace: Israel."

My Hebrew cranks into gear as old language synapses snap back to life, springboarding off nursery-school building blocks. Hebrew, like Arabic, is a language of belonging, welding possessives onto nouns to form one word: our reporter, our country;

---

*Jews all over the world have the automatic right to Israeli citizenship. Israel does not recognize the right to return of Palestinian refugees from 1948, and this remains one of the key sticking points in all negotiations between the two peoples.

tribal languages. In a country that deals with a constant influx of Jewish migrants, my Hebrew accent is swiftly clocked as Anglo-Saxon, but it's not quite strong enough to be new. It jams the filing system and prompts a front-end discussion. One doctor cuts short my symptoms description to announce, on the basis of the bothersome accent: "But you didn't grow up here!" and we have to clear up this malaise before dealing with the real one. It's always the same text: yes, raised in England; no, my parents spoke Arabic between them in the home; yes, Iraqi, on both sides; no, I don't look it.

Mostly, the reception is a kind of "welcome back to the clan" that operates at all levels, from officials who are "personally glad" to see a returning Israeli, to cab drivers who round down fares because we are "all family." The English liberal response would be to protest this fatal clannishness, the precedent of "us" and "them"; to stand up for the cosmopolitan magic of mingling tribes. Still, it's a flattering pull, this lure of belonging, this "You're one of ours," reassuringly repeated, "of ours" forming one word in Hebrew, one people claiming me. But sometimes full membership in this family requires signing up to a national text about who started what in the Israel–Palestine conflict, of who did what to whom and who deserves what they get. Sometimes running off-script can turn "one of us" to "get away from us." In the Palestinian territories, meanwhile, Iraqi roots give rise to similar statements—of "Oh, so you are like us," or sometimes "one of us" again, or if it was "between us," then there would be no conflict. Voices of the Israeli enemy, in my mother's tongue.

"But this is all passé," I am told, once I explain that I'm researching relations between Middle Eastern and Ashkenazi Jews in Israel. Yes, people say, there was some bad stuff in the begin-

ning, but that's all over now. Look, I'm patiently informed, the
Ashkenazi Jews pioneered the nation and so, by the time the
Middle Eastern Jews arrived, all the power structures were already in place. It wasn't deliberate or, heaven forbid, discrimination. Those who do concede a shade of ethnic inequality in
those early power dynamics insist that this is definitely not the
case today. Which means that the entire subject is ancient history. Irrelevant history at that, because now everyone is simply
Israeli and it doesn't matter whose parents came from where.

Israel officially came into being after a war in 1948,* just before which there were around 650,000–711,000 Jews (figures
vary) and twice as many Arabs in the land. Pre-Israel, the country had been called Palestine and had been presided over by a
succession of rulers, culminating in a British Mandate that took
over from the Ottoman Empire in 1920. The Jewish count in
Palestine was around 7.5 percent of the population until 1882.
But from 1882, European Jews began to settle in Palestine. They
are what Israelis call "the pioneers"—the nation-builders, a
revered, almost mythical group seen as possessing physical grit
and political vision, the ones who fought for the land and then
made it a country. They had, during the Mandate period and
with the blessings of the British, set up agencies and institutions

---

*David Ben Gurion, Israel's first prime minister, declared independence in May
1948. In 1947, the UN suggested a partition plan for Palestine which gave two
thirds of the land to the 30 percent Jewish population who by then lived on it.
The League of Arab Nations rejected this plan and, in 1948, declared war on
Israel. It lost. During this period, the majority of Palestinians were driven out
or fled or "left," according to the Israeli version of events. Recently Israeli
"New Historians" such as Ilan Pappe have documented that the expulsion of
Palestinians was official policy. The events of 1948 are described as "the war
of independence" by Israelis and as "the catastrophe" by Palestinians.

that morphed smoothly into state organs after 1948. This is what
the "passé" camp means about the organically developed order
of things: European Jews had established and were controlling all
these official bodies by the time the Middle Eastern Jews came
on board Project Israel. In 1948, Oriental Jews formed 20 percent
of the Jewish population. In 1950, the country passed the Law of
Return, granting citizenship to any Jewish person who requested
it. By 1951, the Jewish presence in Israel had more than
doubled—and half of those immigrants came from the Middle
East. By the 1970s, and through to the early 1990s, this Middle
Eastern population comprised the majority. Then, during the
early 1990s, the figure was nudged down to its current 40 percent
ratio by the migration of Jews from the collapsed Soviet bloc.

Israel comes over as a kind of big Jewish family, where the talents of each are valued equally and where no child gets all the
attention just because it has the loudest voice. We are not, for the
moment, talking about its 20 percent non-Jewish population—
Palestinians who stayed in what became Israel after the 1948
war.* This population of Arab-Israelis, defined as a "minority,"
is supposed to have equal citizenship rights, although in reality
there are limits to that. But the pluralistic, egalitarian vision of a
Jewish Israeli society is declared to be on show everywhere.
There's the intermarrying (between Jews with differing roots)
going on all over the place and spawning mixed-origin Israeli
children. Everyone knows that this is the true mark of integration,
anywhere. Granted, Middle Eastern Jews were once not to be
found in Israeli government and other high-level or professional

---

*Around a quarter of this population are classed as "internal refugees," having
been displaced from original homes.

positions due to that natural, organic development of things. But now they staff those same offices in droves. An Israeli of Iranian origin was until recently the nation's president. Another Iranian Jew has just vacated his seat as Army chief of staff. Scores of members of the Israeli parliament are not Ashkenazi—how does that square with claims of inequality? Fingers point to the number of Middle Eastern-origin Jews in white-collar professions—doctors, lawyers, bank managers. More fingers direct to the many university-degree students with parents from the Middle East. All of this is intended as testimony to an equality which may not have been a feature of the nation's formative years but is self-evidently held to be the case now. Or so the dominant narrative would have it.

On a cultural level, the gesturing fingers go into frenzy. What about the plurality that's such a prominent feature of Israeli cityscapes? There's the Middle East in the hummus and falafel fumes pouring out of haphazardly arranged stands and streetside cafés. There's the possibility of hearing "Inta Omri," the best-known song from the legendary Egyptian singer Umm Kalsoum, at least once a day, blasting out of car stereos or nightclub speaker stacks. Middle Eastern music backs Hebrew singers on the radio, while the theme tune for a top-ratings TV current affairs program is a fully Oriental-flavored, Turkish pop hit (the same one, by the Turkish star Tarkan, that an actress from the Australian TV soap *Neighbours* tamed into the British pop charts in 2002 with "Kiss, Kiss"). Streets bear the names of ancient Oriental Jewish poets and rabbis. Hamsas, hand-shaped charms originating from Arab countries, where they go by their Islamic name, "the hand of Fatima," are a ubiquity here in the Jewish state—they are even featured as the logo for one of the National Lottery operators. (They arrived with Jews from Arab countries who, like their Muslim neighbors, had employed this lucky symbol to ward off the "evil eye.") Young Israelis play backgammon—an Oriental game—on the beach, while eating watermelon with white cheese, an Arabic combination, and sucking on nargile pipes, a signature habit of the Middle East.

Culture characteristics ascribed to the Orient also include the informality, the death-wish driving, and the laxity over hygiene shown by café employees who smoke as they serve, or food stalls that let patrons poke their fingers into the pickle bowls. Also assumed to be Middle Eastern is the evident preference for sadistically bureaucratic officialdom and the use of rude hand signals, which are actually described as "Oriental gestures." And there's a perception—voiced by Western visitors and immigrants—that Israel is "backward," or, more politely, "less developed," precisely because it's a Middle Eastern country.

However it gets signposted, this Middle Eastern presence— and the Oriental features of so many Israelis—can be a bit of a shock to first-time visitors who confess they'd been expecting a modern-day *Fiddler on the Roof* style of setting in the Jewish nation. After all, the Jewish Diaspora has a predominantly European character, so it stands to reason that the Jewish state would reflect that. Plus, that's what the country looks like from afar. Israel plays to the world on several screens and at a near constant rate—proportional to its population, it is one of the most intensely reported places on earth. It's one side in a gridlocked conflict forever a feature of breaking news: the cruel military aggressor that occupies, impoverishes, and kills Palestinians; or, the plucky young country that somehow thrives amidst a sea of hatred and fights on the front line in the global war on terror. On none of these screens is the Jewish state Oriental. In the course of my research, I often hear individuals assert that "Israel is in the Middle East!" and eventually end up using the phrase myself. But it's an odd thing to say: it's not as though anyone has to keep insisting that, for instance, France is located in Europe. Israel appears to much of the world to be a European state that somehow took a wrong turn and ended up in the wrong neighborhood. Geographically it's in the Middle East, but really it's a part of the West. So, for instance, it doesn't register as unusual when Israel takes part (with occasional success) in the Eurovision song contest or (disastrously) in the UEFA cup.

But if the Orient is so present at Israeli street level, albeit not on the country's global face, how can some Israelis claim it has been bleached out? For that, the critics say, you need to get past the Oriental baubles and the Orientalist stereotypes. For a start, there's the business of what to call the Middle Eastern and North African Jews in Israel (because nobody wants to keep saying that)—and the multiple appellations for this population speak volumes. Usually the reference is to a split between "Ashkenazi" and "Sephardi." While these names accurately describe two different styles of practicing the same Judaism, they are misleading in any other context. Sephardi Jews originate from Spain (which is what the name means in Hebrew) and the Iberian Peninsula, from where they were expelled in 1492 by Catholic monarchs who had only just finished kicking out the (Muslim) Moorish population of that region. Both Jewish and Islamic communities, who had lived together in a period that would be later described as a "Golden Age" of creative symbiosis, variously found new homes in North Africa, Turkey, Palestine, and the Balkans—all under the Ottoman Empire, which was mostly hospitable to

Jews. In Israel, the category of Sephardi has broadened to include Jews from all Middle Eastern countries. It's frequently used, but a misnomer—Jews from Iraq, Iran, Egypt, Libya, Lebanon, Yemen, or Syria don't have Hispanic roots.

Also widely used within Israel is the label "Mizrahi"—"Easterners." This term doesn't conform to the logics of geography: How can Moroccan and Egyptian Jews, whose countries of origin lie west of Israel, be described as Eastern? And why are Jews who come from Russia, east of Israel, not defined as such? "Mizrahi" is used in the same way that we might use the words "Oriental" or "Middle Eastern," a categorization for something that is from that region; "not Western." This appellation created a bloc identity for populations that came from disparate countries but who were lumped together as one type. Because Jews from Arab countries shared a common (and mostly negative) experience in Israel, they also came to define themselves as a uniform group. The "Mizrahi" label actually started off as a wider term encompassing Jews from all "not Western" countries: "the Eastern ethnicities"—although the flexible Hebrew is translated as "communities," perhaps to forestall a discussion of "ethnic" subgroups within a singular Jewish race. So there are "Eastern Communities" and "Children of the Eastern Communities." And other terms, too, like "Frank," a derogatory Yiddish word, and "Schwarz," German and Yiddish for "Black." Sometimes you can still hear these in use, and not in an ironic or reclaiming way. For the purposes of this book, the term most used will be "Mizrahi."

Looking at these labels, what is striking is that there are no "Ashkenazi Communities" or "Children of the Western Communities" in Israel. "Ashkenazi" is widely used, but not really expanded in that way. "Of course, because in Israel the sun, the moon, the weather, the air, and the sea is Ashkenazi!" says Rafi Shubeli. Of Yemeni origin, Shubeli is a member of the Mizrahi Democratic Rainbow (MDR), a social-justice organization of Eastern Jews. MDR is received as a radical, oddball outfit in the Israeli mainstream—as it would be, its members say. It's a small voice deemed not worth listening to—although, of course, neither were those who first started talking about Zionism in Europe. By MDR's analysis, the Ashkenazi stamp on Israel is so thorough that it has become invisible—a part of the furniture. There is no need to bloc-label the identity that is both dominant and definitive. National templates in Israel were originally set to an Ashkenazi tune, and if the Oriental seeps in, it is via the subcategory of "folklore"—something cutesy and ethnic and not a defining state hallmark. Tasty morsels of the Orient—the food, the traditions of hospitality, and the knickknacks—are welcome, but the bitter truth of the whole—the Arabness of the Middle Eastern Jews—is not.

According to Israelis who grew up in the years during which the nation was forging a collective identity, Mizrahi culture was deemed inferior, not something that should come to represent the Jewish state. For years, because of public derision, this culture was enjoyed only in private. The very term "Mizrahi culture" was considered an oxymoron. Many Israelis still perceive it as such. These days, it's not politically correct to say so—but you still hear it, especially if you have an English accent and "don't look" Mizrahi.

Cultural arguments can go on forever, with each side compiling lists of items that prove or disprove plurality. In part, it's an ongoing debate because, only sixty years after statehood, the question "What is an Israeli?" is still a work in progress. But it's also a live issue because, despite the "sababa" pronouncements, long-standing battles are still being fought over the continued absence of Mizrahis from the national definitive. Scores of Mizrahi writers, musicians, and actors struggle to find a place on a national platform. Scores of Mizrahis report that they still can't see or hear themselves in the national space.

And the argument about "ethnic whitewash" goes far deeper than a discussion of national symbols and cultural preferences. It doesn't take long to realize that there is a Jewish class split in Israel, running on ethnic lines. The majority of university professors and students, TV presenters, and Supreme Court judges (all but one, in fact) have Ashkenazi surnames; the glaring majority of university cleaners, market stall traders, TV buffoon characters, and blue-collar criminals are Mizrahi in origin. The majority of residents of high-status city areas—the north of Tel Aviv, certain suburbs of Jerusalem—are Ashkenazi, while the neglected or outright slum parts are populated mostly by Mizrahis and, more recently, other low-status migrants.

And beyond the big cities there exists another yawning divide—between the predominantly European-origin members of Israel's communal farms, which form the respected kibbutz movement, and the mostly Mizrahi residents in what are known as "development towns" or "the periphery." These towns were created in the 1950s specifically to absorb the mass influx of Mizrahi migrants, and they are notoriously neglected. These, and the slums, and the Mizrahi population in general are what the Israeli media by the 1970s referred to as "the second Israel": a low-status, low-income, underachieving location (or population) that nobody wanted to be in. It's in these spaces that you find a simmering rage over discrimination that's considered nei-

ther fictitious nor historic, a mute anger at a system that's accused of bringing Mizrahis to Israel on false pretenses and
screwing them ever since. How can the racism be over, goes the
charge from these quarters, when it is embedded in the social
weave?

Statisticians, meanwhile, have reports that prove the evidence
of our own eyes. Ashkenazi students, the grandchildren of immigrants, are still about three times as likely to hold university de-
grees as their Mizrahi equivalents. Men of Ashkenazi origin are
likely to be thirty-nine points above the state wage average,
while Mizrahis hold fewer white-collar positions and score six
points below it. By the late 1990s, 88 percent of upper-income
families were Ashkenazi, while 60 percent of the low-income
families were Mizrahi. These figures stir up furious disagreements in Israel. Some argue that the statistics are based on faulty
research criteria and present other figures, a brighter forecast.
Some say these politely labeled "gaps" in attainment are a product of a difference in aspiration or attitude. An alternative, but
similarly loaded, theory is that Mizrahis are unavoidably playing
catch-up, coming as they did from Arab backwaters with low
professional and academic standards. These organic gaps, it
is supposed, will iron out once a few generations have gone
through the same system of education in Israel. But some sociologists have shown that over two generations of children born
and bred in Israel the gaps have stayed the same. Rather than accept the disparity as unavoidable, academics and campaigners
have argued that the Israeli schooling—and consequently the
labor market—are stacked against Mizrahi skin.

"Why are you even talking about this? Don't you have racism
in England?" one Moroccan-born Israeli asks me furiously.

"There is discrimination in France, in the United States, every-where! Why are you focusing on Israel?" The rage is not about the racism itself, so much as it's about the idea of giving the nation's dirty laundry an international airing. Israelis, with a specific narrative of the Palestinian issue, keenly feel themselves to be the victims of a constant and unjustifiable global condemnation. Exposing Israel's internal problems is perceived as a gift to the enemy: another hard bat with which to bash the Jewish state over the head. Moreover, national unity is paramount and, over the years, has overruled internal divisions. But the social issue—which, because of Israel's class structure, is also the ethnic issue—has combusted in the public sphere. Large-scale Mizrahi protests have been contained, while government leaders and prime commentators called for national unity. Passé? There's a thick scab on this wound—and it is frequently outmatched by bigger battle scars—but pick it just a little and the blood starts flowing.

As it turns out, the accusations of divisive "ethnic organizing"—aimed only at Mizrahi organizing—are usually enough to turn the public taste against any picketing. Everyone, Mizrahis included, wants to subscribe to the national goal of social integration (for Jewish citizens). This unity is crucial, because Israelis perceive their country to be constantly at war. Or constantly under attack. Or under the constant threat of it. Social issues are routinely pushed off the national agenda in a practical enactment of an old Arabic proverb: "Me against my brother; me and my brother against my cousin."* Effectively, the

---

*"Cousin" is how Palestinians and Israelis sometimes refer to each other, on account of Islam and Judaism having the same biblical father, Abraham.

nation is told: So long as there is no peace in the region, social justice is going to take a back seat. Mizrahi campaigners have argued that, as long as there is no social justice, one that by definition would create a more region-friendly national consciousness, there can be no peace.

The conflict between Israel and its cousins is what attracts the global news radar and, being both more important and more deadly, causes it to glide over the tensions within Israel, between brother and sister. It's rarely considered consequential—especially since majority Israel proclaims it no longer relevant. It's rarely viewed as the interfamiliar, softened-for-the-same-faith side of the same coin; a manifestation of the same set of values and assumptions. The absence of the Mizrahi face from the global snapshot of Israel feeds back into a polarized position, serving those on both sides who favor the dichotomous formula of Arab versus Jew. So at one end of the pole, Israel is wholly part of the West, its vanguard in the Middle East. Terroristic violence from its neighbors isn't just anti-Israel, it is anti-Western. This position glosses over an inconvenient fact: that if Mizrahi Jews and Arab-Israelis were joined together as one group—let's call them "of Middle Eastern origin"—it would comprise two thirds of the population. The West is in the minority in Israel. Dichotomists on the Arab side of the formula, meanwhile, overlook the Mizrahi population with pronouncements of the Jewish state as "alien" and an "implant" comprising "European colonizers." That position, with equal convenience, glides over the Jewish presence in the entire region of the Middle East for the last several millennia.

This book is focused on the stifled, small-voice analysis seeking to break this stalemate formula. It does not intend to replace one dichotomy with another: the idea is not to subdivide a nation into "good Israelis"—the Mizrahis, who deserve our sympathies—and "bad Israelis"—the Ashkenazis, who can still be condemned but now on two counts of oppression, internal and external. Neither should it fuel any in-vogue theories about Jewish incompatibility with the idea of nationalism. Israel comprises a fusion of Jewish migrants from East and West. That makes it visible as a particular sort of "case study" with a series of assumptions at work. But there is nothing unique or case-specific about concepts that create Western superiority or cultural intolerance. The same concepts governed the British Empire; dictated relations between the French and its colonies in North Africa and Lebanon; and continue to pretext the American-led "civilizing" missions in Iraq. It's the motor running the modern-day clash of civilizations: the "modern," secular West versus the "backward," religious-fundamentalist East. It's not, in other words, just Israel. It's us.

The founders of the Jewish state did not imagine that it would comprise citizens from both sides of this modern-day divide. The Hungarian Jew Theodor Herzl is credited with laying out the first vision of a Jewish state in Palestine in his 1902 novel *Altneuland* ("old–new land"), which depicts the country before and after Jewish development. Herzl, the architect of Zionism, ended his fictional work with the words "If you will it, it is no dream." Zionism was conceptualized as the political expression of that will, to build a Jewish nation.

In *Altneuland*, Herzl portrayed the Jewish people creating an advanced Western country, definitely facing Europe. All the anti-Semitic slurs hurled at Eastern European Jews during the eighteenth and nineteenth centuries—parasitic, greedy, filthy, all

that—were based on the overarching assessment of this community as "unfortunate Asiatic refugees."[2] They were cast as "miserable darkened Hebrews"[3] and "a piece of Oriental antiquity
in the midst of an ever-progressive Occidental civilization."[4]
Such appraisals were sometimes made by Jews in central Europe,
who encountered Eastern Europeans migrating west to escape
persecution. One Austrian Jewish writer described his brothers
from Eastern Europe as "Stooped, despondent, living in filth . . .
no wonder everyone thinks of them as Asiatics."[5] Zionist
thinkers, including Herzl, naturally wanted to banish the ugly
stereotypes in the new Jewish country. Upon the soils of their
own state, the Jewish people would no longer be despised or depicted as filthy Asiatics. Herzl thought that the Jewish state in
Palestine would "form a portion of a rampart of Europe against
Asia, an outpost of civilization as opposed to barbarism."[6] A key
Zionist of that time, Ahad Ha'am (the pen name of a Russian
Jew, Asher Ginsberg), once said: "What Herzl understood is that
only by leaving Germany and settling in the Jewish state could
the Jew finally become a real German."[7]

Was the Iraqi, Moroccan, or Egyptian Jew to become a real
German too? Back then, nobody had thought about that, quite
simply because nobody had thought about Middle Eastern Jews
at all. Their mass migration to the new Jewish state was dictated
by history, not written into the original plan. Zionism was born
in Eastern Europe, both a reaction and a solution to the rampant
anti-Semitism of the region. It was based on nationalistic ideas
at that time sweeping across the continent and transforming its
countries. There are no Oriental Jewish names on a list of key
Zionist thinkers precisely because there was at that time no nationalism and no murderous anti-Semitism in the Middle East.

Ashkenazi Jews had experienced a centuries-long history of pogrom- and persecution-dodging migration: from Germany to Poland, from there to Russia, and then back to Germany. Jews of the Orient, for the most part, had stayed put.

Israel's first prime minister, David Ben Gurion, was clear that when Herzl wrote of the "Jewish people," he had meant "The Jewish people in Europe, that did not and could not want to stay put, the people that bore the Zionist movement on its shoulders."[8] After Hitler had systematically murdered six million intended subjects of the Jewish state, Ben Gurion wrote: "The State was formed, but could not find the people who had expected it."[9] Such a view came from the Jewish Agency, too. Established as a Zionist representative body in Palestine under the British Mandate in 1923, the agency became the state department for economic development and for locating and absorbing Jewish immigrants. Back in the early 1950s, the Jewish Agency's migration department director wrote: "So long as millions of European Jews were alive, no attention was given to the Jews of the East, and to half a million Jews in north Africa, to the Jews of Asia . . . they were a Jewish tribe ever so forgotten, outside consciousness . . . Zionism was a response to the hardship of the Jews, anti-Semitism, whose focus was, in fact, in Europe, and naturally it did not direct its mind, nor its heart, to the African and Asian Jewry."[10]

Only after the horrific extent of the hardships of the Jews in Europe became clear, he adds, did Zionism remember the Middle Eastern Jews.

Chapter 2

MEET THE FAMILY

IN A BOOK for Israeli third-year pupils aged nine to ten, there is a story about "The Little Yemeni." It's a history textbook of early Zionist settlements in Palestine, issued by the Israeli Ministry for Education and Culture in 1992. "One day a little boy appeared in our alley. This boy was darker and thinner than any of the children I had known until then," the story's girl-narrator, Mira, tells us. "This boy wore a long, gray dress called a galabiya, he had lots of curls on his head, small, black, thick crowded curls and two peyot* curled around his cheeks . . . He would go from house to house shouting, '*Gibne! Gibne!*' [Arabic for], 'Cheese!' in a strange accent, a bit Arabic, a bit Hebrew, something unclear. All the neighbors closed their doors to him and not one of them bought anything from him."[1]

Mira, of Hungarian origin, asks her mother about the strange, dark child and discovers him to be a recent arrival to Jerusalem along with a group of two hundred claiming to be Jews from Yemen—which nobody believed. "All the people spoke against him," narrates Mira. "They said he was an Arab, that he was in

---

*Forelocks worn by religious Jews.

disguise, they said all sorts of other things that I can no longer remember. The rumors about him were so scary and so terrible that Mum double-locked the door that night, to be on the safe side."[2] A few weeks later, there's good news from Mira's neighbor: Rabbis had tested the Yemenis' knowledge of religious practices and found them to be bona-fide Jews. So, the neighbor proclaims, she could buy cheese from the Yemeni child with a "clear conscience." At this point, Mira's mother feels bad about ignoring the obviously poor and sad-looking boy and wants to help him. We learn that the still nameless little Yemeni's family migrated to Palestine because they'd heard that free land was available to Jews, and were living in caves outside the walls of Jerusalem's Old City.

This is what children, right into the 1990s, would learn about the early Yemeni community in Israel. Campaigners protested the negative stereotyping of the chapter, pointing out that it portrayed Yemeni Jews as being primitive (cave-dwellers), opportunistic (free-land grabbers), and generally lowly, weird, and scary. The education ministry seemed to take the point and responded by removing the offending story altogether. This had been the only section of the book to feature any Oriental Jews, and so the message Mizrahi campaigners understood from this was: you can exist in this period of Israeli history on these terms, or not at all. But the Little Yemeni story, told from one standpoint and loaded as it is with racial typecasting, doubtless reflects one facet of the initial encounters between Yemeni and Eastern European Jews—it was a stark shock, for both sides. That period, pre-Israel and during the state's infancy, contained a series of jolting introductions between East and West as the Oriental Jew met the Occidental. If ever there was a romantic vision about the "ingathering of the exiles," the reassembly of the scattered Jewish tribes in their biblical homeland, those first meetings swiftly spat in its eye. Such encounters took place between various groups in different contexts, but were spiked with the same prejudice. An example of it is to be found in the writings of Arye Gelblum, a reporter for the Israeli daily newspaper *Haaretz*. In 1948 he visited a camp set up to absorb Jewish immigrants and containing large populations from the Middle East.

> We have here a people whose primitiveness sets a record. Its level of education borders on total ignorance, and even worse is the incapacity to absorb anything spiritual . . . They also lack Jewish roots. On the contrary they are entirely given to the play of savage primitive instincts . . . in the Africans' [North African Jewish migrants] living quarters in the camps you will find filth, card-playing for money, drunkenness and prostitution . . . Have we considered what would happen to the state if this would be its population? . . . What character will the state of Israel have and what shall be its level with such populations?[3]

This was just one in a series of startled, inauspicious comments made about the Mizrahis at various levels—even at the highest. David Ben Gurion, for example, described immigrants from the Orient as being "without a trace of Jewish or human education."[4] Such opinions among authority figures were aired privately, since nobody wanted to do anything to sabotage the project of building a united, integrated nationality. But even behind closed doors, such comments did not bode well for future relations.

A religious Zionist, in a Jewish context, is defined as someone who cherishes Jerusalem especially and the Holy Land more generally, and moved to Palestine to be close to it. This sort of migration might not especially be bothered with statehood—technically it wouldn't matter who controlled the land, as long as Jewish access to the holy sites was not curtailed.* Religious Zionism later added a messianic adjunct, which viewed the Jewish state in the Holy Land as fulfilment of divine prophecy. Political Zionism is secular, nationalist, and driven by a kind of revolutionary calling to create a Jewish homeland in Palestine. Some† argue that this distinction between religious and political is an anti-Zionist formulation. Others note that these two differently motivated immigrant groups were among the first to meet in Palestine with the encounter described in the schoolbook chapter on the Little Yemeni: between state-builders from Eastern Europe—who formed what's known as the "New Settlement"—and the first Yemeni Jews to settle in Israel, in their thousands, often spiritually propelled.

A different East met the same West as the "Old Settlement" of Jews in Palestine, predominantly Oriental and long-established, greeted the migration waves of the New Settlement. In the 1940s, Zionist emissaries of the New Settlement were dispatched to Middle Eastern countries to reconnoiter and to recruit Jewish

---

*This early, religious impulse to move to Israel is distinct from the Religious Zionist movement that began in Eastern Europe. A faction of the greater Zionist movement and led by Rabbi Avraham Kook, this group justified the political settlement of "Greater" Israel (including the West Bank) on religious terms. They are the modern-day supporters of the Religious Nationalist Party and the Jewish settler movement.

†Such as the historian Ilan Halevi (who was also one of the few Jewish members of the PLO).

communities to the cause—and the letters they sent back to base in Palestine reveal their impressions of Jews from Morocco, Egypt, Iraq, and Iran. For example, Enzo Sereni, who was sent to Baghdad, Iraq, in 1942, had this to report about the Jewish community he met there: "This material is not the material of Europe; rather, it is material that is quick to become impassioned but also quick to despair . . . inability to keep a secret, inability to keep one's word . . . There is deep water and that water isn't bad . . . but there is foam on the surface of the water and it is bad; it is the Levantine-Arab kind . . . They can be made into 'human beings,' but we won't be able to do it without help from the people in Palestine."[5] This French-coined term "Levantine" referred broadly to the region of the Middle East and was by then a negative assessment—indicating a place of backwardness and moral lassitude. Israel is, of course, located in the Levant.

Finally, a mass meeting between Eastern and Western Jews came about when the New Settlement received big-volume migrations after 1948. With the creation of Israel, Jews arrived from all over the world, more than doubling the Jewish population in the course of three years. There would continue to be a steady stream of Jewish immigrants thereafter, but nothing so large or concentrated—not until the influx of eight hundred thousand Jews from the collapsed Soviet Union during the early 1990s.

In 1855, before any sort of political migration to the area, ten thousand Jews lived in it. They were Palestinian Jews—a label that history has consigned to the dustbin of incongruity. Later defined as the "Old Settlement," these communities clustered around the holy sites of Judaism. Hundreds lived around the Wailing Wall in Jerusalem, while others lived in Hebron, site of the tomb of the patriarch Abraham—the biblical father of both Muslims and Jews. Hebron, in the West Bank, is nowadays an ugly flashpoint of the conflict between Israel and the Palestinian territories, but back then life in it was friction-free. Other Jewish communities lived around Safed in the north and Tiberias, perched on the Sea of Galilee—both towns containing tombs of significant rabbis that drew pilgrims, who stayed.

Some of these Palestinian Jewish communities are thought to have arrived after the Islamic ruler Saladin (Salah al-Din) liberated Jerusalem from an intolerant Crusader rule in 1187. The Crusaders had killed or banished both Muslim and Jewish inhabitants of the holy city. The Islamic fighter welcomed both Jewish and Christian faiths, defined as "People of the Book," monotheistic believers whom Saladin was religiously duty-bound to protect. Other Jewish communities arrived later, in the thirteenth century. A few families in the Galilee region apparently claim to be descended from biblical Jews. But overall, and at least until the mid-nineteenth century, Palestinian Jews defined themselves as "Sephardim Tehorim," meaning "pure Spanish"—collectively, then, their roots are the same as those other Sephardi Jews who, having been expelled from Spain in 1492, ended up living in North Africa, the Balkans, and Turkey.

Communities of "pure Spanish" Jews were swelled by other Jewish arrivals from the Arab region—from the Maghreb or Egypt, for instance—and from Europe, too. These were holy settlers, drawn to the land by the concept of *aliyah*—originally the Hebrew term for religious migration, although it now means Zionist-nationalist migration. The point about the Old Jewish Settlement in Palestine is that it was treated—and saw itself—just as any other community in the region. It had, under the

Ottoman Empire (1299–1922), acquired a solid set of rights, effectively autonomy. The Ottomans accepted the authority of the Hakham Bashi—a Hebrew-Turkish amalgam name for the chief rabbi—over the Jews in Palestine. There's a legend about this period, illustrating the stature of Judaism under Ottoman rule: "Upon the death of a Turkish Sultan, the Turks would lock the gates of Jerusalem, sending the keys to the chief rabbi for a blessing, only opening the gates after the blessing was given."[6] Sephardi Jews filled the ranks of the Ottoman civil service in Palestine.

When the new British administration took control in the 1920s, it saw the New Settlement as representative of the region's Jewry. The British distrusted the Sephardi community because of its affiliation with the Ottoman enemy; also, European Jews of the New Settlement were culturally more in line with the British. The Jewish Agency became the prime coffer for Diaspora donations and the prime body for Jewish administration: land, education, religion, all aspects of Jewish life in Palestine. The New Settlement was by all accounts enamored with the Sephardis in Palestine, who were so well-established, spoke Hebrew, and practiced Judaism at the source—indicating a vital regional continuum. But respect for the Old Settlement did not extend to consulting with it over crucial matters during this period in Palestine.

The details of those early relations were documented by Elie Eliachar, a prominent Palestinian Jew from a long-standing, influential family in Jerusalem. To be clear, Eliachar—who later became a member of the Israeli parliament, the Knesset—defined himself as a Zionist and welcomed the Jewish newcomers to Palestine. Eliachar's beef was with the New Settlement's attitude toward the natives, by which he meant both Sephardi Jews and Palestinian Arabs. His perspective, a polar opposite to Zionist pioneer thinking, was that resident Palestinian Jews possessed the default Jewish culture, from which European Jewry had strayed. He wrote: "We Jews are of Semitic-Oriental origin despite the extensive sojourn of a considerable number of our people in the West. The Land of Israel lies in the Orient and our first duty on returning is to regain the Oriental characteristics which we lost while in the West, without in any way relinquishing all the positive traits we acquired there. Jews and Arabs are Semites and hence related. The Hebrew and Arabic languages stem from a common source, as do our religious beliefs; even many of our basic characteristics are alike."[7]

Eliachar was alarmed by the animosity the New Settlement stirred up in Palestine. He believed that European pioneers should have watched and learned from the Sephardi Jews of the region, who had well-established business and social connections with other Palestinians. He recounts several initiatives proposed by Sephardi leaders and rejected by the New Settlement. On one occasion in the early 1920s, Eliachar's father met the Zionist leader Menahem Ussishkin and advised him to explain the Jewish national interests to the native Palestinian population. Ussishkin dismissed the proposal, responding: "You are speaking of an Arab problem. I know of no such thing. Our problem is the Jewish problem!"[8] Eliachar's father continued in his endeavors: "He defended Jewish immigration rights to the Arabs, but demanded and established financial bodies to aid the Arab needy, and called for a bank for Arab farmers . . . his countless memoranda to leading personalities and organizations can still serve as blueprints for mutual understanding, and reveal how well he foresaw the grave developments of the future."[9]

At a time when New Settlement leaders seemed not to heed the existence of a native population, whose ignored rights to the land would cause grave problems in the future, Eliachar had a different take: "[The] arguments which purportedly prove that there is no Palestinian entity and no cohesive community which could become the Palestinian Arab people and country, are totally unacceptable to me," he wrote. "As a native of this country I know that in Turkish times Palestinian Arabs were a separate body, to a large degree different from the Arabs of Syria or Egypt. Historically, the Arabs living in Palestine had an ethnic background entirely different from that of Arabs in other countries."[10]

There were disagreements within both the New Settlement and the World Zionist Organization (WZO) about the treatment of native Palestinian Arabs. But Eliachar's position was informed by something beyond a sense of fair play: he believed that the Zionist movement's drive to build a state that was not "Levantine" foreclosed a possibility for coexistence. Pre-state and Israeli leaders feared the "corruptive" regional forces to which the Jewish settlement was exposed. Such concerns were present in the missives that the Zionist emissary, Sereni, sent back from Iraq. They were also voiced by Ben Gurion: "We do not want Israelis to become Arabs," he said, by the 1960s. "We are in duty bound to fight against the spirit of the Levant, which corrupts individuals and societies, and preserve the authentic Jewish values as they crystallised in the Diaspora."[11] He must have meant only the European Diaspora.

Eliachar also thought that this fear of the Levant was souring inter-Jewish relations. Sephardi leaders, according to his testimonies, were excluded from institutions pre-state but dissuaded from forming their own organizations on the grounds that this would be separatist and divisive. This tendency continued as the process of building a bureaucracy took shape, following the declaration of Israeli independence. Despite the Sephardi majority in the civil service until then, "the new government offices were staffed almost entirely without them," he wrote. "Not one Sephardi was to be found in any position of influence in the political, economic and cultural ministries . . . No Sephardi judges were appointed to the Supreme Court, and only a few members of the distinguished group of Sephardi judges from Mandate times were given posts in the lower courts."[12] This was to have far-reaching consequences. Written into this power structure was not just a control of resources but also a control of historical memory: of who pioneered the nation, building the body of the Jewish state, and who was brought to the land of Israel, passive, needy, and entirely dependent upon it.

The first Zionist-style migration to Palestine was in 1882, by a small group of Russian Jewish idealists known as Biluists. Yemeni Jews had started arriving in Israel a few months before them; by 1914, between 4,000 and 5,000 people from this community, which numbered 80,000 to 85,000, were in Palestine. But their presence in Israeli history, which deals with waves of Jewish migration, is minimal—as slight as "The Little Yemeni." Once, I meet a Yemeni Israeli, Shuki, a retired police officer from the south, who talks about his community's presence in early Palestine. "Until twelve or thirteen years ago, I never saw any sentences about these Yemenis in any history book," he says. "And then they corrected the mistake, so what did they write? 'The migration of Yemen, 1886, a number of Yemenis arrived in Israel.' Three lines! And I thought, 'How much more would it be possible to belittle the migration of the Yemenis?'" Chatting to me in a supermarket, this upbeat man looks momentarily crestfallen. "It hurts, yes," he says. "But time heals and we don't want to pass our hate on to our children, who are growing up and mixing here." The hatred that Shuki talks of forgetting isn't just generated by a few lines of text in a schoolbook. It springs from certain aspects of the early Yemeni experience in Israel, dark, traumatic stories that could not so easily be laid to rest.

Legend has it that the presence of a Jewish population in Yemen dates back to the time of King Solomon, in the tenth century B.C.E. He is thought to have sent Jewish traders to the southern Arabian country to stock up on the gold, frankincense, and myrrh for which the place was then famous. There is concrete evidence of a Jewish presence in Yemen from the second century. There is also evidence of a Jewish kingdom of Yemen, in the fifth or sixth century, ruled by aristocratic converts to Judaism. Historical narrators define this Yemeni Jewish community as thousands of years old, traditionally Arab-speaking, religious, and the keepers of an intact Judaism. Yemenis are the only Jews to read the Bible both in Hebrew and the original Aramaic.

It's not totally clear how much they suffered in Yemen under Islam, since it is variously described as either violently intolerant or smoothly accommodating of Jews in that country. Arriving in

Palestine, some Yemenis did live in caves within the old stone walls of the Holy City—they couldn't find, and were turned away from, accommodation elsewhere—and some did hear that Baron Rothschild, a wealthy French Jewish banker, was buying up Palestinian land and giving it away to Jews willing to work it. Yemeni Jews had been struggling under Ottoman rule, which spread to the Arabian Peninsula and opened the labor market to competition from other parts of the empire. The ensuing economic hardship was more acutely felt by Yemen's Jewish community of artisans, goldsmiths, and craftsmen, whose work was now outpriced by foreign imports. The Yemenis also suffered sporadic curtailments of religious rights and saw the holy land as a place where they might pray in peace. Seeking a way out, they found Palestine to be more readily accessible, since the construction of the Suez Canal in 1869 had opened a water route to it.

In Palestine, they were "discovered" by the New Settlement, which saw in the Yemenis a solution to the entanglements of "Hebrew labor." One of the guiding tenets of the Zionist movement, "Avoda Ivrit" (Hebrew labor) called for the employment of exclusively Jewish workers in the settlement of Palestine, with the double goals of establishing the Jewish community in the region and straightening the "hunched backs"* of the Diaspora Jews with some honest manual work. If in the Diaspora the Jewish people were destitute and parasitical, as those hateful slurs would have it, then in Palestine they would be strong, self-sufficient tillers of land. In practice, those European Jewish settlers who worked as agricultural laborers wanted

---

*A hallmark, anti-Semitic insult.

higher wages but were less efficient and less experienced that their Arab counterparts, so farmers still recruited beyond the same-faith pool.

The Yemeni community—like most Diaspora Jewry—was not known for its work in agriculture. But still, they provided the New Settlement with a ready-made solution: easygoing Jews who would work for close to Arab wages. One regional Jewish newspaper described the community like this, in 1910: "This is the simple, natural worker, capable of doing any kind of work, without shame, without philosophy, and also without poetry. And Mr. Marx is of course absent both from his pocket and from his mind . . . [they] can take the place of the Arabs."[13] Otto Warburg, who was then chairman of the World Zionist Organization, broadened beyond Yemenis the concept of who would do the manual work in Palestine: "The Jews of the Orient, known for their low level, are fit to take the place of the Arab in the colony."[14]

A similarly founded conclusion was reached by the head of the Palestine Office* of the World Zionist Organization, established at the port of Jaffa in 1908. Dr. Arthur Ruppin thought that the Yemeni population "had the lifelong habits of the Arab" and had "a better chance of holding its own in the moshavot [Jewish farming communities] against the competition from the Arabs."[15] There was opposition to that idea at the time, expressed by one New Settlement leader who declared it "an absolute prohibition to deliberately bring Jews to the land for servitude, to become hewers of wood and drawers of water in the farms of idle, noble Ashkenazim [Hebrew plural]."[16] Still, Dr. Ruppin packed off an

---

*Also known as the Office of the Land of Israel.

emissary disguised as a rabbi to Yemen, to urge migration. Samuel
Warshavsky, whose surname was changed to the more Oriental
"Yavnieli" for the purposes of his 1911 trip, delivered a message to
the Jewish community there. He warned them that tough work
and physical hardships awaited them in Palestine, but his story's
frame was such that the Yemenis, a devout community, heard in it
a messianic calling. "With joy I announce the redemption of our
land. Whatever part of the land that Hebrew hands cultivate is being redeemed . . . The land had begun to bear fruit for its sons, its
cultivators, and this is a sign to us that redemption is close,"[17] he
told them. Israeli historian Dr. Bat-Zion Eraqi Klorman notes that
Yavnieli said this despite having commented that many Yemeni
Jewish communities were doing just fine where they were.
Yavnieli, she observes, realized that "in order to move the Jews to
immigrate, he had to use their metaphor. That is, he had to use
messianic terminology to explain the national, secular movement
in the Land of Israel."[18] Around two thousand of this community
joined the other Yemenis who were replacing Arab laborers in
Palestine. By 1914, the New Settlement was overstretched and
could not cope with more immigrants, and then World War I
broke out, forcing another pause to the project. There was no
more Yemeni migration to the area until it was called Israel.

Relations between the pre-state Yemeni Jews and the New
Settlement were not as equal partners in a state-building project.
Yemeni workers were paid less than their European counterparts
and were given smaller houses and smaller plots of land. Yemeni
opinion of what was happening was voiced at the eighteenth
Zionist congress in 1933, where one Yemeni leader of the time
likened his community to second-class citizens, "like non-
Aryans in Germany."[19] Some accounts report instances of

sympathetic European farmers trying to rectify this inequality and the hardships it created. But there was one particular incident which, although involving just a few families, would create deep scars still talked about today, randomly in supermarkets, by people of Yemeni origin.

In 1912, a group of ten or twelve Yemeni families, guided by their rabbi, David Ben Israel, settled the Kinneret region of land around the Sea of Galilee, in the north of what was then Palestine. This land was held and administered by the Palestine Bureau, which paid the Yemenis for their work in swamp drainage, land clearance, and cultivation: classic "pioneering" work. In 1921, new European settlers arrived and turned the area into a kibbutz. These farms are the flagship of the Israeli project. A product of Zionist principles of a return to the land, agriculture, and Jewish labor, the kibbutz movement was founded on an additional supporting column of secular collectivism. Kibbutz ethos is perceived as a dreamy but driven fusion of socialism and Zionism, associated with blooming the nation and booming the agricultural economy. Today, most kibbutzes have lost the earlier collectivism and the land is often used for retail malls and business parks. But they hold a hallowed place in the collective memory—those who live on or come from them are seen as nation-builders, pioneers, self-sacrificing visionaries, salt-of-the-earth types (albeit with questionable fashion sense). The kibbutz movement has produced dozens of national leaders, including former minister and military commander Moshe Dayan and former prime minister Ehud Barak. The hero label is also applied, though less so, to "moshav" farms, which run the actual business of farming along cooperative lines but not the rest of the lives of their occupants.

Kibbutz Kinneret was among the first, located on prime soil overlooking Lake Tiberias (Kinneret in Hebrew). It features in the Bible as the Sea of Galilee, where Jesus walked on water and then turned water into wine. The kibbutz would become a landmark. But the Yemeni families already farming that land didn't join the collective. Instead, there began a campaign, lasting six years, to get them *off* the land. It was waged by a minority of the new kibbutzniks, the rest of whom opposed such action. "A small group of Ashkenazis started to do a lot of awful, really awful things to the Yemenis," says the Israeli historian Professor Yehuda Nini, who in 1996 wrote the first book about this incident. "They cut off water to the Yemeni homes, forbade them to build, didn't let them cultivate their lands. They did everything in their power to make their lives as miserable as possible." Exhausted, and with high rates of malarial illness, the Yemeni community left and were resettled in a quarter of Rehovot, in central Israel, where the streets are named after the Galilee region that they had tended for eighteen years.

According to Professor Nini, the eviction was not orchestrated at the official level of the Palestine Bureau, which had simply caved in to the demands of the kibbutz, perceived as a stronger, more knowledgeable outfit in the hierarchy of the time. But Smadar Cohen, a doctoral student specializing in this incident, cites documents showing an interrelation between the kibbutz members who pushed for the Yemeni expulsion and the Jewish authorities. "Those kibbutz members also had high-level jobs in the agricultural department at the offices of the Land of Israel," she says. "It is naïve to believe that they did not exert an influence." Why weren't the Yemenis simply absorbed into the new kibbutz group? "They were so different. They were religious,

they had a different culture," says Cohen. "They looked like the
enemy." Professor Nini believes that the Yemeni Jews did not
qualify for kibbutz membership because they didn't have the necessary training in political Zionism—they could tend land, in
other words, but not in such a way as would build a state. "As a
Marxist, I think they [the kibbutz group] were right, but as a Jew
I say they were wrong."

Today, the Yemeni community in Rehovot still makes annual
visits to the graves of forebears buried in the Kinneret cemetery,
proof of the community's past presence there. Those grave-
stones, recently renovated, lie in separate, self-contained lines
within a serene cemetery on the banks of the lake, famously the
resting place of founding members of the Zionist Labor movement: Berl Katznelson, Ber Borochov, Moses Hess. The Yemeni
section is pointed out to me by Amiram Edlman, a member of
Kibbutz Kinneret. "I was exposed to their story by chance," he
says. "I never heard a thing about it when I was growing up
here." Edlman searched for documentation of the whole story,
visiting archives of the Labor movement and the Yemenis in
Rehovot, families of those who had once lived on the lands of
his kibbutz. He wrote an award-winning final degree paper on
the subject and later helped publicize the issue, to the disapproval
of other kibbutz members who thought that he was shaming the
collective. Still, in part a result of his efforts, an exhibition at the
farm's historic pump house, where the Yemenis once lived, now
contains a section about this early community.

Edlman directs his protest not at the substance of the story,
but at the fact that it was erased. "I'm not arguing over whether
they should have been moved or not," he says. "What matters
to me and is painful is that there were Yemenis here who were

wiped off the platform of pioneers. If you don't enter the pioneer story, you are considered a type B citizen."

That distinction is expanded by Israeli historians Gershon
Shafir and Yoav Peled, who argue that it was employed to legit-
imize New Settlement practice. " 'Idealistic workers' . . . were
the stuff pioneers were made of, blazing the trail and setting
moral standards for the nation. 'Natural workers,' on the other
hand, were to be foot-soldiers in the Zionist campaign, adding
'quantity' to the pioneers' 'qualitative' efforts."[20] Yemeni Jews,
who in those days were a sizable population in Palestine and were
frequently employed for work defined as pioneering, do not
share in the pioneer glory of the kibbutz movement.

The Yemeni community in Israel grew exponentially in 1949,
after the exodus of 49,000 Jews from Yemen, in what was nick-
named "Operation Magic Carpet" (so called because Yemenis had
never seen a plane before). Yemenis prefer to call it "Operation
Eagles' Wings," from the biblical description of the Jewish exodus
from Egypt. This gets described as a welcomed community, flown
into Israel en masse and at some cost—an estimated $4 million.
An Israeli newspaper of the time described them as "a fabulous
tribe, the most poetic of the tribes of Israel. Their features bear
the ancient Hebrew grace, and their hearts are filled with innocent
faith and a fervent love for the Holy Land."[21] More than the
Sephardis of the Old Settlement, the Yemenis were in possession
of the sort of authentic, ancient Judaism that the Zionist movement adored. An American pilot on one of the planes bringing
the Yemenis to Israel best voiced that sentiment when he described them as "prophets stepping out of the Bible."[22]

But if they were special, they were also strange—at least to
the Western eye. The Yemenis had made long, grueling treks,

by foot, to reach the Jewish Agency camp for migrants in Aden, "Camp Redemption," whose name fitted both religious and political concepts of Jewish settlement in Palestine. Making it to Aden; boarding the planes; arriving in Israel, which was a few centuries ahead of Yemen technologically—this community was doubtless in a state of shock. One doctor who had contact with them in Aden wrote that they resembled "a flock of sheep." He added that, even though the high intellectual capacities of the Yemeni Jews were known, "their expression is a bestial one."[23]

Perhaps it was their passivity that emboldened veteran Israelis to remove treasured possessions from the Yemenis, as their rabbis now say occured in some cases. There were no printing presses in Yemen, so its Jewish population preserved a collection of handwritten manuscripts, centuries old. These were packed up for the trip to Israel—ancient Bible scrolls, poetry, astrology, and historical writings that dated back seven hundred years, and original documents from the Babylonian period, a pivotal era in Judaism. Before the Yemenis boarded the planes, their luggage was, in some instances, taken away from them with the assurance that it would be shipped separately. They never saw it again, except when individuals would happen to stumble across various manuscripts, still bearing family signatures, in bookshops, libraries, and institutes. Their original owners were told that the documents had been destroyed in a port fire.

If the Yemeni community was in anguish over its manuscripts, the loss of which stripped them of a diligently preserved heritage, it was in absolute despair over rumors of a much darker theft. Partly because there had been a famine in Yemen, partly as a result of those long journeys to the Jewish migration camp in

Aden and the months-long wait in overcrowded conditions there for Israel-bound planes, many Yemenis arrived sick and in need of care. Babies arrived in the same state. In 1949, Amnon Hever's parents reached Israel from Yemen via Aden, with their nine-month-old daughter, and were placed in a migrant camp. "One day a nurse came to the camp and said, 'Your baby is very ill and if you don't take her to the infirmary she will die,'" relates Amnon. His mother didn't know what the nurse was talking about, because the baby was eating and smiling, and generally seemed fine. But the infant was taken to an infirmary and, two days later, her parents were told that she had died. "My mother and father went to the camp manager and asked to see the body of their child," recounts Amnon. "They were told that there was no body, that the baby had been buried in a mass grave." Amnon was in his twenties when he first heard this, from his mother. Until then, he hadn't known there had been a sister. He was told that she had green eyes and pale skin—unusual features among a more typically dark-skinned community.

Variations of this tale were repeated over and over again, hundreds of times. Babies were pronounced ill, taken to the hospital or to the camp infirmary, and were never seen again. Demands were made to see bodies, death certificates, more information— but there were no answers. Distraught parents had to accept that their babies were gone. And it might have stayed that way, a silent question mark burned into hundreds of hearts, but for the citizen-tracking efficiency of a national military based on compulsory enlistment. Years later, as the Israeli historian and journalist Tom Segev has documented, hundreds of army-aged men and women were called up to serve—Yemeni Israelis who were supposed to be long dead.

In 1967, a commission was set up to look into the cases of 342 missing Yemeni children. By this time terrible suspicions were circulating, that the supposedly deceased babies had actually been stolen and put up for adoption, within Israel and overseas. The commission found that most had died (producing death certificates for these), although more than twenty cases couldn't be accounted for. It put the disappearances down to the chaos of mass migrations to Israel in the early 1950s. After large, angry protests on the subject, a further commission investigated in 1994 and reached the same conclusion: there was no evidence of criminal activity. A final panel, set up in 1995, authorized the exhumation in 1997 of twenty-two child skeletons, which were sent to Britain to be DNA-tested. The British scientists reported that they could only test one set of bones with any accuracy, which was greeted with skepticism by the Yemeni community. Also during that period, one allegedly stolen child, now the adult Tzila Levine, claimed to have found her natural mother, a Yemeni named Margalit Omessi—having been separated from her at birth and raised on a kibbutz by adoptive parents. British DNA testing showed that Levine and Omessi were indeed related, but later tests using "newer methods" at a forensic institute in Tel Aviv refuted the English findings. Yemeni parents, who feared their babies had been snatched and handed over to Ashkenazi couples, thought that the facts, just like their children, had been whitewashed. This final inquiry that began in 1995 reached the same conclusion as the one preceding it: nothing criminal or untoward.

For the Yemeni Jewish community—and beyond it, too—the case is far from closed. The stolen children remain a live, unresolved issue, a lie; and discussion on the subject easily resurfaces. Avi, a Yemeni-Israeli in his fifties whom I met randomly in Tel

Aviv one day, tells me his sister was one of the babies who died in the hospital during that period—although he doesn't for a moment believe it. "Nobody will admit what they did," he says. "And now I look at the history of our country and I see our leaders who were all involved in stealing Yemeni children—and they are described as heroes. So what am I supposed to make of those history books?"

The period from 1948 to 1951 saw migrations from all over: first the Holocaust survivors that the British had been keeping in camps in Cyprus,* then Iraqis, Iranians, Libyans, North Africans, Poles, Rumanians, Hungarians. Tens of thousands of Jewish migrants lived in camps because there was nowhere else to put them. Camps started off as tents and later developed into wooden huts. Conditions were poor: overused communal showers and toilets, shortages in medical supplies and schooling facilities, minimal employment, food and fuel rations. My mother, whose family spent three years in transit tents and huts in Israel upon arrival in 1951, would later joke that the chickens were kept in better conditions than the humans in those camps. Another Iraqi Jewish immigrant has these recollections: "If there was a plane going back to Iraq that same second, I would have taken it," he says. "Take me back, please God! We stayed there five years, in a tent and then a hut. Once there was two weeks of rain with no break, in 1950 I think. We brothers each grabbed ahold of a pole so that the tent wouldn't take off. You could see someone's shoe, a saucepan, personal belongings passing in the water, and I was standing in a vest up to my knees in sand."

---

*During the 1940s, Britain operated a quota on Jewish migration to Palestine. Those caught illegally migrating to the country, in excess of the quota, were sent to prison camps in British-controlled Cyprus.

When the history of the transit camps was written, it was assumed that all new immigrants had gone through similar experiences. In three years of mass migration, 650,000 people arrived
in Israel. Around half of those were from Arab countries. By
1952, 80 percent of transit camp occupants were Mizrahi—if
Ashkenazi migrants at first populated the camps proportionally,
they must have gotten out faster. Or perhaps some of them had
bypassed the transit stage entirely. Speaking at a Jewish Agency
executive meeting in 1949, member Itzhak Refael said: "The
immigrants from Poland are not like the others . . . If we spare
them the camps and give them priority in housing, they will
manage better in Israel than most of the Oriental inhabitants in
the camps because many of them have the skills that are needed
for the economy. It will be a blessing to the country."[24] The
Jewish Agency decided to house the Jews from Poland, whose
migration had just been okayed by that country, in accordance
with Refael's proposals.

Dvora Elinor, a social services supervisor during the transit
camp period, later said: "An entire generation, about a hundred
thousand people, actually we broke them, their values, their
ability to make their own decisions. That is the worst damage
we've caused by our paternalism and by this entire operation of
discrimination, and more transit camps and more transit
camps—it broke them down . . . We felt that if we don't give
them all our values, in every aspect, they would be lost. We felt
so arrogant and superior, as if we knew everything, and they
nothing."[25] In personal narratives describing this period,
Mizrahis relate feeling shocked, disappointed, confused—and
crying a lot. In narratives about Mizrahis during this period, it's
often reported that Mizrahis got stuck in transit camps because

of a different, somehow less aspirational outlook, or felt disappointed because they had unreasonably high expectations. Today, Mizrahis who still complain about ethnic discrimination are labeled as "crybabies," the tears now a slur associated with a community that needs to get a grip and get over it.

To corroborate the "get over it" theory, it does seem like the New Settlement was mean to all newcomers. Collectively concerned only with building the new state, it was cultish, tough, snooty, and short on manifestations of either compassion or sympathy. These, at any rate, are labels ascribed to the pioneer movement by present-day, Zionism-supporting Israelis, some of them children of those veterans. These adjectives are chosen to backhandedly salute the single-minded grit required at the time. In theory, the arrival of thousands of Jews was a good thing, but in practice, new arrivals appeared alien, needy, and dependent. Tom Segev has documented that the New Settlement was contemptuous of the Diaspora and would often discuss the elimination of it. This scorn, Segev relates, also contaminated the compassion felt toward Holocaust survivors arriving in Israel after 1948. The New Settlement's sympathies were streaked with shame and disdain for the survivors, so fatally emblematic of the Diaspora Jew.

Officials back then had a tendency to describe all new immigrants as "human material." Not just Oriental Jews but all incoming Jews were viewed as component parts of an overall project and defined as having collective traits. One agency inspector filed a report after visiting Jewish immigrant camps in various countries: Jews from Europe, including Rumania and Hungary, "have no pioneering spirit at all . . . view the Jewish Agency with contempt"; the Yugoslavians, Bulgarians, and

Czechs were "of a high cultural level. Productive and healthy";
Iraqis, Iranians, and Tripolitans were "generally healthy"; Turks
were "good human material." North Africans were written up
as "mostly destitute, hot-tempered, unorganized." All these nationalities were additionally categorized as willing or not willing
to do agricultural work.[26]

In public circles, name-calling and character-labeling could
be seen as little more than a steam-releasing string of verbal insults, practically unavoidable among a new and motley population. Certainly Mizrahis have their own jibes for Ashkenazis,
stereotyped as cold, over-cerebral, joyless consumers of bad
food. But what happens when East is ascribed a series of negative characteristics by West, and West happens to be holding the
reins of power at the time? The anthropologist Raphael Patai
catalogued the ethnic stereotypes associated with Oriental Jews
in the early 1950s and compiled a list of traits: "Instability, emo-
tionalism, impulsiveness, unreliability, incompetence, habitual
lying, cheating, laziness, boastfulness, inclination to violence, un-
controlled temper, superstitiousness, childishness, lack of cleanli-
ness."[27] In general, he says, a concept of "primitivity" had formed
about Mizrahis, implying that they were culturally inferior. According to Israeli sociology professor Sammy Smooha, prejudice
had become asymmetrical by the 1970s—Ashkenazis had more
negative things to say about Mizrahis than vice versa. Mizrahis,
Smooha also noted, shared in the negative stereotyping of
themselves—they had, in other words, internalized the prevalent
social messaging.

By the 1980s—when Mizrahis were a majority in Israel—
there was mounting anxiety over a perceived clash of cultures.
In 1983, Amnon Dankner, then a journalist with the Israeli

liberal newspaper *Haaretz*, gave vent to his animosity for Mizrahis: "These are not my brothers and not my sisters," he wrote, in the context of warnings over a civil war between Mizrahi and Ashkenazi communities in Israel (where civil war is termed a "war of brothers"). "Leave me alone, I have no sister . . . They [those toeing the official integrationist line] lay down the sticky blanket of the love of Israel and ask me to consider the cultural lack, the sentiments of authentic neglect . . . they put me in a single cage with an enraged baboon and tell me, 'OK, now you are together, start having a dialogue, there is no other choice . . . speak nicely to him, toss him a banana, after all, you are brothers.' "[28]

Dankner, who later became the editor of the popular midmarket newspaper *Ma'ariv*, apologized for and retracted these words, publicly, on several occasions. But it was too late. Attitudes such as his had helped to inform an entire system of allocation, clung to the structural premises of a schooling system that would hobble Mizrahi Jews, and would send large populations of them into backwaters of isolation.

Chapter 3

DEVELOPMENT TOWNS

Haim is idly toying with a collection of hundreds of red and yellow roses, individually cellophane-wrapped, piled outside his family-run supermarket in Sderot. It's December 2006, and this town, on the northern tip of the southern Israeli desert, is suffering a wave of Qassam attacks, homemade rockets fired from the nearby Palestinian Gaza Strip. Haim's eyes are bloodshot and he jumps at rogue sounds. There are rocket-shaped dents in the tarmac only meters from his store. His two-year-old can say the words "Code Red," the early-warning signal for incoming missiles. Haim, in his early thirties, hands me one of the roses, to which is attached the message "Thank you for your empathy with the people of Sderot." Thousands of people were expected to pour into the town today for a kind of shopping and solidarity visit, promoted on the regional radio station. Nobody came. Haim's neatly tagged roses go to waste.

In the ledger book of suffering collated by these two nations, the Palestinian Gaza Strip has many more reams of pages than its Israeli neighbors in Sderot, population 20,000, and the surrounding inhabitants of the Israeli northern Negev desert. Gaza is home to 1.4 million Palestinians, three quarters of whom are

registered by the UN as refugees.* Amnesty International, the
UN refugee agency, and Human Rights Watch all report an
unprecedented blockade of the Gaza Strip since the Islamic
party Hamas came to government in January 2006, following
the Palestinian elections that year. Increasingly urgent reports
from aid organizations warned of an impending humanitarian
crisis in Gaza. In one of the most densely populated areas on
earth, 87.7 percent of households live in poverty.

Between June 2005, when Israel removed its troops and settlers
from the Gaza Strip, and October 2007, 739 Palestinians were
killed by Israeli fire. Of those, 388 did not participate in hostilities
and 153 were children. In June 2007, Hamas ousted the Fatah-
controlled Palestinian Authority from the Strip, after weeks of
infighting that killed 118 and injured 550 Palestinians. During
that same period, five Israelis were killed in or near Sderot, while
hundreds more were injured. An estimated two thousand rockets
fell on the area. Comparing death tolls is a sinister business, but
there is no way that anyone looking at this bloody scorecard
would conclude that the Palestinian side is less deserving of sympathy. Unless you presupposed that Gaza has brought the misery
upon itself. "We gave them [Gazans] everything they want and
they are not satisfied," says Haim. He is referring to the Israeli
disengagement of 2005. Another resident of Sderot gives a similar verdict: "You see that they are looking for war, and we gave
[them] weapons, we gave food, we gave land and we gave medi-
cines, water, electricity, money, everything, and they don't do
anything for us, they continue to shell us." You hear this sort of
analysis beyond Sderot, too; it's like the national line.

---

*Palestinian refugees from the 1948 war.

Israel's disengagement was not a complete withdrawal. Pulling settlers and troops out of an area are two in a list of criteria to be met by a nation withdrawing from an occupied territory; other conditions include returning control of borders and air and sea-space to the occupied population (Israel still commands all of these around Gaza). International law holds the occupying force responsible for the free passage of people, trade exports, and essentials such as food, water, fuel, and medical care in the areas it has occupied. The passage of everything and everyone has for years been severely restricted across Gaza's borders. Israel cites security considerations for this state of affairs.

In Sderot in late 2006, the streets are dead, businesses are folding, marriages are falling apart, and everyone is breaking, snapping, collapsing under the strain of dealing with sometimes daily missile barrages. Even if the rockets rarely hit humans, the fear is the same. The Israeli government says the need to defend its citizens in Sderot is the motive for launching aerial and ground attacks on Gaza. This has in the past prompted critics of the policy to dismiss the impact of the Qassams—short-range pipe-rockets with no guiding device. In June 2006, months before I meet Haim, the vice premier, Shimon Peres (now Israeli president), had this to say about the rockets in Sderot: "This hysteria over the Qassams must end . . . We must tell the Palestinians, Qassams, shmassams, we'll hold firm. We won't move from here."[1]

By early 2008, the situation had deteriorated even further. Israel tightened its blockade of Gaza; supplies, including electricity, ran dry. Scores of organizations, including the UN, Amnesty International, and the European Commission, denounced this as collective punishment. Israel, meanwhile, continued its policy of "targeted" assassinations of militants—which frequently kills noncombatants. Rocket attacks into Sderot intensified; Grad missiles with a longer range reached Ashkelon, seventeen kilometers from Gaza. Israel launched a week-long military attack on the Strip in February, leaving hundreds injured and killing around 120—a third of them children. Thousands of Palestinians vowed to avenge them. A week later, an armed Arab-Israeli killed eight students at a religious seminary in Jerusalem. Then there were more signs of solidarity with Sderot: food parcels, shopping trips, Internet donor links, pop song dedications, an awareness-raising concert in the States. Haim describes this as the equivalent of "giving Acamol to a dying patient."

The residents of Sderot aren't comparing their suffering with that of their Palestinian neighbors. Their reference point is the rest of Israel, which they feel both ignores and underestimates their misery. In Sderot, an often-voiced perception is that, if the same rockets were falling over Ramat Aviv, a well-heeled suburb of north Tel Aviv, it would be a different story. "They would give everything [to defend it]. Ramat Aviv is like the seat of the prime minister, so hurting that would hurt his family," says Haim. "Here, Sderot, it is the back yard." Haim isn't talking about simple geography, a proximity to the center. What would happen if the majority population in Sderot was from Poland— like Peres—and not Morocco, the origin of 70 percent of the town's residents? "Polish people, they wouldn't let it pass in silence. They are Ashkenazi, so they are strong and they are connected to the country, to our government." This isn't entirely accurate, since Sderot is surrounded by Ashkenazi-populated, powerful kibbutzes, also within Qassam range. But there is something about Sderot, according to this view, that makes it expendable, just like its population—whose plight under the Qassams is by far the worst in a series of adverse experiences.

Sderot is one of twenty-seven officially termed "development towns," founded between 1952 and 1964 to absorb migrants during that period. These towns are nearly always peripheral: Sderot and Ofakim in the Negev desert in the south; Kiryat Shmona bordering Lebanon in the north; Bet She'an located close to the eastern border with the West Bank. They were created as part of a government policy of population dispersal. Just after 1948, most Israelis were based in the big cities of Haifa, Tel Aviv, and Jerusalem, which left vast stretches of empty land in the new state. By the early fifties, there was mounting international concern, voiced through the United Nations, that Israel do something about the 711,000 (UN figure) Palestinians made refugees following the 1948 war. Israel sought to settle its newly won ground. Perhaps also a factor was a post–World War II consciousness over not centralizing populations too much. With the Jews of North Africa in mind, the Israeli government launched Operation From the Boat to the Town, whereby immigrants would be taken straight from the transporting vessels to the areas marked as development-towns-to-be. They wouldn't be given a choice of where to go; that decision had already been made for them by the Jewish Agency.

Sderot, like other development towns, started out as a transit camp. Aharale Cohen, a Sderot-based historian, relates that the camp's manager was still in the process of setting it up on the eve of Passover 1951 when a truck rolled up to the camp, its driver requesting a swift signature for a delivery, wanting to get home in time for the festival dinner. The manager, who was not expecting any deliveries, duly signed, and the driver tipped out the content of his truck. Five Kurdish families landed on the ground. Along with other Kurdish and Libyan Jews, they helped to set up the tents of a camp that would a few years later be replaced by thin huts and then by the buildings of Sderot.

By the mid-fifties, Jewish migration from Morocco, mostly, but also from Tunisia was in full swing. Many of the residents of Sderot—and other periphery towns like Kiryat Shmona in the north—still remember those first few hours in Israel. They left Morocco by boat from Casablanca to the French port of Marseilles, waited for sometimes months at an overcrowded absorption center, and then boarded another boat to the port of Haifa in the Jewish state—like the trip to France, a week-long journey. From Haifa, they were loaded onto trucks, "like cattle being taken to the market," says one of the older residents of Sderot who made the journey. Like cattle, they were sprayed with disinfectant—something that remains a visceral memory today. The trucks were bound for Sderot and other peripheral areas, always at night and often with the reassurance, once the destination was reached, that it was a small distance from big cities like Tel Aviv and Haifa. Yitzhak Triki, the manager of the camp in Sderot, explains that this method of transportation was official policy: "They called me, the Jewish Agency, and said, 'You are going to be the manager of the transit camp. And what do we want from you? It's very simple: we are sending you migrants only at night. Not in the day, so they won't see the shape of the camp. Try to convince them, in French, in Moroccan, in any language that you can understand, Yitzhak, get them off the trucks . . . the moment that everyone has got off, you release the truck, so that it goes and people do not try to climb back on it and leave with it.' "[2]

The Jewish populations of North Africa were by this stage caught up in rip currents hitting the broader Middle East: Arab nationalist calls for release from Western rule, coupled with rising hostility to Zionist nationalism. Algeria, Tunisia, and Morocco were all under French rule—in the case of Morocco, it became a French "protectorate" in 1912. On paper, the Moroccan Sultan Mohammad V still ruled, but in practice the French took control of the country. Morocco at that time had the largest Jewish population of any Arab nation. During the Second World War, the pro-German Vichy government in France tried to enforce anti-Jewish laws in Morocco. But Mohammad V was having none of it: "Just as in the past, the Israelites will remain under my protection. I refuse to make any distinction between my subjects,"[3] he said. Some Israelis of Moroccan origin still have framed portraits of the sultan's son and successor, Hassan II, in their homes and sing his praises at ceremonies and religious festivals. When King Hassan II died in 1999, the royal protectorate of minority citizens passed to the current king, Mohammad VI—who has often pronounced his intolerance for any mistreatment of Morocco's Jews. In May 2003, following suicide attacks on Jewish targets in Casablanca, the king visited the sites of attack, urging the Jewish community to rebuild, and organized a mass rally of support for them. Today, there are an estimated five thousand Jews still living in Morocco.

In 1948, that figure was over 265,000. Morocco was not one of the Arab nations fighting Israel in 1948, which may explain why interfaith hostilities were not as pronounced as they might have been. That said, tensions flared immediately after the war, when forty-four Jews were killed and hundreds more injured in Djerada and Oujda, both near the Algerian border. This frightened around ten thousand of the Jewish community into emigrating to Israel. These were the Moroccan Jews that the journalist Arye Gelblum encountered in the Israeli transit camps and wrote about so scathingly. Mohammad V, reflecting the mood of his nation's Muslim community at large, backed the Arab side in Palestine, while the Jewish population of Morocco broadly reacted with enthusiasm to the news of the new Israel. This reaction, historians note, was a religious one: It was viewed as the fulfillment of a divine promise that Jewish exile would one day end.

Happiness over the creation of Israel did not translate into a wish to live there—in the years immediately after 1948, most Jewish Moroccans stayed put. There were no good enough social or economic reason for them to go. French rule-by-proxy had privileged the Jewish population and significantly elevated its status. At that time, several Jewish charity outfits were operating in Morocco, including the French Alliance Israelite Universelle* schooling system and education or welfare projects set up by the American Joint Distribution Committee.† Also, Moroccans who had already emigrated to Israel were writing letters back home putting people off the idea of joining them. In any case, both the French and the Israeli governments were restricting immigration from Morocco: Israel was overburdened with new immigrants (and, some argue, was allocating quotas on an ethnic basis); France didn't want to rock the Moroccan boat by green-lighting Jewish departure. Its control of this country was based

---

*Founded in 1860, this organization was committed to the education and development of Jews around the world.

†A U.S. Jewish charitable organization set up in 1912.

on the standard "divide and rule" principle of colonialism. Broadly, the French favored the Jewish population in Morocco, but not so much as to antagonize the sultan and jeopardize their right-to-rule agreements with him.

By 1955, things had changed. The Israel–Palestine battlefield was polarizing two movements that often, in the Middle East, operated in the same country: Zionist nationalism on the one side, and pan-Arab nationalism* on the other. The Zionist movement had been organizing in Morocco—which didn't go down too well, not just because it was geopolitically charged, but also because the Moroccan leadership didn't want its Jewish community to go. Jews were seen as natives and, as such, a part of the independence movement—some Jews were members of Moroccan nationalist parties. But most of the Jewish community was anxious about how Moroccan independence might affect them. Between French colonialism and Arab nationalism, the Jewish community was again stuck in the middle: loyal to their colonial patrons, but equally sympathetic to the Arab community with whom they shared so many ties—and a country. Both sides wanted the Moroccan Jews to take sides.

When neighboring Tunisia secured independence, it was read by Morocco's Jewish community as a harbinger. In 1954, France granted Tunisia home rule as a precursor to self-rule, achieved in 1956. Tunisian Jews, who numbered 105,000, were equal citizens in the newly independent nation, on paper. But in practice they experienced a severe curtailment of rights. Their rabbinical

---

*A secular, nationalist, and socialist ideology that calls for unification of Arab peoples. It is anti-Western and anticolonialist. In this context, it is opposed to Zionism, which is viewed as another Western colony on Arab soil.

court, a long-running legal system arbitrating on personal (not civil) matters, was abolished. Various community councils were similarly dissolved and fused to form a single Jewish body. A Jewish cemetery was turned into a public park, and a Jewish district was torn down in the name of slum clearance—thereby also demolishing a historic synagogue. The reasons for these actions were subject to interpretation. Depending on your filters, it was either under a wave of measures striving for equal citizenship (no religious separatism) and progress (no slums); or because Islam is inherently anti-Jewish and Islamic rule in Tunisia couldn't help but reflect that; or because Tunisian Jewry, so obviously loyal to the former colonizer, France, was seen as a potential fifth column. But in Morocco, the Jewish community worried that, without the French to protect them, they would face the same future.

Jewish emigration was read by the broader Moroccan population as a product of colonialist or Zionist schemes to deprive the country of an integral and productive segment of society. The Moroccan government put a legal freeze on Jewish emigration from 1956 to 1961, but that didn't totally stop it. By then, a third of the Moroccan Jewish population had left—the ones that Israel dispersed into the development towns. Some have argued that pan-Arab sentiment encouraged a stop to Jewish migration in order to block the supply of manpower to Israel. Conversely, others say that the Arab countries mass-released their Jewish citizens so they would flood Israel, harming it that way. Such disparities suggest a dead-end theory, that Arab nations were running their affairs solely on the basis of how best to crash the Jewish state.

The Moroccan Jewish exodus of 1954–1956 was doubtless prompted by myriad individual reasons. But all were in some way a combination of two polar forces at work, one pushing and the other pulling: fear in the home country, attraction to the new one. Moroccan Israelis old enough to remember this period offer no single narrative, because there is no unified Jewish experience of life in Morocco—or life anywhere in the Arab world, come to that. Also, people choose what they remember. Some recall fear, curfews, thefts, murders, and a breakdown in trust between neighbors. Some say they didn't experience a single day free from the worry that they would suffer some sort of attack. Some describe the moves for Moroccan independence as an "intifada," an uprising, which directly threatened the Jewish locals. But there are many different recollections, too, of living very well with their Arab co-nationalists, a hospitable bunch—much more so than these Ashkenazi Jews in Israel, some Moroccans lament. One woman recalls that her Muslim neighbor would offer to fetch a portion of meat from the kosher butcher so that she, a child playing with the neighbor's children, could also eat with them.

There are vested interests in presenting each side—harmonious or hateful—of the Jewish experience in North Africa and the greater Arab region. Some dismiss what historian Salo Baron labelled a "lachrymose" interpretation of Jewish history, whereby this period is cast as a "morbidly selective tracing the dots"[4] of a series of terrifying and bloody incidents creating a persecuted whole. In this setup, according to a critique presented by Mizrahi academics, "Zionism claims to have 'saved' Sephardi Jews from the harsh rule of their Arab 'captors.'"[5] At the other end of the spectrum, the view is of a former Muslim–Jewish coexistence that was only harmonious and happy. This picture consolidates the theory that Jews from Arab lands were unnecessarily uprooted by the forces of Zionism, in order to then serve it. Some historians point out that this discussion is irrelevant, given that by the late nineteenth century the Arab countries in question were in any case under imperialistic rule: France and Britain in Egypt; France in North Africa; Britain in Iraq. Colonizing forces in each case promoted Jewish communities above the standards of their compatriots, thereby causing intercommunal hostilities as nationalist independence movements developed.

People's allegiances are contradictory and not always driven by religion or race. In Algeria, for instance, the anticolonial Communist party had a Jewish presence. Among them was Henri Alleg, who edited *Alger républicain*, a nationalist newspaper, and was captured and tortured by French forces as a suspected Algerian national liberation movement member. Jews in both Tunisia and Algeria had suffered cruel anti-Semitism during the Hitler years, as neither country resisted the persecuting dictates of the French Vichy government. But when Algeria gained independence in 1962, 90 percent of its 140,000 Jewish population, given French citizenship in 1870, migrated to that country, not Israel. Two thirds of the 105,000 Jews of Tunisia, who were not French citizens, nonetheless did the same.

In the Spielberg Jewish Film Archive of the Hebrew University in Jerusalem, there's a clip from 1956 called "Nobody Runs Away."* Made by the American United Jewish Appeal and clearly a fund-raising production, the film features big-name

---

*It features within a modern-day Israeli documentary film about Sderot, *The Pioneers*.

American actors Cameron Mitchell and Virginia Grey as new Israeli migrants. A beautiful couple, impeccably turned out, they live with their children on one of the settlements of the Galilee. They discuss, with the film's narrator (another screen name, Joseph Cotten), the thousands of Jews in Morocco and Tunisia for whom the time had come to leave: "While they still have a chance, while the doors are still open," says Mitchell, the husband character, who is wearing a silk necktie and gesticulating with a pipe to emphasize the point. Why, Cotten asks; what's wrong with Morocco? "You'd have to come from there, like I did, to really know," the polished blonde wife, played by Grey, says in a perfect American accent. "To live in a ghetto in Tunisia or Morocco is meant to live like a ghost. No rights, no acceptance, no status before the laws . . . no vote and, worst of all, no future."

Raquel Uliel, now in her seventies, was one of the first arrivals to Sderot from Morocco in 1955. She was housed in one of a cluster of huts, provided by American donors, which had no running water or electricity and no doors or windows. "We didn't have any financial problems," she says of her life in Fez, Morocco, prior to migration. "Yes, we had rights, free access to schools and hospitals, voting rights," she continues. "We had good relations with them [Muslim Moroccans]; they never caused us any harm." First-generation Moroccan Jews in peripheral towns often do not define their migration as Zionism. "Do you think we knew what was Zionist and what wasn't?" asks Uliel. "We loved Jerusalem, and that was it."

Once I ask a Moroccan in Ashkelon, a coastal city south of Tel Aviv, a question beginning "When you migrated to

Israel . . ." using the Hebrew word aliyah, or "ascent."* He immediately cuts in, angrily: "I didn't ascend! I was brought here!"
It's an expression of the extent to which some Mizrahis feel disconnected from their own fate, lured to Israel at the mercy of
the Ashkenazi-dominated Jewish Agency. The man in Ashkelon
arrived in Israel aged five, young enough to forgive and forget.
He is furious that the fabric of Israeli life is still steeped with
inter-Jewish discrimination.

In the fifties, residents of development towns and transit
camps were optimistic. They believed that everyone was in the
same situation and that it would collectively improve. There was
great hope for the new country, which meant that new citizens
put up with circumstances they might not otherwise have tolerated. But, as it transpired, not everyone developed at the same rate.
Mizrahi immigrants were disproportionately sent to the periphery,
as documented by several sociology professors, including Aziza
Khazzoom at Israel's Hebrew University in 2005. Using Israeli
census figures, she showed that during the period 1953–1959,
when the two biggest immigrant populations were Moroccan
and Polish, 30 percent more of the former were sent to development towns. "The chances that a high-status Mizrahi with a
small family would be sent to the towns were about the same as
those of a low-status Ashkenazi with a large family,"[6] she reported. During the 1970s, another sociologist reported similar
results; Professor Sami Smooha showed that between October
1956 and April 1958, 22.5 percent of Polish as compared with 8.5
percent of North African migrants were sent to coastal strip

---

*If Jews are meant to be returning home to the Holy Land, then "migration" is
a problematic word for it, hence the Israeli usage of the verb "to ascend."

accommodation (not usually development town locations). What's more, according to other researchers also using census figures, an Ashkenazi family was more likely to leave a deprived area and re-house in a better one. By the mid-seventies, more than 90 percent of foreign-born residents in development towns were Oriental Jews. In eleven of those towns, Orientals comprised more than 80 percent of the population. In 1998, the development towns housed 18 percent of the Israeli population, of which about two thirds were of Mizrahi origin. The remaining third were predominantly migrants from the former Soviet bloc or, less so, from Ethiopia. More often than not, the former Soviets come from the "stans" of Central Asia—Muslim states.

But there was another cause for optimism back in the 1950s: the prioritization given these towns at government level, reflected in the level of investment the periphery received. The idea was that these towns would develop into thriving hubs, providing services—schooling, banking, retail—to the agricultural settlements that surround them. It didn't really work out that way. The collective farms that often form geographic rings around development towns stuck to their own schools and had centralized purchase structures that bought in bulk and bypassed regional retail. Development towns became dependent on the kibbutz network for casual labor—they served the farms that way, rather than in the more empowered manner envisaged. But with the development of employment in mind, the government took on a crash program of industrializing the towns. It wanted to create immediate work for the floods of unemployed new immigrants now living in Israel's peripheral belt. The quick fix was labor-intensive industry. Shlomo Swirski, head of the Israeli policy analysis center, Adva, has written books and research papers on development towns and provides much illuminating information about the periphery's economic growth—or lack of it. For ten years starting in 1955, a hefty majority of all government loans and other incentives was awarded to the textile, food processing, metal, and chemical industries, to set up factories in development towns. That solved the problem of unemployment. But it created another one, as these towns turned into giant production lines. Swirski points out that companies were run and managed by private investors who did not live in the development towns, whereas town residents were stuck in the unskilled bottom rungs of the employment ladder. They were stuck with low wages that kept falling, compared to the national average for the same work. They were stuck in precarious, low-skill employment, the survival of which was dependent on national forces that they couldn't control and the profits of which leaked out of the towns, back to the power center, in the national center. Then the next generation repeated the work patterns of the first, since it had been educated in "vocationally guided" schools, of a lower standard than the national average and with a slant on non-academic training.*

On top of all that, the local population was not in control of its own economy. During the fifties and sixties, local council leaders came from the ranks of the central Labor party, dominated by Ashkenazi politicians with little connection to the towns. Later, when that grip loosened and locals became town mayors, they didn't have much power either, because the periphery was overdependent on central government allocations.

*For more details on education, see chapter 7.

Three quarters of the income of local councils in development towns comes from central government, as compared with 43 percent in the big cities. With no infrastructures for running a local economy, the development towns have limited means of generating income through local taxes. For instance, those factories that employ the residents of development towns are often located on kibbutz land, which means that the farms collect the business tax imposed on them. Council tax is the main means of raising independent municipal revenue. You could say that this outcome—of Mizrahi-dense, low-income, low-skill towns— was not part of a deliberate planning strategy, but simply an accident of timing, geography, and decision-making under pressure. Many reports argue this position. It is not, however, the opinion of the residents stuck in them.

I first meet Shlomi, in Ofakim, a few days after Israeli Independence Day, in May, which is celebrated with barbecues everywhere, followed by fireworks, roof parties the night before in Tel Aviv, Israeli flags flapping proudly for weeks before on the streets, draped out of home windows, fluttering atop cars. "My children will never raise the Israeli flag, never!" Shlomi declares—an unconventional statement. "Do you need to ask if there is still discrimination here? Of course there is! Look at this place!" Ofakim is the Hebrew for "horizons," but there are none here, only sand and dusty red air and an unshakable feeling that people have been cast into the desert. Ofakim, population 24,000, lies thirty kilometers south of Sderot, deeper into the Negev. It is the third poorest place in Israel, after two Arab villages. The average salary in Ofakim is well below the national level, and the percentage of the population dependent on income support is way above it. Less than half of the children here pass high school matriculation exams. Residents talk of problems with depression and crime, drink and drugs.

Shlomi is thirty-six; his parents came to Israel from Morocco. His wife, far more stoic than Shlomi, thinks him too sensitive. Unlike her—even though she has similar stories to tell—Shlomi feels so hurt by Ashkenazis in Israel that he wants to lash back. "The Holocaust? They brought it on themselves," he says. "They built the hatred . . . anti-Semitism doesn't come from nowhere, something causes it." Holocaust-mangling is a surprising occurrence in Israel. Mizrahis, reportedly, have said things like "Hitler left *these* Ashkenazis alive so that we would understand why he murdered the rest of them." And in 1982, after a Yemeni Jew was killed by police during a housing protest on the outskirts of Tel Aviv, Mizrahis daubed the walls with graffiti reading: "Ashke-NAZIM" (Hebrew plural). But these expressions aren't representative; a far more common sentiment is to identify with the suffering of Ashkenazi Jews (and certain Jewish communities in North Africa) in the Holocaust.

Shlomi doesn't want to be identified by his real name, because he thinks his stance will attract unwanted attention. On one occasion that we meet, he has just picked up his kids from school. He asks at what time they had eaten lunch before allowing them an ice cream, thus ensuring their adherence to Jewish dietary laws of not mixing meat and milk products in the same stomach. I think of Prime Minister Ben Gurion's comments in the 1950s, about Oriental migrants having "no Jewish education," and can't guess at how insulting this must be for someone like Shlomi. "There is racism here, in no uncertain terms, and nobody can weaken it," he says. "When you are Mizrahi, you suffer, just like that, *halas*. They [the Ashkenazis] screwed my parents, who came from Morocco and were thrown to the dogs here, promised houses and given tents, given black jobs, while the Ashkenazis took the office jobs."

Shlomi describes discrimination experienced at work, at school, and in the Army. His sister saved up to send him to a good boarding school, which he left early—the majority of pupils there were Ashkenazi, he says, and made him feel a failure. The Army was just as bad. Everything in his world is seen through this prism, of being tricked and trampled. Everything is mired in racism and corruption and greed—qualities that he associates with Ashkenazis; icy people with bad hearts, he says. Is he a Zionist? "No way, I told you I hate Israel! Write it: 'Shlomi hates Israel.'" He pauses, looks away. "You know, it really hurts to hear it, but you can't run away from reality. You love the country and you want to be here and you can't." Shlomi's biggest hope is that his children will leave. He says that he is raising them with full knowledge of discrimination in Israel so that they won't harbor any false hopes, or want to stay.

By the mid-sixties, the development towns were a half-completed project, in need of investment. But after the Six-Day War, in which Israel occupied the Palestinian territories, the towns were pushed to the back room of government policy. At that point, the priority was to settle the Occupied Territories of the West Bank, formerly under Jordanian control, and (to a lesser extent) the Gaza Strip, formerly in the hands of Egypt. Settling the territories began in the late 1960s and came into full force in 1977 when the right-wing Likud party won the elections. That put the Labor party, Israel's only government since its creation, into opposition. One of Prime Minister Menachem

Begin's biggest vote-winners was his courting of the Mizrahi populations.* The Labor party understood this and contributed to the ethnic nature of the next elections in 1981. A Labor leaflet from the 1981 campaign carries a picture of an Oriental-looking crowd with the taglines: "This time you must choose between this sort of a reality or an enlightened government" and "The real choice: Hooliganism or Zionism."[7] Begin understood that this sizable Mizrahi voting community felt embittered by discriminatory experiences under the Labor party. He needed only to talk to that grievance to earn their allegiance. He did just that, traveling the development towns talking of an end to racial discrimination. In 1981, on the eve of elections that would secure an even bigger majority for the Likud party, Begin addressed a crowd at a central square in Tel Aviv. A day before, the popular Israeli entertainer Dudu Topaz, appearing at a Labor party convention, had described the Mizrahis as *chah chahim*. A still-used Hebrew derogatory term usually reserved for Mizrahis, this is understood to mean "wild" and "uneducated." Begin responded directly to the insults from the Labor-campaigner comedian: "Our sons of the communities of the East were heroes and fighters . . . There are martyrs among them who until the very last minute of their lives sang Hatikva [the Israeli national anthem] and astounded the world with their exceptional heroism . . . Is it right that a hired actor of the Labor party stand up and abuse and desecrate their name? . . . No one has hurt the pride of a whole tribe of Israel like the Labor party did in this place yesterday."[8] At one stage, a rumor was circulating among

---

*Begin was previously the leader of Irgun, the militant Zionist group that employed terror tactics against the British Mandate during the 1940s, and against the Palestinian population from 1947 to 1948

the "communities of the East"—whom he so honored—that the Polish-born Begin was in fact Moroccan.

Coming to power, Begin unveiled an urban regeneration project, aimed at development towns and city slums. But Shlomo Swirski at Adva documents that far more of Begin's attention—and the national budget—was awarded to the settlement project. This enterprise was initiated by the Labor party but continued and was accelerated by Likud under Begin. Settlers were perceived then as being the "new pioneers"; they came from the ranks of the National Religious party. Mizrahis do populate the Palestinian territories, but less so: statistics from 2003 show that Mizrahi-origin Jews comprise 21 percent of the settler population.

At this stage, postwar, Israel had increased resources at its disposal, its coffers swelled by Palestinian taxes—both income and custom tax, a result of the Palestinian territories turning into a captive market for Israeli goods and of the many Palestinians now employed in Israel. That money could have been plowed into the development towns, to bring them up to speed: to build public transport lines and invest in schools, housing, and employment opportunities. Instead, the new cash was used to construct new settlements—a major undertaking in terms of the resources needed to set up populations and infrastructure such as roads, electricity, water, and security systems in often remote locations. Between 1990 and 1999, the government budget for settlement local authorities was over double that for regional authorities within the borders of Israel. A study from Tel Aviv University in 2004 showed that councils like Hebron and Emmanuel (both in the occupied Palestinian territories) continued to receive double the government aid.

What all this means in practice is that a settlement like Ariel, illegal under international law, positioned deep inside the West Bank, is much better disposed with far better amenities than somewhere like Ofakim. Begin's urban renewal project, the one that was intended to reward the Mizrahi vote, didn't receive enough government funding and was left to rely on foreign donations. This preference was clocked in some quarters long before Adva and the Tel Aviv University reported it. In 1981, an election flyer from the left-wing Jewish-Arab party Hadash read: "150 billion for settlements! The sum is four times more than is needed to eliminate all the poor neighbourhoods in Israel!"[9] That same year a flyer from the Ohalim [tents] movement, a social protest group, accused the government of burning millions on settlements while residents "rotted in the distress of the slums" in Israel. Jump forward to October 2002 and five ministers, including the Labor leader and defense minister, Benyamin (Fuad) Ben-Eliezer, quit the National Unity government, in protest at Prime Minister Ariel Sharon's funding of settlements in the West Bank at the expense of social-welfare programs within Israel.

During the years right after 1967, the development towns were struggling as textile and other manufacture-based industries were in decline. This same period began Israel's heavy investment in high tech, which would create a dynamic industry located in the country's center. Having been geared to supply labor for low-skill industries, the development towns did not attract the investors, private or government, in this new business. When they did, the jobs were at the lower end of the high-tech spectrum. For example, in 1999 Intel opened a chip factory in Kiryat Gat, a development town, while basing its research and development operations in Israel's central cities. The white-collar component—a high-investment, high-yield, high-growth sector—bypassed the development towns entirely.

"You know what you remind me of?" Shlomi in Ofakim asks when we first meet. "You're like one of those people you see on National Geographic [channel], who spend days in the mountains looking for elephants. What for? What use is it, you coming here and writing about us? You know what we say in Moroccan [Arabic]? *'Dy ma und dush al- fluss—klamu mi shush.'* It means: The words of the poor are worth nothing." He refuses to talk any further and, wanting him to continue, I feebly suggest that his situation might change if foreign donors knew about it. Shlomi knows better than to believe this. But he looks as though he might.

Months later and several worlds away, I'm at the tranquil, botanically blessed Hebrew University on Mount Scopus in Jerusalem, with its prized views over the Judean desert, a scene that has inspired centuries of paintings and prose. I put the question of foreign funds to an analyst of charitable donations to Israel. Why is none of this money reaching places such as Ofakim? I ask the specialist during an informal conversation. Despite the blinding evidence of our own eyes, he responds, there is no way to prove that funds from overseas organizations, philanthropists, and communal and private donors stop short of development towns in the desert. Some Israeli charities that collate foreign funds do deal specifically with development towns and deprived areas. Some foreign cities are twinned with these underdeveloped areas. But if you mapped money allocation, it would show up at big-city charity HQs, where the money is received, not at the final destination in which it is spent.

The specialist, in the absence of statistical information, switches to analysis. He says that the Mizrahi populations of Israel were historically done over, but that Israel did the best it could at the time under constant, external pressures and with overstretched resources. He thinks there are more relevant issues in Israel today, such as relations between Arab-Israeli and Jewish-Israeli citizens and the (Jewish) secular versus the national-religious. In any case, he concludes, all these issues are far exceeded in importance by the ever-present physical threat that Israel faces over its very survival. The trump card, the catch-all answer to any question or criticism of social policy—this constant, choking existential terror seemingly inhaled with every breath of being an Israeli. How real is that threat, I ask, when the Arab League, just as an example, has recently repeated its 2002 offer of peace and normalized relations in exchange for Israel handing the occupied territories over to the Palestinians?

That's the wrong question and a dumb move. Have I not been listening, the charities expert wants to know, to the lethal threats pouring out of Hamas leader Ismail Haniyeh's mouth? Or to Iranian Prime Minister Mahmoud Ahmadinejad, for that matter? Have I not been paying attention to the rain of deadly and entirely unprovoked Qassam rockets falling on Sderot? Two Israeli children were murdered in Sderot as a result of those rockets (in an attack that injured thirty-one others, in September 2004); do I not consider that important? Oh, God. Obviously, the murder of children on both sides is important, I respond. There is no way to stop the existential fear; there is only a way to talk yourself out of the club. "Wait a minute," he checks. "How long did you say you have lived here?" The doorstop pulls out. Let's not forget the Jewish people's history, the Holocaust, he cautions, just before the conversational door closes, politely, with me on the outside, having blown it. Blown it, that is, for Shlomi in Ofakim, who for a moment had believed that the pointless, National Geographic–style reporter might at least find one concrete explanation for the beaten-down life he and his Moroccan-origin neighbors lead. Something he might be able to fight, rather than a series of terrifying, cast-iron national beliefs, against which he doesn't stand a chance.

Chapter 4

BABYLON CALLING

DAVID YOSEF IS not Or Yehuda's mayor when we meet, but it is obvious that he will be. We are walking around the Israeli town sometimes dubbed "Little Iraq" for its density of citizens from that country, and Yosef is introducing me to all whom we meet as "Iraqi, from England." Then people invariably respond: "Ah, so you're one of ours."

Or Yehuda (located on land that that used to be the Arab village of Saqiya) is about five miles east of Tel Aviv and, although not peripheral, still counts as a development town. It was once a transit camp, with thousands of tents and, later, tin huts. Today, you can still see row upon row of the boxy, two-roomed housing-project flats that had replaced the huts by the late 1950s. There's bigger, better housing in sight, too, more so on the outskirts. In recent years the town has received an influx of Russian and Ethiopian Jewish migrants, but it is still predominantly Iraqi in flavor. There's Iraqi-Jewish dialect on every street corner, often spoken by twenty-somethings and always called "Iraqi," not "Arabic." There's Iraqi food everywhere: *sambusak*, cheese- or meat-filled triangle pastries; *ba'aba b'tamar*, date-filled flattened round pastries; *kubba*, herbed meat and semolina dumplings in sweet–savory sauces of either beetroot or okra. There's *amba*, the spicy mango pickle that Iraqis are addicted to—although this radioactively bright orange condiment can now be found all over Israel. Or Yehuda is home to the Babylonian Jewry Heritage Center, which narrates this community's history in Iraq. The town might be better known for its Middle Eastern restaurant, Sa'id, named after the owner, about whom a waitress there tells me: "He's Iraqi. I mean he's Jewish, but everyone thinks he is Arab because of his name."

David Yosef, himself of Iraqi origin, is a kind of devotee of the Jews of Babylon. He clearly respects this community, and it respects him right back—everyone greets him with a genuine smile. His stand-up comedy and theater routines affectionately send up Iraqi Jews; he has written a book about the early days in Israeli transit camps, *Nostalgia for the Primus Stoves* (used in those camps), and a dictionary of Iraqi-Jewish slang. A critical assessment of this output might pronounce it a somewhat schmaltzy line in Iraqi-Jewish folklore, a hued rendition of a narrowly defined cultural heritage. But, whatever; the locals are happy. Yosef is conducting a street poll for my benefit, asking the people we meet if they feel Iraqi or Israeli—and most of them, even the ones obviously born in the Jewish state, choose the former. There's Shafiq: "Iraqi and proud of it." There's Sali, thirty years old, Israeli-born, but he feels Iraqi. A couple of late-twenty-something women, who don't give names but have the sort of pale makeup and lightened hair that might signal an attempt to hide Oriental roots, reply that they're Iraqi too. We sit at the central bakery and eat warm pastries that might have come out of a Baghdadi kitchen, suffused in the steamy smell of *huwayij*, an aromatic blend of spices used to flavor dough. Back then, in late

2006, Or Yehuda feels slightly off-kilter, like a stalled Iraqi-Jewish theme park. Its characters look small. They don't match the Iraqi Jewish that I know from childhood, when visiting relatives from around the U.K. would conduct all-Arabic catch-up sessions late into the night, music- and meze-fueled gatherings, punctuated by singing and storytelling, politics and laughter. That seemed more like a little Iraq, incongruous in our English living room.

The vague feeling that something is awry takes hold in the Babylonian Jewry Heritage Center, the national keeper of Iraqi-Jewish history. Schoolchildren are regularly bused in to see the exhibition here, which begins with this placard: "After 2,600 years in the Diaspora, Jews of Babylon returned on masse to Eretz Yisrael,* settled here and have integrated into all spheres of life in the State of Israel."† This text stands next to historical pictures of hard nation-building labor and transit-camp milieus. If the frame is not clear enough, the next placard helps set it: "From the days of the first exile in 8th century BCE until today, the Jews of Babylon never lost their love of Zion, nor their urge to return to Eretz Yisrael . . . the Jews of Iraq joined the Zionist movement at its inception and set up local Zionist organizations." So the Iraqi Jews were twiddling their thumbs for two and a half millennia, waiting for Zionism to be invented before they helped it take them back "home"?

What speaks loudly from these texts is the wish that Iraqi Jews be counted as vital to the Jewish homeland project, be considered active agents of its realization. The collection was put together by

---

*The Land of Israel, an early Zionist term.
†The Babylonian Jewry Heritage Center has since been renovated; exhibition texts may have changed.

a committee of Iraqi Jews, some of them members of the Zionist movement that helped Iraqi Jews migrate—at first dangerously, illegally, and then en masse to Israel. And while the exhibition covers other aspects of Iraqi-Jewish life, a large section of it deals with the activities of this underground organization.

"Is this your history?" I ask overseas relatives who had reached early adulthood in Iraq. "No!" several members of the American family branch fire back. "Lies, damned lies!" proclaims a cousin, taking issue with lines I quote from the exhibition placards. A few days later, another e-mail arrives, announcing the impending visit to Israel of an uncle from Europe who is keen to meet with me, "to dispute the adverse propaganda." Their outrage is understandable. Relatively speaking, there's nothing wrong with the protagonists of Iraqi Zionism wanting their deeds honored on a par with other Zionist leaders. But that doesn't justify skewing the history of all Iraqi Jews—within Israel and beyond it—to this purpose.

When King Nebuchadnezzar II invaded Judah in 597 B.C.E., he conquered Jerusalem, torched the Jewish First Temple, and exiled around forty thousand Jews to his royal seat, Babylon. Home to biblical father Abraham until God instructed him to leave it, Babylon, since its absorption of those Judean exiles, has been a Jewish address for over two millennia. That, by a long way, is the longest record of Jewish residence, anywhere. In the early 1950s, the majority of the Jewish population of Iraq—as Babylon came to be known—left, at once, to Israel. Today, there are fewer than a dozen Jews in Iraq. Every time you read something historical on the subject, it's always noted that Babylonian Jews were the most well established, the best positioned, and the least likely of any Jewish community to uproot and go.

Trying to console those banished to Babylon, the prophet Jeremiah wrote to them from Jerusalem: "Build houses and settle down; plant gardens and eat what they produce. Marry and have sons and daughters . . . Also seek the peace and prosperity of the city to which I have carried you into exile. Pray to the Lord for it, for if it prospers, you too will prosper."[1] Babylonian Jews took his advice. Historians have this exiled community adjusting swiftly, establishing itself socially and financially in this lucky, lush land fed by its two famous rivers, the Tigris and the Euphrates. They didn't lose their faith, because, shortly after their arrival, the similarly exiled prophet Ezekiel gave planning permission for a place of worship. That was the first synagogue in history—built in Babylon.

In 538 B.C.E., the Persian king Cyrus took over Babylon and told its Jewish community they could go back home, to Jerusalem, if they wanted to. Several thousand did, and set about restoring Judaism to the city, building the Second Temple. But most remained in Babylon; the Jewish community was thriving in the Fertile Crescent, which in those days was a financial and trade center. To the vast majority, Jerusalem didn't seem an attractive relocation prospect. It's with reference to this period that my father lampoons the legend, versed in song, of Iraqi Jews weeping by the rivers of Babylon as they remembered Zion. "They weren't crying," he says. "They were singing and dancing and drinking arak*!" Iraq saw the rise and fall of countless empires, but the Jewish community stayed put throughout.

In 69 C.E., the Romans ruined the Second Temple, and scholars from the sacked Jerusalem poured into Babylon, fortifying its

---

*A clear, aniseed-flavored Middle Eastern alcoholic drink.

Jewish community. Then Hadrian arrived and collapsed Palestine as a Jewish center. Wanting to assimilate the Jews, the Roman emperor tried to shut down their religion, introducing a swath of anti-Jewish laws to that end. The Jewish community in Palestine was left impoverished, ineffective, and in decline. That's when Babylon took the spotlight. Already a Judaism hothouse, the region boasted a high number of religious community leaders—"Exilarchs"—and two academies of Jewish thought: at Sura, in the south, and at Pumbedita, the modern-day Fallujah. This Mesopotamian Jewish center was about to produce its greatest work: the Babylonian Talmud.

More widely used than another version written in Palestine, this Talmud is second only to the Bible in the Jewish holy-book charts. It covers the entire doctrine, practice, and moral and mental commitments of Judaism. It's as big a deal to Jews as the hadith, the Prophet Mohammad's instructions on Islamic practice, is to Muslims. By the time the Babylonian Talmud was being written (it took 130 years and was completed by 500 C.E.), Jewish communities were on the move, scattering across the world, mostly escaping Roman persecution. Cut off from former centers, this was a new phase of Jewish life, placing people in unfamiliar situations in which they were crucially dependent on the Talmud for guidance. Babylon, in other words, kept global Judaism going.

The armies of Islam conquered Babylon in the seventh century, but its rulers didn't meddle with the region's operation as a kind of Judaism HQ. Having taken custody over people who didn't fight or want to convert to Islam, Muslim rulers created the category "Ahl al-Kitab," People of the Book: the monotheistic Christian and Jewish subjects. Their legal status was as *dhimmi*, lower than Muslims but protected if they accepted the distinction and paid taxes to receive it. Some historians are highly critical of this dhimmi status, pointing out all the degradations and persecutions inherent—and suffered—as a result of this second-class label. Others say that the concept changed dramatically according to which ruler was enforcing it and that, apart from some specific suffering in places such as Yemen and North Africa, dhimmi really did mean "protected"—a liberal measure in the context of the time. It's a contentious point, with each side of the debate raising happy or horrible examples as proof. In any case, dhimmi status didn't stop what's described as a golden age of Jewish Responsa, a religious Q&A correspondence system, between Babylon and world Jewry, maintained until 1250. That's when the Islamic empire declined, as did the Judaism practiced within its realm. Babylon diminished in importance, and the Jewish faith focus shifted to a Sephardi base in Spain, then an Ashkenazi base further east in Europe. It's at this point that some commentators have Middle Eastern Jews falling off the map of history. European Jewry was multiplying, coming into its own, and Oriental Jewry became the global minority population.

But Middle Eastern Jewry didn't ossify just because Europe wasn't looking at it. Like other Jews in other areas of the Ottoman Empire (which began in 1299 and conquered Iraq in 1534), the Babylon branch did well under it. Certainly, they fared better than coreligionists in Christian countries, who were exposed to a virulent anti-Semitism that made pogroms, persecutions, and forced relocations routine. Christianity, which invented religious anti-Semitism, labeled the Jews "God-killers," and pronounced them cosmically evil, had effectively sanctioned an open season of abuse. By the latter stages of the Ottoman Empire, Iraq's Jewish community was thriving as a result of the modernization brought about under this rule. Mahmud II, who came to the Ottoman throne in 1808, announced that new liberalization laws applied to everyone: "Henceforth, I recognize Muslims only in the mosque, Christians only in the church, and Jews only in the synagogue," he said. "Outside these places of worship, I desire every individual to enjoy the same political rights and my fatherly protection."[2] Two decrees from later Sultans confirmed that minorities were no longer "dhimmi" but "millet." People of the Book had religious and educational autonomy, and the dhimmi tax was replaced by a military tax for those who wanted service exemption.

From 1849, the Iraqi Jews had an elected leader, the Hakham Bashi (just like the Sephardis in Palestine). Between then and the eve of the First World War, this Jewish community dominated trade in Iraq, mainly because it was mobile—many Iraqi Jews migrated to India or England—and fluent in foreign languages. It also dominated the spheres of banking and money-lending. These successes fed into and were inspired by an education spurt around the same time, with the establishment of independent Jewish schools running alongside those operated by Alliance Israelite Universelle, the system of French-inspired education in the Jewish Middle East.

Things only got better when the British conquered Iraq in 1917. By then, the Jewish community comprised 3 percent—around 87,488—of the total population and was concentrated in the main cities: Baghdad, Basra, and Mosul. An estimated one in four or five Baghdadis was Jewish; the Iraqi-Israeli writer Nissim Rejwan comments that he has always considered Baghdad a

Jewish city in the same way that you might think of today's New York. Iraqi Jews perfectly fitted the requirements of a British colonial power reliant on support from a favored minority community. Educated, good with English, business-minded, the Jewish population featured disproportionately in private businesses—oil and banking especially—as well as public works such as railroad management, the postal system, and the customs office (strategic national assets as far as the British were concerned). In the late 1940s, around 25 percent of the Jewish population was employed as clerks, civil servants, managers, and other white-collar workers. Sasson Yehezkel was Iraqi minister for finance during the early 1920s, and another Iraqi Jew, Ibrahim al-Kabir, was the director general of the finance ministry for around twenty years, until 1948. Salman Shina, a high-profile Jewish attorney and newspaper editor, said: "Commerce blossomed and flourished, the Jews made fortunes, and gold descended upon them like rain on grass."[3]

By the 1920s, Jewish writers and poets were composing in Arabic, active in music and theater, committed to national aspirations, and proclaiming themselves loyal Iraqis. Some Iraqi newspapers and magazines were founded by Jewish journalists who had contacts and working relations with writers in other Arab countries. Jews held four seats out of eighty-eight in the Iraqi parliament of 1924, and had one out of twenty senate members. Reviewing this situation, the Israeli historian Haim Cohen wrote: "The Jews felt themselves to be Jews by religion and Arabs by nationality, believing that Jews and Arabs were members of the same race."[4]

British presence in Iraq cleared a path for Zionist activities, as officers stationed there were frequently Jews from Palestine.

Most sources state that during the early 1920s, Zionism in Iraq was limited and manifested itself mostly in fund-raising and teaching Hebrew. Breaking with this assessment, the Babylonian Center in Or Yehuda ties Iraqi Jewry to Zionism "at its inception"—which would be during the late nineteenth century. U.K. rule in Babylon nominally lasted only until 1920, but in effect carried on as a British Mandate was imposed, with King Faisal—son of the Sharif of Mecca—as its first ruler.*

By then, Iraqis were calling for self-determination and nationalism, which took two forms: a pan-Arab variety that emphasized Arab unity, and a national-democratic branch that stressed rights and social reform. Initially, Iraqi nationalism of both flavors viewed the Jewish population as comrades to the cause. Later, this frayed: the Jewish community was increasingly seen as allied to the increasingly hated British occupiers. But in the 1930s, a Nazi branch took hold in some nationalist quarters in Iraq and seeped into the government. It was, some argue, Nazi only insofar as it was anti-British and anticolonial and thus saw a natural ally in the Germans. Recent history shows that occupation can produce stomach-turning alliances. Still, that distinction may have been lost on the Jewish community. Some Iraqi Jews, like the writer Nissim Rejwan, assert that they remained friends with Muslims in Baghdad, who self-defined as pro-Nazi but clearly weren't anti-Jewish. Others recall the terror with which they greeted the news that the Mufti of Jerusalem, a Muslim leader and Nazi sympathizer, had arrived in Iraq during

---

*King Faisal had just been expelled from Syria by the French, who took over from British rule there.

the Arab revolt in Palestine in 1936–1939,* and the declared pro-
German sympathies of Prime Minister Rashid Ali al-Gailani.

In Iraq, the period up to the Arab–Israeli war in 1948 was
characterized by political instability, as a series of pro-British
governments tried to crush nationalism. At the heart of these
power struggles, a landmark incident shattered the Jewish community's sense of belonging. In 1941, the Nazi-leaning, ultra-
nationalist Rashid Ali al-Gailani took hold of Iraq by coup,
banished the British-appointed regent Prince Abdul-Ilah and
Prime Minister Nuri al-Said, and declared the country an ally of
Germany. That gave Britain the excuse to reoccupy Iraq. With
the prince regent under their protection in the Gulf, U.K. forces
landed in Basra in May 1941 and reached the outskirts of Baghdad a month later. Defeated nationalist leaders fled by the end of
May, while the regent reclaimed his seat on 1 June. For two days,
nobody was in charge of the country.

The Baghdadi Jewish community, dressed in its finest on the
last day of a religious festival, thought it would be okay to go and
welcome the returning regent—not knowing that his return had
been delayed. Nationalists, having just been defeated by British
forces, were incensed by that. They were already angered by Zionist operations in Palestine and turning against the Jewish community in Iraq. Rioting quickly spread to the looting of homes and
properties and the killing of hundreds, mostly Jews. An official investigation puts the death toll at 110, including 28 Muslims, with
204 injured. The head of the Iraqi Jewish community says 130

---

*Revolts over British-approved Jewish immigration to and land purchases in
    Palestine. Thousands of Arabs, Jews, and British were killed; precise figures
    vary.

were killed and 450 injured. But other estimates vary: 160 to 180 deaths were cited by the British writer Marion Woolfson; 900 Jewish deaths were cited by the Iraqi Zionist underground member Heskel Haddad. Many report that Muslim neighbors had defended Jews against mob attacks. Accusing fingers are pointed at the British, whose decision to delay the regent's return is seen as a tactic to divert anger while completing a takeover of the country—sacrificing the Jewish community to this end. The British journalist Tony Rocca co-edited his Iraqi-Jewish mother-in-law's recent memoirs and reports newly discovered documentation showing that the army's entry into Baghdad was delayed at the behest of one man: the British ambassador to Iraq.

Things calmed down, helped by the government bringing al-Gailani agitators to trial and paying compensation to the Jewish community. Nine months after what became known as the "Farhud,"* a visiting Zionist emissary sent a report back to the Jewish Agency in Israel, astonished at the "lack of enthusiasm amongst the Baghdadi Jews for Palestine,"[5] and the speed with which this community seemed to forgive and forget. Eight new Jewish schools were built during this period—not the behavior of a people in flight. World War II created prosperity in Iraq (a supply base for the British Army), and for Iraqi Jews in particular, doubtless helping to heal the wound. But Iraqi Jews were shocked by the Farhud; something had ripped. It was the first time in a long history that anything like that had happened.

The Babylonian Jewry Heritage Center portrays this incident as "awakening" the Jews of Iraq to Zionism. It is true that the

---

*Farhud is Iraqi Arabic for looting, accompanied by an absence of order; the event is now often referred to as a pogrom.

Farhud made young Iraqi Jews think about their own precariousness, and Zionism provided one solution. But the dovetailing of problem and cure might also be due to the fact that, by the early 1940s, Zionism had woken up to the Jews of the Middle East. In 1942, as Nazi horrors were unfolding in Europe, Ben Gurion announced the Million Person plan to bring Oriental Jews to the Israeli homeland. Without them, he argued, there wouldn't be enough Jews in Palestine, and Zionism would collapse. Along with other leaders, he was worried about what might happen to Jews in Arab lands, given what was already happening in a "civilized" country like Germany. Planning to bring them to Israel, Ben Gurion warned: "If we do not do away with Iraqi Jewry in the Zionist manner, there is a danger that it will be done away with in the Hitlerian manner."[6]

Historians deem this an unfair and unfounded comparison between Nazi Germany and Arab nations. Judging from the minutes of meetings held during the time, Jewish Agency leaders knew that officially and publicly linking Middle Eastern Jews to the Palestinian issue would compromise those Jews in their homelands. "The very same day that brings redemption and salvation to European Jewry will be the most dangerous day of all for the exiles in Arab lands," said Eliyahu Dobkin, head of the Jewish Agency for Immigration, in July 1943. "When Zionism enters the stage of fulfilment and we are engaged in our campaign for the Zionist solution in Palestine, these Jews will face great danger, danger of terrible slaughter, which will make the slaughter in Europe look less terrible than it looks today. Our first task therefore is to save these Jews."[7] In other words, the escalating conflict in Palestine would imperil Jews in the Middle East; but the Zionist leadership committed to saving them, by bringing them to Palestine. Since Jewish migration to the homeland was seen as self-evidently a good thing and the purpose of Zionism, its leaders saw no problem with this self-perpetuating loop of logic.

Just as predicted, hostilities in Palestine took their toll in Iraq. The Jewish population was damned either way: those who opposed Zionism weren't believed by their co-nationalists; those who didn't oppose it were considered traitors. Those who kept in touch with relatives who had already migrated to Palestine— illegally—were accused of having contact with the enemy. The fragile Iraqi government, under British control and terrified of the constant, popular calls for nationalism, liberalism, and democracy, took the easy way out: it shifted the focus onto Palestine, a unifying cause that deflected attention from pressing internal matters. It compromised its own Jewish community.

By 1948, ceding to demands from the right wing, Iraq declared itself at war with Israel and sent five thousand troops to Palestine. Military rule was declared; a collection of new anti-Zionist measures affected the whole Jewish community and were seen as anti-Semitic. Jewish freedom of movement was restricted in Iraq, with travel outside the country allowed only in extraordinary circumstances, such as illness. Wealthy Jews were arrested on pretexts and fined. Martial law was exploited by the government to round up Zionists, communists, nationalists—anyone, in fact, perceived as contributing to the extreme political instability, anti-government activity, and regular protests of the time.

In July 1948, the Iraqi government made Zionism an illegal offense, like communism and anarchism, with a penalty of death or seven years' imprisonment. But it didn't properly define Zionism. Numerous Jews were arrested, especially rich ones, as the law—wide open to abuse—was used as a means of extortion. Later that year, Jewish bank permits were canceled, curtailing trade in foreign currency; officially, this was to prevent illegal smuggling of funds to the Israeli enemy. For similar reasons, the Ministry of Defense told government bodies to dismiss Jewish employees. Young Jewish graduates struggled to find work, while others weren't admitted into higher education. Then a wealthy Jewish businessman, Shafiq Adas, was accused of treason and hanged. It looked like the Iraqi government was taking revenge on its Jewish population for the defeat suffered in Palestine at the hands of other Jews. Ades, who had friends in high places and gave funds to the Palestinian (Arab) cause, became symbolic of a likely Jewish fate in Iraq.

In late 1949, wartime emergency restrictions eased (in any case, Jews had found ways to get around them with bribes and favors). But by then, the number emigrating to Palestine was on the up, and the Iraqi government was determined to bring it down. From the government's perspective, Jewish emigration amounted to people-smuggling carried out by a traitorous organization. After a war that created 711,000 Arab refugees in Palestine, the Iraqi government had to be seen to be dealing with Zionism, especially since Iraqi right-wing nationalists were routinely demanding the expulsion of the Jewish community. In this climate, anti-Jewish demonstrations could easily turn into anti-government riots.

In March 1950, Iraq passed the Draft Law, by which any Jewish citizen who wanted to leave could now do so, but would be stripped of Iraqi nationality. The government announced that those who wished to go would do the country harm if they remained. The administration, increasingly embarrassed by illegal

Jewish migration across the border with Iran and overland to Israel, thought the new law would enable the exit of troublemakers: Zionist activists and their protégés. Everyone saw it as a
liberal measure. The government figured that around eight to
ten thousand of the Jewish population would take advantage of
the law. By July 1951, 90 percent of the Jewish community had
left Iraq, on planes commissioned by Israel in what was dubbed
"Operation Ezra and Nehemiah."*

On 8 April 1950, the last day of Passover, "The Jews of Baghdad were strolling, as was their custom, along Abu Nawas street
besides the river Tigris," wrote British-Jewish journalist Marion
Woolfson. The riverside was flanked by cafés, and one of them,
Dar al-Baida, was especially popular with "young Jewish intel-
lectuals." At around 9 P.M., a bomb exploded near this café, injuring four people. On 15 January 1951, another bomb went off
at Baghdad's Masouda Shemtob synagogue, killing a seven-year-
old sweets-seller who was outside the building and injuring
twenty-two or twenty-seven Jews, two of them fatally. There
were three more bombs with no more casualties: an explosion in
March at the American cultural center in Baghdad, a favorite
meeting place for young Jews; and explosions in May and in
June, both seeming to target Jewish businesses in the capital.
There was a surge in signatories to the registry of Jews who now
wanted to exit Iraq.

Historians and writers roughly agree over the final number of
Jews signing up to leave the country during 1950 and 1951. But

---

*These two prophets led Jewish communities in exile back to Jerusalem during
the pre-Christian era. Ironically, they did not manage to persuade Babylonian Jews to do so.

different sources give different figures for the numbers register-
ing to go and the dates that they signed up. There's a reason for
the disparities: If the bombs were the final impetus, terrifying the
Jewish community into leaving Iraq in such absolute numbers,
who planted them? The Jewish community at the time assumed
the attacks to be the work of anti-Jewish forces. Then, in December 1951, the government brought three individuals to trial—
all of them Jewish. The bombs, it was claimed, had been planted
by the Zionist underground, with the express purpose of terror-
izing the Jewish community and precipitating its exodus. The
defendants were found guilty; two of them, Iraqi nationals, were
hanged, while the third, an Israeli, was given a life sentence.
Shlomo Hillel describes the conviction as the result of "a deep,
pervasive and, to all appearances, insatiable desire to see Jews
hanging from the gallows."[8] He argues that the only convincing
evidence the Iraqi court could come up with was that its Jewish
witnesses had been tortured. Israeli historians Moshe Gat and Dr.
Esther Meir-Glitzenstein, both authors on Iraqi Jewry, also conclude that the bombings were not the work of the Zionist underground. Others have a different take. In the mid-1960s, the
Israeli magazine *Ha'olam Hazeh* ("This World") published an account connecting the Zionist underground with the explosions,
based on a testimonial from an Israeli operative in Iraq. Then in
the early 1970s, an Iraqi lawyer who had been in the country at
the time of the bombings told the Israeli *Black Panther* magazine
about a jarring occurrence immediately after the incident at the
Dar al-Bayda coffee house. "The day after the explosion, at 4:00
A.M., leaflets were already being distributed amongst the first
worshippers at the synagogue," he said. "The leaflets warned of
the dangers revealed by the throwing of the bomb and recom-

mended the people to come to Israel."[9] According to the Iraqi Criminal Investigation Department, a handwritten leaflet advised Jews to return "to your natural homeland, Israel" and ended its delivery like this: "O sons of Zion, inhabitants of Babylon, free yourselves . . . O brother Jews, Israel is calling you."[10]

Neither British nor American reports from the period think the Iraqi trial of the alleged bombers a sham. Wilbur Grane Eveland, a former adviser to the CIA, in Baghdad at the time, wrote: "In an attempt to portray the Iraqis as anti-American and to terrorize the Jews, the Zionists planted bombs in the US information service library and synagogues, and soon leaflets began to appear urging Jews to flee to Israel."[11] Israel has never claimed responsibility for the bombs, although some say that it has been implied by officials. In 1954, when the Israeli government was reeling from the Lavon affair, in which intelligence officials were accused of planting bombs in Egypt, an IDF minister said: "This method of operation was not invented for Egypt. It was first tried in Iraq."[12]

In Or Yehuda, it's hard to find someone who doesn't believe that the Iraqi bombs were the work of the Zionist underground; many are convinced down to the naming of names. There is a story that when the Iraqi Jews, in their transit camps of the 1950s, heard about the hanging of the two Jews sentenced for throwing bombs in Baghdad, they reacted by saying that it was divine retribution against the Zionist underground for bringing them to Israel. Some commentators suggest that this stems from an embittered need to find someone to blame for the disappointing conditions those Iraqi Jews found in Israel. There were two good reasons for resentment. One was that Zionist activists in Iraq had painted enticing images of Israel, where migrants would be assured homes, jobs, and an altogether better life. Another, more concrete, was that a day after the denaturalization law expired in March 1951, the Iraqi government passed another law that froze the assets of all departing Jews. Stripped of their nationality, harangued in the crossfire of the Palestinian conflict, and now deprived of their material wealth, Iraqi Jews arrived in Israel as destitute dependents. It was quite a drop. "We were in the skies and fell to earth," says one of my Israeli uncles. *"Itfanu ala il shen il sowenanu!"*—"We cursed ourselves over what we had done [coming to Israel]," says another.

The five thousand Jews who stayed in Iraq were mostly middle- and upper-class. They lived well, especially under Prime Minister Abd al-Karim Qasim, whose famously clement leadership lasted from 1958, when he took over the country by force, until 1963, when the Ba'ath party deposed and killed him. The Jewish community wasn't allowed to leave the country, except during Qasim's rule—which was exactly when they didn't want to. Many lived to regret that, as Saddam Hussein's rule unleashed brutality in all directions. Scores of Jews from Iraq recall the imprisonment, torture, or murder of loved ones during that period. The 1967 Arab–Israeli war didn't help Arab–Jewish relations in Iraq; neither did the public hanging of fourteen Iraqis, nine of them Jews, on spying charges in 1969. Most of the remaining Jewish community left when they could in the 1970s, although few of them went to Israel. In 2003, Ezra Levy, one of the last remaining Jews of Baghdad, was secretly flown to Israel, courtesy of the Jewish Agency. He seems ambivalent about his presence in the Jewish state, in a nursing home, today.

According to several sources, the Zionist underground comprised no more than two thousand members on the eve of the

1948 Arab–Israeli war. But the Babylonian Jewry Heritage Center in Or Yehuda talks of "tens of thousands" of members "subjected to arrest, torture, imposition of fines, and imprisonment." By exaggerating the volume and significance of the movement, the center blocks other narratives about the Iraqi Jews of this period—most pointedly, that there was vocal Jewish opposition to Zionism in Iraq, from the start and right up until Israel's creation. Back in 1922, Menahem Saleh Daniel, a landowning Baghdadi notable, wrote to the Zionist Organization: "The Jews are already acting with culpable indifference to public and political affairs, and if they espouse so publicly and tactlessly* as they have done lately, a cause which is regarded by the Arabs not only as foreign but actually hostile, I have no doubt that they will succeed in making themselves a totally alien element in the country and as such they will have great difficulty in defending a position which . . . is on other grounds already too enviable."[13] In 1936, thirty-three Jewish community heads in Iraq wrote to the British Colonial Office and to the League of Nations in protest over Zionist policy in Palestine that year, asserting their solidarity with the Arab side of the riots. Zionism was publicly attacked by a prominent Baghdadi Jewish lawyer, Yusuf al-Kabir, in the *Iraq Times* in 1938. He wrote that he considered the Balfour Declaration a solution to a European problem and that he was against the Jewish claim to a historical ownership of Palestine. The prominent Iraqi Jewish poet Me'ir Basri put his opposition in blunt terms: "If Israel had not been established, nothing

---

*Iraqi Jews had welcomed the Balfour Declaration committing to a Jewish homeland in 1917—a welcome that was based far more on theory than the actual desire to move to Palestine at that stage.

would have happened to the Iraqi Jews. They could have stayed as any other religious minority."[14]

Young Iraqi Jews were attracted to the ideas put forward by the Zionist movement—of independence, equality, and a better life in Israel. Women comprised 30 percent of Iraqi underground members; it wasn't just based on national liberation, but on social liberation too. But young Iraqi Jews were also attracted to other nascent movements, such as the Communist party and the National Democratic party, the friendlier of nationalism's two branches. The Zionist organization in Iraq seemed unimpressed by this development. The emissary Enzo Sereni wrote: "There are already some who say that there is no need for Palestine, that everything will work out locally at the end of the war with the victory of Communism. Enlightening informational activity will be needed in this regard to show the rightness of our path and the socialist value of our Zionist solution."[15]

He was right to be worried, because Zionism and communism were fishing in the same pond: young, educated, secular Jews seeking a solution to their threatened status. Communism offered a socialist-nationalist solution in Iraq; Zionism presented a socialist-nationalist solution in Palestine. Formed in 1934, the Communist party gained momentum; by the 1940s it was organizing openly. In 1946, the party, excluded from parliamentary politics, set up the Anti-Zionist League (AZL), comprising Jewish members. One account of that period notes: "A Zionist meeting in 1946 was attended by three dozen people while *al-Usbua* [the AZL's daily newspaper] was printing six thousand copies a day."[16] The AZL generated a public debate in Iraq, clarifying a distinction between Zionism and Judaism, something that the Zionist underground seemed intent on blurring—part of its modus operandi, as an illegal organization, was to store arms caches in synagogues. The Jewish general secretary of the AZL called Zionism a "colonial phenomenon" and said "Jews have no cause other than that of their surrounding societies."[17] One AZL leaflet accused the British, collaborating with Zionist leaders, of wanting to "divert the Arab struggle against the colonialists to one against the Jews, and to create a rift that would enable them to go on exploiting the Arab people."[18] But then Russia's sudden, about-face decision to support the UN's 1947 partition plan (and therefore support the creation of a Jewish state) undermined communist parties in all Arab countries, who were as a result seen as obliquely serving the Zionist cause. That was the excuse that the antidemocratic government used to crack down on communists and, ironically, on the Anti-Zionist League, too.

In December 1949, the *Jewish Chronicle* in Britain surmised the Iraqi position: "Sassoon [Khedouri, chief rabbi] and those Baghdadi Jews with anything to lose dislike Zionism because it has brought them misery," an editorial on 30 December read. "They and their kind would like to stay. They are attached to their homes, traditions and the shrines of their Prophets,* and would not like to leave them in order to begin once more in an immigrant camp in Israel, where they believe people are not particularly friendly to Oriental Jews."[19] Despite the restrictions of the war period, Jewish community leaders thought their

---

*The Jewish prophets Ezra, Ezekiel, and Daniel are thought to be buried in Iraq.

difficulties in Iraq would dissipate, especially since they expected that there'd be a peace agreement between Israelis and Palestinians. Even during the worst of it, some Iraqi Jews remained reluctant to prize their two identities apart. The same year that the Jewish businessman Shafiq Ades was hanged, Ezra Haddad, a Jewish scholar and translator, wrote a front-page article in *al-Bilad*, declaring: "We are Arabs first and Jews second."[20] The director general of the Finance Ministry, Ibrahim al-Kabir, had a few years earlier, in 1946, said: "The Jews of Iraq do not feel that they have a problem which must be solved through outside assistance . . . They do not feel the need to emigrate to Palestine, to America, or to any other country."[21]

On several occasions, the Zionist underground sought the assistance of the Jewish community and was refused it. In the summer of 1944, Iraqi officials intercepted letters to Palestine that contained damning information about the Zionist movement's organization in Iraq. This was the first concrete proof that Iraqi authorities had on the underground movement it suspected of inciting against the Iraqi people and smuggling individuals into Palestine. The Iraqi police began a sweep on the basis of the new information, arresting and interrogating Zionist members. Amid accusations of police torture, the Zionist movement asked the well-positioned Jewish lawyer Yusuf al-Kabir and other community notables to help. They didn't. The Zionist emissary Yehoshua Givoni wrote: "Our demand . . . was that the chief rabbi go to the Interior Ministry and demand that he put an end to the whole business. The community decided not to intervene; in its opinion, this was not a general Jewish matter at all, but a political Zionist one."[22] Then the Zionist movement tried to place its teachers in Jewish schools, but community leaders endeavored to block it. One Halutz* member wrote: "The community executive is opposed to Zionist work among the Jews and the Jews themselves are not interested in it."[23] The movement did not have much success in this respect: thirty out of four hundred Baghdadi teachers in 1948 were Zionist supporters.

In 1949, an informer gave more incriminating details to the Iraqi police, who came down heavily, arresting dozens of Jews. The Zionist movement again appealed to Jewish community leaders for help and was initially refused, but then the chief rabbi, Sasson Khedouri, did get involved. If police unearthed the movement's arms cache, it would have devastating consequences for the entire Jewish community. By then, the community perception was of a police system persecuting Jews, a view encouraged by Zionist action. Halutz literature in circulation at the time read: "In the name of Arabism and Islam, behind the screen of nationalism and slogans, and on grounds of Communism and Zionism [Prime Minister] Nuri al-Said is acting . . . to tighten the noose around the Jews in Iraq through humiliation, beatings, and all sorts of tortures, for no wrongdoings or sin other than being Jewish." The chief rabbi was perceived as being old-school and out of touch—again, perhaps a view perpetuated by underground activists. Rabbi Khedouri resigned in December 1949, to be replaced by the Zionism-friendly Heskel Shemtob.

In the Babylonian Jewry Heritage Center in Israel, there is a large, detailed re-creation of a Baghdad street, where Jewish and

---

*The Zionist movement in Iraq had two branches: Halutz was for information and educational activities; Haganah was the defense wing.

Muslim shops are located side by side, testimony to a shared life. But this jars with the overall exhibition text theme, which intimates that Jewish life was forcibly separate. Jews, one section of the display reads, set up institutions for education, health, and social services because the Iraqis denied them such services. "What's this about no Jewish access to education? Your father and uncles graduated from government high schools," one cousin in the States points out. "Your uncle and aunt went to the Royal College of Medicine in Baghdad, both tuition-free. Your uncle and two other Jewish graduates (the top three graduates that year) were sent to England to specialize at government expense. Two more of your aunts graduated from public high schools." Of all the lies about life in Iraq, pronounces my cousin, this is the worst. For while there were harsh restrictions on education in 1948, prior to that the Jewish community was an integral part of the state school system.

When a community is portrayed as isolated, discriminated against, and reliant on its own resources, something gets lost. In the binary narrative of Arab and Jew—polar opposites, permanent enemies—there is no space for the voices of those who experienced something different. And voices don't have to be insulated by privilege, former communists, or otherwise members of the left wing to speak of difference. Emmanuel Paamon, a seventy-seven-year-old from Or Yehuda, was old enough when he left Baghdad to have gone through the Iraqi state education system. "I would sit in the class and read the Koran with them," he says. "And when the teacher would tell me that I should go outside [because Jewish pupils did not have to study Islam], my classmates would say, 'Leave him alone, he is one of us, a boy of our house.' So I learned the Koran, I would say, more than the

Hebrew Bible. I learned their mentality, and I would say they loved me." Years later in Israel, the son of a friend who was a Hamas leader from Gaza was leaving to study abroad and presented Paamon with a parting gift: the Koran. "He told me that I would remember him with it, because I had learned and loved it." Paamon defines himself as Jewish and a Zionist ("heart and soul") even back in Iraq. But this doesn't sever his consciousness from an essentially Arab childhood, nor does it foreclose an appreciation of the Koran as a linguistic, cultural, and theological work—which is perhaps also why Paamon doesn't view the gift as an attempt to convert him. He just doesn't recoil from this affinity between himself and the Arab world: Paamon watches Arabic cable TV until the small hours and was recently gripped by an Arab poetry contest broadcast from Abu Dhabi. He's also a big fan of the Arabic version of *Who Wants to be a Millionaire?* It is hard not to smile at the vision of Paamon, a composed-looking man, shouting the correct answers to Arabic history and culture questions at George Kurdahi, the program's suave Lebanese presenter, on the Saudi MBC channel.*

This is not uncommon for the older generation of Iraqis in Or Yehuda, who turn on to Arabic culture sometimes more than Israeli. And, despite the Farhud, the pro-Nazi sentiments of the ultra-right, and the pre- and wartime persecutions in Iraq, Or Yehuda residents do not always try to then "write history backwards"† and tar the rest of their experiences in that country.

---

*Started in 2002, the show is a big hit on cable TV and noted for its inclusion of veiled female contestants, a new thing for Arab TV.

†Sociologist Sami Zubaida's phrase, although he uses it in the context of the history of political Islam.

"Believe me, it was excellent," says Naima, who was seventeen when she left Iraq in 1951. "We got along, and how. Believe me, it was a pleasure. They would come and make tea for us on the Sabbath!" Several Iraqis in Or Yehuda mention religious events in this context, of Muslim neighbors aiding the process of keeping Jewish customs, while both faiths shared in each other's weddings and holy celebrations.

Naima is another one of those Iraqis who, still fluent in Arabic, tunes in to the neighborhood's TV channels. "What do the Israeli channels have, except crying?" she asks. Iraqi-Israeli writers such as Haim Khattan and Nissim Rejwan describe a Baghdad that moved to the rhythms of the Jewish calendar, market traders shutting shop on the Jewish Sabbath, the city involuntarily closing down completely for the Jewish Day of Atonement. These accounts give the impression that the Jewish community did not function as an isolated adjunct, but rather as an integral part of Baghdadi life. It sounds like the sort of unselfconscious plurality to which modern cities aspire.

What's also missing from the isolationist narrative is the intellectual blossoming of generations of Iraqi Jews, in part as a result of integration into the wider community. That experience is encapsulated by someone like Sasson Somekh, professor of Arabic literature at Tel Aviv University. He began his linguistic career writing Arabic poetry in Baghdad, where he was born in 1933. He is living testimony to the period of modernization that swept sections of the Jewish-Iraqi community and smoothed a cultural and intellectual integration with non-Jewish contemporaries. Once cultural sensibilities are set, they can't always be switched off just because your new nation is at war with your old one. Professor Somekh remains immersed in Arab literature, translating hundreds of works into Hebrew, reviewing them for Israeli newspapers. He counts the now-deceased Naguib Mahfouz, Egypt's most respected fiction writer, as one of his great friends. The two were bound together by literary passions that pole-vaulted over testy national boundaries, much to the annoyance of the wider Egyptian public that did not approve of Mahfouz breaking the unofficial cultural boycott imposed on Israel.

Similar intellectual imprints are alive and well within Shimon Ballas, an Iraqi-born writer, engrossed during his childhood in the literary traditions of both West—which he read in English and French—and East, in Arabic. A proud product of that, Ballas doesn't place anything beyond a geographic and linguistic significance on his current nationality. "I came from the Arab environment and I remain in constant colloquy with the Arab environment," he says. "I also didn't change my environment. I just moved from one place to another within it . . . I see myself as part of that [Arab] world while at the same time being deeply involved with life in Israel. I just moved from Arabic to Hebrew." Critics have noted that Ballas is essentially an Arab writer, now writing in Hebrew.

That the Iraqis might not have been dancing in the streets following the exodus of the Jews is a theme employed by Ballas in several of his works. Right at the beginning of his first novel, *The Transit Camp*, set in Israel, its protagonist recalls a Muslim acquaintance from Baghdad: "Hajji Hussein is a man the like of whom are not many," the Iraqi Jewish character says. "May Allah bless his memory! He told me: 'Oh Abu Fuad, don't go! You will regret it!' "[24] A short story, "Iya," is narrated entirely from the viewpoint of a Muslim maid to a Jewish family, who nursed and loved children whom she then saw pack up and leave for

Israel. The story depicts Iya living within, and being intimately familiar with the customs of, a Jewish environment. Through her eyes, the sudden mass departure of Baghdad's Jewish community is strange and saddening. She can barely bring herself to watch her adoptive Jewish family pack up to leave, "preparing for a new life, journeying far away from her, and she is only watching them from the side and no longer has a place in their world."[25]

These fictional characters appear to have real-life equivalents. Naima in Or Yehuda says that her parents left Baghdad ahead of her, since her husband wouldn't sanction her migration to Israel along with them. "I saw an Arab woman in the street, my mother used to sew her clothes," says Naima. "She said to me, 'Your mother has gone to Palestine and our hearts hurt.' And she started to cry." Even as the situation for Jews in Iraq became practically untenable, that didn't always manifest itself in personal relations between Muslims and Jews. "There was no fight between us over what was going on in Palestine," says Naima. "We didn't feel anything in our village—they respected us and knew that we were not to blame." Another Iraqi-Israeli, Avner, talks of how his Muslim friends—with whom he went on trips and played sports—would try to discourage him from leaving: "They would say, 'Don't be stupid, there is nothing for you to do in Israel,'" he recalls. "They tried in every way to get us to stay—it was easy for them to work and prosper with us."

Despite everything—the unraveling of lives in Iraq, the mass, impoverished departure, the relations since between Iraq and Israel, the brutal descent of Iraqi life from dictatorship to a postwar terror zone—Jews who once lived in Babylon have a stubborn loyal streak. "Of course I still love Iraq," says Najad. "If you told me tomorrow that I could go, I would do it." Najad re-

minds me of my father's "I am Iraqi!" declarations, although he
and Najad are a world apart. Their sentiments stir deeper than
exilic longing; illogical, but somehow more substantial than nos-
talgic mist. These former Iraqis are fundamentally tied to their
birth country. I can't find a better word for this sentiment than
"patriotism."

Past the vibrant Baghdadi street replica at the Babylonian
Jewry Heritage Center, there's a room-sized mockup of Baghdad's Great Synagogue, the largest in the city. It's a captivating
work, beautifully rendered, and around its sides are glass-cased
displays of objects from the tables of Jewish religious festivals, in
the Iraqi tradition. One of them details the all-important
Passover festival, which is when (optionally from Basra) date
syrup comes into the spotlight for Iraqi Jews. The exotic dark
syrup is mixed with crushed walnuts to create the haroset of the
Seder table, symbolizing the mortar that Jewish forebears used to
build pyramids during their Egyptian slavery. Admittedly, this
nutty brown cement is a tricky foodstuff to re-create in plastic.
On display behind a glass case in Or Yehuda, the fake date delight is sad and musty-looking—and it appears to be covered in
a film of dust.

Chapter 5

TALK THIS WAY

COLLEAGUES WOULD TELL me that, whenever one of the producers at my former station heard my programs, she would grimace at my accent," says radio journalist Yael Tzadok. She's currently on the air for Reshet Aleph, one of the Israel Broadcasting Authority (IBA)'s public service radio stations. "Had I been speaking in the Ashkenazi accent, my way to radio and television programs could have been easier," explains Tzadok. "But I've chosen not to do so." That hasn't prevented her success in broadcast journalism. Still, an Israeli of Yemeni origin, Tzadok thinks that she may be the only serious national radio host to speak "Mizrahi" Hebrew: "My accent reflects who I am: an Israeli Mizrahi woman. I wouldn't like to blur that." Tzadok airs a highbrow program on Reshet Aleph comprising interviews and literary reviews. Her accent, although quite mild, is distinctly audible on the radio—Oriental tones, rolling over the airwaves.

Upon arriving in Israel, I check into a Hebrew literacy class, intensive for those who can already speak the language, at a local *ulpan*. These are city-wide language schools, free to the stream of Jewish immigrants arriving from all over the world. They are in constant use; only half of the population of Israel speaks Hebrew as mother tongue.* It's at this school that I first hear an explanation for the standard Israeli pronunciation of the national language. Picking out certain letters, a teacher explains: "The Mizrahi communities, they pronounce this letter the right way. But it is not the way it is pronounced in Israel today." By the time native Israelis learn the alphabet, there is no need for such distinctions. Children, by the age of five, speak in the only accent that qualifies as Israeli Hebrew. And this accent has no remaining trace of the guttural Oriental sounds that are an acknowledged part of the original Hebrew language, as the ulpan teacher says, but which seem to offend people like Tzadok's former producer. Mizrahi Jews, at very least the ones who were born in Arab countries, do still speak Hebrew studded with gutturals. But to be honest, this accent has become something of a joke.

Gutturals are the letters that signpost Hebrew's roots as a Semitic language. They feature in Arabic, the exact same letters, called gutturals because they sound as though they originate somewhere deep in the digestive tract. Coming from the back of the throat, like swallowing while speaking, for the letter *ayin,* which starts the word "Aman"; more gently, as though trying to mist a mirror, for the letter *het* (its Hebrew name), which begins "Hamas" and ends "Fatah." These letters, which remain a part of Hebrew script, have been flattened out of the pronunciation. These days the *ayin* sounds like a regular "A" and the *het* is spoken hard like a German "ich" or a Scottish "loch." There's a rolled "R" in Arabic, but its sister language has swapped the same letter for a flat French-speaker's consonant. And the

*This figure includes Israel's Arab population.

guttural "Q" sound, heard in Arabic, has completely disappeared from the Hebrew.

The result of all this swallowing of sounds is that there is no longer a tonal similarity between these two languages, as there should be. There's another loss, too—of sound variety within the Hebrew language itself. Originally a phonetically distinct language, Hebrew writing is now taught systematically, although the spelling would, in its correct pronunciation, be self-evident.

Linguists lament another outcome: If words with different meanings—denoted by different spelling and pronunciation— are spoken as one, they eventually come to be used for the same purpose. So a nuanced vocabulary gets stunted. "The Ashkenazi accent flattens Hebrew, narrows it and, worst of all, makes it confusing and vague," says Tzadok. "Hebrew has become a crippled language that needs crutches in order to be understood by its own speakers. Only a society with no self-dignity can cause its language such damage, such a deformation in order to pretend to be what it has never been, what it will never be." But whatever the complaints, the immediate upshot of all this is that Hebrew is not widely considered by those who hear it to be a beautiful language. Tzadok's speech is melodic and easy on the ears, but within Israel it registers as an archaic oddity, even while at the same time it is acknowledged as correct. The sort of Semitic soundscapes that people romanticize—much as they do actual Romance languages—are now held to be the exclusive territory of Arabic. And the final twist in all these linguistic contortions is that Israel's founders really wanted the nation to talk using Tzadok's tones.

"We have a garment with a few stains, but after all it is a beautiful, good garment, it warms and covers the body," one Israeli linguistics professor responds to my seemingly undue preoccupation with the accent—the stains. He urges that, despite the erasure of the gutturals, one should not forget the wonder of the Hebrew-language revival in Israel. Supposedly lying dormant (beyond its use in synagogues, to read the Bible) and vying with Latin for dead-as-a-dodo status, Hebrew, the legend goes, was revived by Zionist pioneers who returned the Jewish tribe to its ancestral home replete with its ancestral language. It's a comfortable legend, using broad brush strokes to paint the Hebrew language renaissance into an overall picture of a kind of authentic Jewish resurrection in the mother land. But it is not entirely accurate, since Hebrew was in use before its supposed year zero: "pure Spanish" Sephardi Jewish inhabitants of Palestine spoke Hebrew long before the first wave of Zionists arrived in Israel; the Jewish renaissance in Western Europe in part comprised the learning of Hebrew.

Still, like one of those dusty robots that suddenly goes sentient in sci-fi movies, the Hebrew language rapidly multiplied its composites during the period of revivalism. Today, the once sparsely used language is employed in composing reams of poetry and literature, rhyming hip-hop, teaching yoga, posting to Facebook. And those ulpans, meanwhile, are bringing Babel-like classrooms at least to the level of ordering falafel or getting a job waiting tables in the national tongue. But the trouble is that these, like the nursery schools and like the overarching linguistic environment in Israel, are ensuring that in the space of a few generations, the original Hebrew accent will be erased completely. Then the language revival will have suffocated the Hebrew that belongs to the region, part of a Semitic family that has been disowned.

Israelis who spoke their first words in Arab countries do still pronounce Hebrew gutturals. Sometimes their children do too, especially in peripheral areas where the vast majority of inhabitants came from the same country. In mixed-origin, more central locations, children might talk in the Mizrahi accent at least until they get to school, and then they cut it out. Tzadok, for instance, remembers that in her youth, she perfected a modern Hebrew accent: "I went to a school with many Ashkenazis and I felt very strange talking the way I used to talk," she says. "I felt like I had to hide my gutturals." Tzadok just wanted to speak like everyone else did. "And I guess it was a process that took months or years," she says. "Until one day my father said to me, 'Why do you speak without the *het* and *ayin*?'" Tzadok reverted to her original Oriental accent after completing university, reclaiming the pronunciation that she had previously tried to obscure. "I met a Yemeni girl who had just come to Tel Aviv from some village," recalls Tzadok. "She spoke with guttural Hebrew that sounded to me like a beautiful, rich music. I suddenly became aware of the treasure I had thrown away, and immediately I decided to reclaim my original accent. It took me some time to relearn the guttural sounds, but I persisted until it became natural to me again."

Tzadok's daughter does not talk like her; the grandchildren of Middle Eastern–born Jews almost without exception do not speak with a Mizrahi accent. It is not just that the accent is now the "wrong" one for Israelis; it has also been marked as inferior: low-class, comedic, common. On one Internet forum, a poster seeking information on the Mizrahi Hebrew accent is informed by an Israeli respondent: "This pronunciation, although proper, is not common, and native Hebrew speakers who use it are

often labelled as 'Arsim.' " That's from the Arabic for pimp,
used to denote a chunky-gold-chain-wearing, near–trailer-trashy
type.

But for a long time, the Mizrahi accent was desirable. Israel's
founders thought it authentic, rootsy, and biblical—acoustically
consolidating the claim to the land and a return to the source. At
the turn of the twentieth century, inhabitants of Palestine spoke
Yiddish if they were Jews from Europe, or Arabic if they were
anyone else (and also Ladino if they were Sephardi Jews). The
official national language, under Ottoman rule, was Turkish.
The Brits, naturally, shifted the region to their native tongue—
which is maybe why you can sometimes find elderly Palestinians
speaking perfect Queen's English. Jewish state-builders first
agreed that the national language would be Hebrew and not
German—as Herzl had wanted—or Yiddish.* Then Eliezer Ben
Yehuda, the man credited with reviving the Hebrew language,
insisted that it be spoken in the correct, original accent. Under
consideration were the accents in which Hebrew was spoken in
a religious context—there had developed a distinct Ashkenazi
pronunciation of Bible readings, which was closer in sound to
the languages of Eastern Europe, and, conversely, the Sephardi
reading which, immersed in the Middle East, hung on to the authentic Hebrew sounds.

Ben Yehuda and other purists pushed their preference at the
Committee for Language meetings which, in 1913, declared that
the Sephardi (Mizrahi) accent would be officially adopted. There
were reportedly protestations from other committee members

---

*Language revivalism was then a component of nationalism across Europe,
   although clearly Hebrew fared much better than, say, Breton or Irish.

that the guttural accent was unnatural and unpronounceable. But this was dismissed as rubbish—there is no accent that cannot be learned, assuming the desire to do so. The mouth is configured to create certain sounds by the age of twelve, at the latest, settings that are precise to the millimeter. Switching these is, granted, an onerous task, but mouth muscles can be reconditioned just like any other. So, for example, while the language committee was discussing the issue, there lived in Palestine an achingly puritanical group of European Jewish settlers who had already practiced the accent until they had it down pat. This same group, which settled in the Galilee region, also learned Arabic and wore Arabic-style dress—wanting, they had claimed, to be a part of the region and assuming that they would be sharing it with the Palestinians already living in it.

The declaration in favor of the Mizrahi accent meant that all officials would speak it. So during Mandate times, IBA's predecessor, the Palestinian Broadcasting Authority, would not let anyone near its microphones unless they talked guttural Hebrew. The preference for this accent is still written into the IBA's mandate, although nobody, except for Yael Tzadok and a few veteran newsreaders, still uses it.* However much Mandate-period Jewish officials wanted to enforce the Mizrahi pronunciation, it just wasn't feasible to dictate it from above. Jewish migration during those pre-state years was coming mostly from Russia and Germany. These populations couldn't pronounce the gutturals and wouldn't learn them, either. In part a result of the constant, mounting collisions with the Arab region, hostility to

---

*Talk show presenters on commercial channels do sometimes speak in the Mizrahi accent.

all things "Arabic" developed and began to prize the Hebrew accent away from its Semitic sister. Vladimir Jabotinsky, the founder of right-wing revisionist Zionism,* made this pronouncement in an essay on Hebrew in the 1930s: "There are experts who think that we ought to bring our accent closer to the Arabic accent. But this is a mistake. Although Hebrew and Arabic are Semitic languages, it does not mean that our Fathers spoke in [an] 'Arabic accent' . . . We are European and our musical taste is European, the taste of Rubinstein, Mendelssohn, and Bizet."[26]

This distinction gained more resonance when Mizrahi Jews—those annoyingly non-Europeans—arrived in Israel, en masse, after 1948. Coming from Arabic-speaking countries, they spoke Hebrew with its native gutturals. In some cases, Oriental Jews would write Arabic using the Hebrew alphabet, since the latter was more familiar to them from religious schooling. Guttural Hebrew, with the mass migration of Mizrahis, soon became a marked accent—it acquired certain associations. If Mizrahis were deemed to have come from countries of an inferior culture, their accent naturally fell into the same category: uncivilized, low-quality, and low-class. If there was a climate of derision of the Mizrahi communities at that time, the accent too was mocked.

Aspects of the Sephardi style of speech have been preserved in modern Hebrew: the choice of which syllables—first or final—to stress, for instance. It is also true, as linguists hold, that there is nothing inherently wrong with accent changes—language is fluid and should adapt to its users rather than force them to conform.

---

*More militant, more territorially expansionist than the mainstream Zionism of the time.

Still, cutting Hebrew from its Semitic origins disconnects the language from its genealogy. It also disconnects Mizrahis—from themselves. What does a child think about her origins when her grandfather's accent is laughed at? What would happen if Yael Tzadok just went with the flow and abandoned her troublesome accent? "I would be lying to myself," she says. "I would be denying my identity, or lose a part of it."

The marking of the Mizrahi accent occurred through a series of social forces, just like those operating in other countries to similar effect—we form impressions about accents according to what we absorb from media and social and cultural outlets. And we are all hypersensitive to accent: it is the first trick used by comics and parodists the world over, precisely because accent usually has unambiguous associations. In Israel, one of those opinion-forming forces, the national theater, did not have much good to say about the Mizrahi accent. Founded in Moscow in 1918, the Habima theater company settled permanently in Tel Aviv in 1928. Since 1958 it has been Israel's official national theater—the title affording not just prestige but also public funds. In this capacity, the theater initially turned away Mizrahi actors who possessed the "wrong" accent. One of them was the Iraqi-born Arye Elias, who studied acting at an academy in Baghdad and was a regular in classical theater performances in Iraq thereafter. The Habima theater did give him one role—as a judge, who said nothing throughout his performance.

Elias, who feld from Iraq in 1947, was told that his accent was "inappropriate," and especially so for Shakespeare's plays. The actor wanted to play Shylock, but the theater deemed that this Jewish character should speak Hebrew in an Eastern European accent. It was apparently the same story at the Cameri, a well-known repertory theater in Tel Aviv: they loved his acting, but not the accent. He was given one role as a muezzin—the mosque official who chants the call to prayer—and another silent role. The Cameri Theater has a reputation for reaching out to Israel's Arab population, putting on many performances with simultaneous Arabic translation, setting up a "Peace Experience" project that brings Arab and Jewish audiences under one roof, a cultural step toward coexistence. This liberal-minded theater naturally does not object to Arabs speaking Arabic; but it considered Semitic stresses inappropriate for Hebrew—and did so precisely at a time when cultural establishments such as theater were shaping a common, accepted accent. If a certain pronunciation is absent from a "high-culture" forum, this practically marks the accent, by default, as low-culture.

Yossi Alfi, who now heads the Community Theater, a multicultural touring platform for performances otherwise pushed into the periphery, recalls directing the musical *The King and I* at the Cameri Theater in 1985. A piano teacher of Russian origin was training the cast children, who came from the Mizrahi-dense neighborhood of Schunat HaTikva, a suburb of Tel Aviv. "He was teaching them diction," says Alfi. "He was a newcomer, then in the country for two or three years, and he was teaching this group of Israeli-born children the right Hebrew diction!"

The actor Elias, meanwhile, was employed by the Labor Union, at his own initiative, to take drama workshops in Israeli-Arab villages and cities, and to direct Arabic-language plays.. He later became a star of Israeli cinema, where he is still to be found performing today. Cinema in the 1960s was not so uppity on accent and had far more roles for Mizrahis, requiring its actors to utilize the gutturals. Quite commonly at first, Ashkenazi actors would be cast as Mizrahi characters, thereby proving, perhaps unintentionally, that adopting the guttural accent wasn't so tough after all.

Film is a hefty tool in the kit-box of a country trying to forge a common language. (Song, arguably the multifeatured power tool in this context, is discussed at length in the next chapter.) The Israeli professor Ella Shohat wrote a comprehensive book about Israeli cinema in 1989, charting how it portrays concepts of East and West. She notes that when the first Hebrew talking film, *Sabra*,* was released in 1933, it was to an enthusiastic reception that acknowledged a symbolic moment in the revival of Hebrew. There was less glee over the screening of films in Yiddish. When *My Jewish Mother* (*Mayne Yidishe Mame*), an American-Yiddish production, opened in Palestine in 1930, Hebrew-language fundamentalists stink-bombed the screen and protested until a compromise was reached: the film was screened with the sound off. Since the goal was to get everyone speaking in the same tongue—this being one of the basic definitions of a "nation," according to Ben Yehuda—linguistic deviations were not tolerated.[†]

Mizrahis were very rarely featured in early cinema, which dealt in the "self-important idealism"[‡] of the pioneer period and depicted this via blond, fair-skinned European characters. Then a new genre of films developed: "bourekas," named after the cheese- or vegetable-filled pastries associated with the

---

Sabra is the Hebrew for "prickly pear" and a description of a native-born Israeli—like the fruit, spiky on the outside but soft and sweet on the inside. Seeing this fruit in situ is almost certain evidence of a former Palestinian village, since those natives cultivated the fruit around their homes.

[†] This concern was still a factor by the 1950s, when the famous Yiddish comedy duo Dzigan and Schumacher initially struggled, despite their popularity, to find platforms in Israel.

[‡] As described by myjewishlearning.com.

Ottoman Empire and brought to Israel by its former subjects. Bourekas films, featuring Mizrahi lead roles, were panned by the critics as cheap, low-quality productions. But they were adored by the Mizrahi population, who attended screenings in droves and created blockbuster ratings. Now considered to be cult classics, the mention of one or two of these films in particular can have third-generation Mizrahis in rapture.

Quite glaringly, this genre was created almost exclusively by Ashkenazi filmmakers. Boaz Davidson, one of them, explained the film material and landscape: "Bourekas films deal with our local folklore in its different colourings . . . Why is it bad to deal with ethnic groups and ethnicity? After all, this is our situation. There are Ashkenazis and Frenks [pejorative for Mizrahis] and they don't like each other. Period. This is a fact and there is nothing we can do about it."[2] Although they represented a breakthrough in terms of having dark-skinned characters take center stage—a big deal considering how absent these figures had been up until that point—Professor Shohat reports that bourekas films did end up perpetuating certain stereotypes. These inevitably forged certain associations between accent and personal disposition; accent and social standing.

Sometimes, watching these films and the exaggerated caricatures they rely on, it looks as though Israel went through something resembling a *Black and White Minstrel Show* period of ethnic-cultural representation.* Bourekas films were created at

---

*The *Black and White Minstrel Show* screened on BBC TV from 1958, for twenty years. It featured white actors "blacked-up" in makeup and was immensely popular for its tightly choreographed song-and-dance routines. By the seventies, the cultural insensitivity and offensiveness of such black caricaturing was made evident and the show was dropped.

around the same time that the Minstrels were on TV. A good
example of a bourekas film—even though it preceded the genre
and was filed as such retroactively—is *Salah Shabbati*, a satire by
Efrayim Kishon. Of Hungarian descent, Kishon was one of Israel's best-loved comic writers; his death in 2006 was widely
mourned. *Salah Shabbati* charts the experiences of a Mizrahi
family in one of the transit camps to which mass immigrants were
initially dispatched. It's not clear from which country this Shabbati family originates, but it is definitely somewhere in the Orient, as denoted by the family's dark features, Arabic dress,
tastes—and, of course, accent. In fact, all the clichéd Oriental
Jewish signifiers are present: a large family, which the father can
barely keep track of; a patriarch who doesn't like work, preferring instead to fritter away his time on backgammon and the
money his children earn on arak. He also possesses a simple, un-
sophisticated logic—a classic stereotype.

This childlike rationale is the cinematic device used to expose
the hypocrisy and corruption of the Ashkenazi characters—the
transit-camp social worker, the neighboring kibbutz members,
and a series of corrupt political-party officials. Such lampooning of the European-Jewish-dominated infrastructure is what
redeemed Kishon from accusations of discrimination: he actually came down on everyone.* The film ends with the redemptive
solution that Professor Shohat reveals to be a feature of other
films of this genre: Shabbati's two eldest children marry kibbutz

---

*According to Ella Shohat, who authored *Israeli Cinema*, Prime Minister Golda
Meir was especially horrified at scenes depicting Jewish National Fund officials taking different U.S. donors to the same newly planted forest, each
time switching the name signs to suit the donor. Meir opposed sending the
film to Hollywood on this basis.

members (Ashkenazis), thereby ensuring that they, at least, will have a smooth passage into Israeli society. At that time, the older migrants from the Middle East were defined as the "desert generation"; for them there was no hope of salvation in Israel, although their children were expected to fare better.

Social climbing is similarly the reward for the eponymous hero of *Casablan*, a popular musical comedy from 1973, in which the lovable rogue Mizrahi hooks up with a beautiful, elegant Ashkenazi woman. This happens after it is revealed to the audience that Casablan, although a dodgy character, has a patriotic heart of gold: He once risked his life to save that of an army superior. Another Mizrahi movie hero, the Moroccan-born Ze'ev Revah, starred in the film *Charlie and a Half*—classic bourekas and a hit. Revah played the protagonist Charlie, a grocer from Jerusalem's open-air market, who has an affair with a high-society Ashkenazi woman behind her doctor husband's back. These, and a dozen other films just like them, establish the Mizrahi character: as petty criminals; bumbling, big-hearted policemen; market-stall traders; jokers; hustlers and hookers. Since they all talk in a Mizrahi accent, the associations become hardwired: low-class loveable rogues; lazy and irrational Orientals; incompetent but good-natured souls. Some of these appellations clearly aren't negative, but so many of them denote inferiority.

Anecdotal research—just watching Israeli TV, as opposed to studying it—creates some immediate impressions. There are few dark-skinned newscasters, anchors, and current-affairs commentators, although Mizrahis do host chat shows and lifestyle programs. If there is negative Mizrahi stereotyping in dramas and sitcoms, then it is no longer denoted by accent. Meanwhile, the standard-bearing, correctly accented newscasters, anchors, and reporters long ago dropped the gutturals. "In the early sixties, the media was almost isolated from the way in which ordinary people speak," says Yaron London, a veteran Israeli journalist, highly regarded and part of the national furniture. "There were no telephones and no recording devices [in the context of phone interviews and reporting], so the people in the markets could speak in their way while we, the 'preachers of the correct Hebrew,' could speak as we wished, as the teachers," he explains. An improvement in communications technology brought broadcast journalists in touch with the hoi polloi. "Now that's not possible—the elite cannot predict or order how the language should be spoken." London comments that he still uses the Sephardi accent to pronounce words over which there might otherwise be confusion, or for public poetry recitals, when he employs "all the treasures of the language, all the possibilities." With a natural actor's command of accent, London immediately switches to Sephardi speech patterns if he is talking with an Arab person, he reveals.

TV satire programs do still mock Mizrahis using that accent, but they poke fun at everyone, and accent is one of the best ways to do that. Curiously, though, Yossi Alfi relates that a top satire program, *Eretz Nehederet* (Wonderful Country), gave the actors playing him and a well-known Mizrahi-origin singer guttural accents even though neither actually speaks in one. Some social theorists say that there is still a gross underrepresentation of Mizrahis—and, come to that, Arab-Israelis, Ethiopians, Russians, and the Orthodox sector—on white, male, Ashkenazi-dominated, elitist TV. Most agree that in the past, the situation was much worse.

TV got to Israel late, in 1967. This is partly because Israel's early years were of austerity, and partly because David Ben

Gurion shunned it for so long. He thought TV would be a bad influence. He also stopped the Beatles playing in Israel on the same grounds. Critics say that he finally ended the TV blockade out of concern that surrounding Arab nations had acquired square-box habits a few years earlier.* Israel didn't want to be the techno latecomers, plus it perhaps wanted to match the propaganda output. Until the early 1980s, Mizrahi faces were barely seen on TV. There was only one public-service channel until 1992; Channel One is remembered as being high-minded, hegemonic TV with education content by day, high-brow European culture by night, and a religious slot closing each day's broadcasting. When the right-wing Likud party came to power in the late seventies, its shattering of the Labor party monopoly extended to the media, which became more representative of the Rightists' voting base, the Mizrahis. That's the odd thing about Israeli politics: leaving aside the impossible-to-leave-aside Palestinian issue, the Left is seen as the traditional, elite, establishment party; the right wing, although typically populist, was the underdog for ages and still carries something of that heritage.

Some argue that the Mizrahi accent, when it came to TV beyond its news content, was habitually marked as negative: "Not one child who is black and spoke with a Mizrahi accent didn't have a whore for a mother, or a father who beat them because he drank too much arak," says Yossi Alfi. "Once, the Mizrahi characters were the idiots, the hoodlums, and the *ar-sim*." During the 1980s, Alfi wrote a children's TV series, *Schunat Hayim* (Hayim's Quarter), which he describes as *Sesame*

---

*Egypt, Syria, and Lebanon got TV in 1959; Jordan a year after Israel in 1968.

Street without the puppets. The way he tells it, the year *Schunat Hayim* took to the screen, as part of an education TV remit, schoolchildren's sick days were at record high levels—the kids were faking illness to stay home and watch their favorite program. The thing about *Schunat Hayim* is that the Mizrahi characters were not negative stereotypes. "We created a lot of noise," says Alfi. "It was the first time children spoke with *het* and *ayin and* were very clever!" A wide stride for the positive promotion of the guttural accent, says Alfi, although he now thinks that it created just a small dent on a landscape that continues to be racist. When teachers were polled for opinions about the program, they expressed dislike because they thought it lacked credibility.

"I would like to strongly protest after watching the Tuvia Tzafir children's video, which I bought about a week ago . . . for my son, aged two," wrote Dorit Algobi to Hed Artzi, the makers of *Grandpa Tuvia*. Starring Tuvia Tzafir, these popular productions, based on a TV series, regularly tour the children's theater circuit too. It's not hard to see why kids can't get enough of the Grandpa. Tzafir is a gifted storyteller who narrates legends and fables, accompanied by a troop of children; there's plenty of song and dance, and it's all set in enchanting environments with all the right attention to costume and scenery. But Algobi's letter points to a problem with at least the first *Grandpa Tuvia* video in January 2004. "During a second, more profound viewing of the tape, I was astonished to discover an ugly, primitive phenomenon, and it particularly upset me to find it in a children's video," she wrote. "Among the range of characters that he presented beautifully, Tuvia Tzafir chose to present all the negative characters as Sephardim." She provides details. There's the ant and the grasshopper, an Aesop fable where the ant spends the summer gathering food for winter while the grasshopper sings the summer away. In Tuvia's version, the grasshopper has a Mizrahi accent and idles his time with Oriental songs and a darbuka (Middle Eastern drum) at the local drinking hole. Similarly, says Algobi, the fox who breaks through a hole into a vineyard, feasts on grapes, and then has to starve himself thin enough to get back out again, has a Mizrahi accent—associating the Oriental tones with a "wily, greedy, and lazy" character. There are other examples provided, all of the same stereotyped and negative use of the Mizrahi accent and all confirmed by watching the videos.

Grandpa Tuvia is so obviously a child-loving production that it is hard to accuse its makers of malicious intent. They probably just didn't think about it. When I ask both Tuvia's manager and PR company about this accent-led character profiling, they both respond that they "do not understand the question." Maybe they don't, but it is doubtless this sort of incidental stereotyping that builds a set of assumptions about Mizrahi and standard Israeli accents, about the Orient and the West. The program is not the cause of, but does contribute to, an ambient environment, so that it's eventually of no surprise to hear ten-year-olds pronounce, for example, a dislike of a character from a popular TV soap on the basis of her Mizrahi accent—even one that the character uses only occasionally, as a sort of knowingly comical device.

On TV and radio today, environments where practically everybody speaks standard Hebrew, the Mizrahi accent is mostly heard on advertisements. Or at least, on certain ads: coffee, hummus,* cleaning products, supermarkets, the national lottery, post office, and national phone company. Advertisers, whose concern for the bottom line outweighs any regard for political correctness, use the Mizrahi accent to denote the common person: decent, honest, and reliable. But there is a limit to what the common touch can convey. "Once a big bank asked me to read for a commercial on the radio, and I used the Sephardi accent because it is clearer," says Yaron London, the veteran Israeli journalist. "The director told me not to speak like that, and I immediately understood . . . if you want to make a commercial for a bank, don't use the Sephardi accent because the Sephardi accent is not respectable enough."

Dorit Dayan of Bar Ilan University put together the first—and, thus far, only—academic research on the subject of stereotypes in electronic advertising, from 1957[†] to 2000. She reports that the stereotyping has remained exactly the same, except for the fact that it worsened with the introduction of commercial TV in 1994. First off, Mizrahis are underrepresented in ads. When they do appear, they are more often of a low status and of low professions; they are more vulgar and dress in louder clothing than the Ashkenazi characters that populate Israeli ads. The latter group are usually of a higher status, more often wear suits and glasses, and advertise cars, banks, educational courses, and other

---

*Yossi Alfi recently took out a court injunction to stop a top hummus brand from running a TV ad he contests is blatantly based on his *Schunat Hayim* show.

†1957 was the date that ads began to be featured during cinema screenings.

high-end products. Just under half of all Mizrahi characters on ads reviewed by Dayan bore a Mizrahi accent, often exaggerated. The Mizrahi product-peddler typically mispronounces words and puts gutturals in places where they shouldn't be, which is just idiotic: anyone who speaks Mizrahi-accented Hebrew clearly knows exactly when to pronounce a *het* or an *ayin*.

To be honest, after a while in Israel these stereotype biases toward the Mizrahi accent begin to creep into my own responses. Because so many people who speak it in public are in the working class, I start assuming it's a low-skilled, laborer accent. Because so many characters who speak it on ads come over as buffoons, I start connecting it with idiocy. Because so many Mizrahi voices I hear are raising social conditions, I connect it with complaining. When my parents visit, I'm mildly shocked and bemused at their Mizrahi-accented Hebrew because they don't fit the stereotypes. An unfortunate form of social orientation has taken hold. Previously, I'd thought the accent melodic and hadn't attached a status value to it. Now the same impression requires a conscious effort.

In a kebab-falafel joint in Tel Aviv, in late summer 2006 just after the Lebanon war, two Arab-Israelis, owner and customer, are talking. A chilled-out, long-haired Tel Aviv sababa type strolls in, orders, moves to the salad bar, and tuts back in their direction: "You shouldn't speak Arabic here," he pronounces. The two men look at him, exasperated, and fall silent. Never trust a hippie, I think, turning to ask him: "Why not? It's the language spoken here, of the region—which, in case you hadn't noticed, is the Middle East." A tiny flicker of irritation flashes across his face before the default setting of ambivalence resumes. "No," he responds, turning back to the salads. "I hadn't noticed."

Arabic isn't just the language of the region; it's the language of the nation's 20 percent Arab-Israeli population. It's also the mother tongue of Mizrahis old enough to talk while they lived in Arab countries. And Arabic is officially the second language in Israel, which means that all official communication, all road signs, all government ministry documents (ID cards, passports, driving licenses), and all national information lines are legally required to be written or spoken in both languages. Also, the two languages are theoretically compulsory at school. In practice, Hebrew is compulsory in Arab schools and Arabic is taught in Jewish schools* between the ages of thirteen and sixteen, with an opt-out clause if pupils choose another third language—which the vast majority do.† It isn't compulsory to sit a matriculation exam in Arabic, as a result of which only 7 to 8 percent of Israeli Jewish students wind up with certificates in the language. That percentage is immediately of interest to the Army's intelligence recruitment department, thereby perpetuating a perception among the Palestinian population, both within and without the borders of Israel, that only spies speak Arabic.

Yacoub (Jacob) Alali, an Iraqi-born Israeli, remembers this about life in the new Israel: "If I was just walking the street or on a bus, and I said, '*Ya'ani*' [Arabic for "So to speak"], people

---

*During the nineteenth century, the Jewish philanthropist Montefiore donated £200, back then a sizable sum, to the teaching of Arabic in Ashkenazi schools in Palestine. The money was sent back; the schools didn't want to teach Arabic.

†English is the second language taught at schools, from the first year. French, Russian, and German are third languages.

would say, 'No speaking Arabic!' " he relates. "Did anyone tell the Russians not to speak Russian? And you hear 'Shhh' when you speak Arabic, like they are talking to a horse! I am asking my friend how do I get to the health center, or how do I get to this or that bureau. How will I ask him if not in Arabic? Suddenly, it's 'Shhh, no speaking Arabic.' "

In areas where Mizrahi communities were concentrated, many did keep speaking Arabic and passed particular dialects of the language on to their children. So Moroccan Arabic, in its Jewish dialect, can be heard among families in Sderot, for instance, and Iraqi-Jewish Arabic in areas such as Or Yehuda and Petah Tikva, both satellite towns of Tel Aviv. It's usually just to conversational level, no literacy skills, a patchy remnant of the language their parents possess fully—and the oldest of all Jewish Diaspora dialects. Their native language survived, people supposed, because in these homogenous areas there was nobody to say "Shhh!" Alali's experience was perhaps more typical in mixed-community areas, where kids didn't learn the language from their parents. Often, children would feel embarrassed that their parents spoke Arabic. So then they became the ones to say "Shhh!"

In those early years, there was a near-fanatical drive to get everyone speaking Hebrew—part of the whole nation-building enterprise. As demonstrated by the cinema stink-bomb incident, Yiddish speakers weren't exactly encouraged to carry on talking in their native tongue, either. And scores of Ashkenazi-origin Israelis recall being raised in an ambience of disdain for that language—something that Yiddish revival groups in Israel are now seeking to redress. But on the other hand, many Israelis still remember the words of Golda Meir, Israel's prime minister from 1969 to 1974, as she greeted new immigrants from Russia in

1973: "You are the real Jews . . . You speak Yiddish! Every loyal
Jew must speak Yiddish."[3] So then what does that make a Jew
who speaks Arabic?

While language fanatics tried to ban Yiddish from public
spaces—and, come to that, tried the same with the Ladino spoken by Sephardi communities—that didn't stem the use of Yiddish in official circles. When Aharale Cohen, the historian from
Sderot, trawled the Zionist archives in Jerusalem seeking early
Jewish Agency records, he found them to be only partly written
in Hebrew. "Some of the protocols of the agency I read were in
Yiddish," he says. "You get to a certain point and then go,
'Oops, I can't read any more.'" It is with this sort of occurrence
in mind, presumably, that Ella Shohat observed: "Yiddish,
through an ironic turn in history, became for Sephardis the lan-
guage of the oppressor, a coded speech linked to privilege."[4]
That perception was laid out earlier by the Iraqi-born author
Shimon Ballas. In his first novel, *The Transit Camps*, a Mizrahi
living in one of these camps despairs that her prayers to leave it
would never be answered because "The God of Israel is also
Yiddish!"[5]

There exists a tangible lack of regard for the Arabic language
in Israel, an air of "Well, unless you work in the security services,
it doesn't really matter." In January 2006, Shimon Peres visited
Doha, Qatar, for a round of World Trade Organization talks, the
first time that an Israeli official had visited the country. Back
then, he was Israel's longest-serving politician, twice prime minister, winner of the Nobel Peace Prize, and founder of the Peres
Peace Center. Now he's also the nation's president. Israeli TV
showed him taking an evening stroll around the night market of
the Qatari capital. A market vendor calls out a greeting to Peres,

who replies, in Arabic: "Good morning"—although it was 9 P.M. Israeli TV commentators joked that Peres probably exhausted his entire Arabic vocabulary in the next, embarrassed-looking relay of words—"How are you?" and "Thank you"—to a stall-keeper.

By his own definition, the eighty-seven-year-old Peres has spent a political lifetime working for peace with the Palestinians and the region. Amir Peretz, the Moroccan-born former leader of the Labor party who does speak Arabic, has been routinely ridiculed for his bad English. During the election campaign of 2006—which, had Labor won, would have put Peretz in the position of prime minister—it was widely commented that his lack of English would be a liability in such a role. It was never observed, as he toured Arab countries and especially Morocco, that Peretz's linguistic range might be an asset. Former French prime minister Lionel Jospin and current president Nicholas Sarkozy do not speak perfect English; former Spanish and current Italian prime ministers José Maria Aznar and Silvio Berlusconi both require English-language interpreters. If nations actually within Europe don't consider it such a big deal that their leaders speak English, why should Israel?

The universal language has cachet—financial, cultural, and professional—whereas there is no perceived advantage to knowing Arabic. The cultural vaults of the region remain sealed shut to all but a few Jewish Israelis who do learn the language and consequently enjoy the myriad treasures laid open to them as cinematic, musical, and literary output from the Orient is decoded. With only three* Arabic-speaking nations having diplomatic relations with Israel, there is limited economic benefit to

---

*Jordan, Egypt, and Mauritania have diplomatic relations with Israel.

fluency in the language. Still, it's a missed opportunity, if only from a practical perspective: professors of both languages hold that Hebrew speakers would find it easier to learn Arabic than would natives of another tongue. The two languages conjugate in a similar manner—the words build, especially the future, in the same way. Both are characterized by words formed using "root" letters—the foundations of a word, built upon according to meaning, tense, and gender. One linguist says that he was astonished to find that 63 percent of words in biblical Hebrew share the same root letters in Arabic. Literary scholars of Golden Age poetry, written in Hebrew by Jews in Spain from the eighth to around the twelfth century, have remarked on the clear influence of Arabic in the syntax, grammar, and composition of these works. Centuries later, the Hebrew-language revivalist Ben Yehuda reestablished this influence: writing the first Hebrew dictionary, he looked to Arabic for grammatical inspiration.

Dr. Meir Buzaglo teaches philosophy at the Hebrew University of Jerusalem, where he initially confused students with the sort of guttural accent they were more accustomed to hearing at the city's open-air market. Moroccan in origin, he says: "It would be easier not to create a contrast between Hebrew and Arabic—there is a different system of phonetics at the moment, and this is not good for life and for being together here." This current system forsakes all the internal relationships that exist between the two languages. "There really is a connection between them," he continues. "So there are a lot of similarities and of course similarities in the pronunciation. Once I create this way of speaking Hebrew [without the gutturals], then I am creating gaps and tensions." The outcome, he says, is this: "I know that when I speak Arabic and turn to Hebrew, or when

I speak Hebrew and turn to Arabic, I have to put in a new system, change the cassette. It is like two different beings." Like many keepers of the Mizrahi accent, Professor Buzaglo does not insist that his children also speak it—to do so would make him "a real fanatic, a fascist," he says.

Some Israelis say that the nation is in fact regional-language–friendly, pointing to the abundance of Arabic words used as part of the Hebrew language. No doubt to the disdain of the purists,* modern Hebrew has absorbed hundreds of foreign words, on long-term loan, into its own collection, borrowing mostly from Yiddish, English, and Arabic. Since the Hebrew language is relatively small and spoken in so many cases as a second language, word-loaning was inevitable. Especially in the early years of the language, according to Rubik Rosenthal, who pens a weekly Hebrew-language column in a popular daily newspaper and has written several books on the subject. "Yiddish became the basis for Hebrew slang in the twenties and thirties," he says. "It was used for humor or slang—Yiddish is a folk rhythm language and so fits this function." Those days, he says, there was an unanticipated trend of using Arabic slang as well. "They were speaking Palestinian Arabic . . . young Israelis wanted to imitate or be influenced by the people who lived here for generations, who are part of the area, men of the field, close to the ground," he explains. "It looks very odd because they were enemies, but until 1948 they were not only enemies but also neighbors."

Nowadays, says Rosenthal, author of a dictionary on Hebrew slang with another one on idioms in progress, Arabic has

*Former Prime Minister Ariel Sharon once had a go at Israelis for using an English-Arabic amalgam to say good-bye, instead of the Hebrew.

surpassed all other languages in its assimilation into Hebrew. Much of that is in the arena of swearing. On a popular enter- tainment program a few years ago, a field reporter polled passersby on what they considered to be the most Israeli of expressions, and one colorful Arabic curse came in first each time. Slang, says Rosenthal, just like foreign word loaning, is a spontaneous phe- nomenon that cannot be controlled from above. The Academy of the Hebrew Language, which guards the native tongue, issues new additions when the need arises—a new word for "hi-tech," for example, or "e-mail." But the population often does not adopt these newly minted words, preferring to stick to the English loans.

Israelis are very comfortable using Arabic as slang, but Rosen- thal suggests that it is telling when and how they choose to do so. Take, he says, the very common usage of an Arabic derivative, *basa*, when a term for "too bad" or "bummer" is re- quired. The original Arabic word means something like "spin on this"—a strong obscenity that, as Arab-Israeli posters to In- ternet talkbacks testified, would never be used with such casual frequency by native Arab speakers. "We don't feel that we iden- tify with Arabs when we speak Arabic slang," surmises Rosen- thal. "We simply feel that it is a fitting part of Israeli slang." In other words, there is a total disconnect between slang and the language culture from which it originates.

There seems to be a sorting system determining the place- ment of loan words from other languages. Rosenthal points out that there is no Arabic slang in arenas of high culture, or high- status professions. Arabic features heavily in the lexicon of drug culture, although, as the drugs become more international in origin—ecstasy, LSD, and cocaine as opposed to grass or hash—

so too does the terminology. German words and idioms are a feature of the construction domain, because the industry was initially dominated by Jewish migrants from that country. English words are used by car mechanics, since the Brits brought the motor engine to Palestine during the Mandate years. Looking at various subgroups within Israeli society, Rosenthal found only one in which Arabic vernacular was dominant: in prison, where majority populations are Arab or Mizrahi-Israeli.

The true status of Arabic in Israel is more accurately revealed by looking at another language, Russian. Following the influx of around eight hundred thousand migrants from the former Soviet bloc in the 1990s, the Russian language is a healthy, thriving feature of Israel. There now exists in Israel one commercial Russian TV channel, one public service Russian radio station, two commercial Russian radio stations, and around ten Russian-language newspapers. Russian culture commentators say that, aside from the sheer size of this community in Israel, one potential reason for this is a strong linguistic tradition, reliant on newspapers and the dramatic arts, at a time when mainstream Soviet sources were rigidly conformist. Although the Russian immigrants of the seventies felt the need to hide their mark-of-origin accents while talking Hebrew, the later ones do not do so. Many help-lines, such as for national travel information, have recorded menus in three languages: Hebrew, English, and Russian; if it's two languages, then the English is often dropped. Cyrillic scripts are seen alongside Hebrew on ingredient lists and instruction leaflets for household items. Needless to say, all this Russian on the scene is a positive development: a reflection of pride in this sizable community's cultural clout. Such public confirmation is glaringly absent in the Arab-language sector, even though they are a larger community than the Russians, more so if we include with Arab-Israelis the Mizrahi Jews who are Arabic-literate. A population that ought publicly to prize a strong linguistic tradition, a language that wordy people rave about for its depth and scope, does not feel a capacity to do so in the Jewish state. Drop into an Internet café in Haifa, and the point really hits home. Frequently lauded as the best example of a mixed Arab-Jewish city, Haifa's Internet café computers have English, Hebrew, and Cyrillic alphabets running on the keyboards, despite the fact that Haifa has the largest Arab population of any Israeli mixed city.

In 2005, the Mossawa advocacy center for Arab-Israeli citizens ran a series of short ads on Israel's Channel Two. A spoken greeting in Arabic was followed by the Hebrew: "We just wanted to say 'Good morning'" or "We just wanted to wish you a happy festival." The ads might as well have said: We just wanted our language to be heard as a neutral form of communication between neighbors, as opposed to a cause for suspicion among enemies. It all depends on where it happens and what type of wind the conflict turbines are generating that day. "If you sit on a bus and talk on your telephone, all the bus looks at you aggressively and you feel you can't talk Arabic," says Jafar Farah, director of the Mossawa center. Israelis who speak Arabic in public places say that, perhaps prompted by a sense of betrayal, the response they receive can sometimes be worse.

Chapter 6

EVERYONE DESERVES MUSIC

A T T W O A.M., mid-June and the middle of a wilting heat wave in Tel Aviv, I'm led through a sticky, pizza-scented restaurant kitchen. Mizrahi chefs are watching cable TV and dealing with the dwindling requests for food. It's the staff entrance to a central city nightclub, past the queues and the scrutiny of the main doors. Inside, we go straight upstairs to a bar overlooking the bigger main one below, and just as we make it, "Fire" by Moshe Peretz starts up over the speakers. There's a whoosh of delight, clapping along to the tune, and a surge of feet onto the floor, tables, and bar-tops to dance to this anthem track. There seem, if looks can be relied upon, a lot of Mizrahi faces here tonight, or mixes—I'm with a fusion Yemeni-Hungarian chef. And they're all going wild for the pop track, a few years old now but still a hit, still described on radio as the song driving the nation crazy, every word known, every beat proposed to. It's the standard euphoria of any bar in the small hours of this city.

Tel Aviv nights are often high-adrenaline, high-volume, and high on hedonism—wanting not just to fit the "unexpected capital of cool" label awarded it by *Time* magazine, but to

morph it into "entirely expected and recognized party central."
It's like a deep wish to be regular, coupled with the intimate
knowledge that this country is not. But on this overheated summer night, when the Peretz track comes on, there is something
else coming up loud over the standard ebullience, another emo-
tion riding high, giddily proud: validation.

"Fire" is one of the iconic tracks of a Mizrahi music explosion, at first blacked out of the mainstream and now, arguably, a
healthy part of it. Arguably, because some industry heads and
musicians say it is still discriminated against and others hold that
the prominence of Mizrahi music in Israeli society signals this
community's biggest breakthrough into the mainstream, proof
that cultural discrimination is firmly located in the past. The
Moshe Peretz track is not too emphatically Oriental in sound,
but it has enough of the requisite motifs to label it "Mizrahi."
Peretz himself is of Moroccan origin—the name, if not the
bleached-out anodyne pop-star CD covers, is a giveaway. But
that doesn't mean much per se, since many Israeli performers
have Middle Eastern roots and give the Mizrahi style a wide
berth. More indicative of the genre is that Peretz's voice quivers
in the style of an Oriental singer's and that his accent is Mizrahi
(other performers of this genre use both Hebrew and Arabic).
He sings over a very faintly Oriental quarter-tone melody—
music from the Middle East utilizes notes in between the ones
on a Western scale, tones that can sound strange to an unaccus-
tomed ear. The Peretz track is played by Eastern instruments
such as the oud (the Middle Eastern guitar) and darbuka drums.
All this is layered over a prominent Greek-style rhythm section
and electric guitar picking out a high-pitched, bouzouki-
inspired lead. This curious, hybrid pop is the Israeli heir, off-

shoot, or best-case survivor of a Judeo-Arab music legacy spanning thousands of years. And hearing this song on the multi-
stacked sound system of a Tel Aviv club represents a victory
moment for Mizrahi music makers and its fans, precisely because
this music was unofficially banned from the national airwaves
and laughed at for so long.

Middle Eastern Jews came to Israel with ears tuned to an
Oriental frequency, set to appreciate the complex half- and
quarter-tone arrangements of the East. They were—and often
remain—dedicated fans of Arabic musical legends such as the
Egyptians Umm Kalsoum and Mohammed Abd-Wahab, and the
Lebanese Farid al-Atrash. The possession of a stack of battered
cassettes by these Middle Eastern performers or the ability to
sing along to the best known of their recordings is a giveaway
mark of origin. Mizrahis share this passion with the nation's
Arab population (and, nowadays, with many European-origin
Israelis who also get this groove). But at one point, the music
was scorned and hushed up, decreed as belonging to the enemy
camp and considered low quality—like all things Oriental. Masters of the music, top-league singers and oud players, composers
and violinists, Jewish immigrants who had once played for kings,
who in Iraq during the 1950s formed 90 percent of the nation's
professional performers—these musicians were overlooked in
the new country, their talents undervalued and underexposed.
The music didn't die, because you can't quash or reconfigure
deep-seated culture settings. But, unable to find it on the national loudspeaker, fans listened to the Oriental cassettes privately, while performers played at local parties—given the Arabic
name *hafla*—and community events. Scores of older-generation
Israelis describe listening to their music in secret, picking up

Arabic stations on backroom radios. Their children recount how they would veto this music, embarrassed by it, urging their parents to turn it off.

Music, the example most often cited of a historic cultural discrimination in Israel, is also a major component of national identity. During formative years, music probably helped forge an Israeli identity and almost certainly helped forge the national language. There are songs that all Israelis know, played on a loop during national holidays, especially sad ones like Remembrance Day (for Israeli fallen soldiers and victims of terror attacks) and Yom Kippur (a religious, fasting holiday), precisely because they signify nationhood and collectivism. Israeli folk songs, also known as Songs of the Land of Israel, are still covered by contemporary pop stars and sung verbatim by teenagers—decades after the tracks were originally released.

Right from the start, pre-state, Jewish settlers to Palestine were strong on song. Singing was encouraged in public and collectively, a way of getting to grips with Hebrew and communicating some core values. In their book, *Popular Music and National Culture in Israel*, Motti Regev and Edwin Seroussi, a sociologist and an ethnomusicologist, respectively, hold it to be widely acknowledged that "Music in general, and popular/folk music in particular, is a major cultural tool in the construction of modern national, ethnic and other collectivities and in the evocation of a sense of place."[1] Some Israeli folk lyrics are simple word plays. Others sing of building the nation, defending it, populating it, of loving the land and making it bloom. Others still reflect the national self-image as a country eternally extending the hand of peace to hostile neighbors. "When peace comes, we'll go by train to Damascus . . . when peace comes to Israel, we'll go skiing in Lebanon," is a refrain from Shlishiat Gesher HaYarkon's "Uksheyavo Shalom." Continuing the theme, these lyrics—"I was born for peace, if only it would get here! I was born for peace, if only it would come!"—are from "Noladeti La Shalom," another catchy, well-known song.* This particular refrain made bizarrely reassuring humming material during the second Lebanon war in 2006, a bitterly ironic coping mechanism pitted against the overwhelming national chorus for attack.

The musical score to these songs ruptured the "melting pot" theory of building a national identity. The goal was to create a new culture, Israeli, a new definition of "Jewish." Everyone's Diaspora heritage would be thrown into a large pot and melded to form this new Israeli culture. But fusion involves a presumption of cultural equality. In practice, the national culture was set to the tastes of the ones in power. And the soundtrack was Eastern European—comprising renovated old Russian, Polish, and Yiddish tunes. It was convincing, this melting-pot theory, so much so that the Israeli actor Asher Cohen (born in Morocco) has said: "I realized how things were one day when I found a record of the Red Army Orchestra. I was stunned to find that the Russians imitate Israelis in their songs. That's when I realized the cultural deception upon which I had been raised."[2] At first he thought, how nice, they've converted Israeli songs from Hebrew into Russian. Only later did he grasp that Israeli songs actually were based on the Russian.

If Oriental music featured at all during this early period, it was to provide an ethnic motif, in particular drawn from the

---

*"Noladeti La Shalom" (I was born for peace) was written and sung by Uzi Hitman, to commemorate the Israeli-Egyptian peace process in 1978.

music of the "authentic" Yemeni community,* which appeared as though it had arrived in Israel straight off the pages of the Old Testament. Several collaborations between Ashkenazi composers and female Yemeni singers made household names of the latter, the most popular of whom was Shoshana Damari, dubbed "the Queen of Israeli song."

The first recording of the new genre Mizrahi music came out of Schunat HaTikva, a satellite city of Tel Aviv, then full of migrants from Iraq and Yemen. Asher Reuveni, who later cofounded the Reuveni Brothers music label, taped his wedding celebration, held just after the 1973 war, so that his friends still serving on the front might share in it. The party, he recounts, went on all night, two hundred people in a two-room flat. The police were called because of the noise, but they just joined in the celebrations, and then the neighbors did too. That tape did the rounds and sparked an entire industry, whose genesis mainstream commentators then used as a way to deride the music. It was dismissed as "cassette music" (privately recorded or amateurish) and "bus-station music"—referring to one of the places in Tel Aviv where the music was sold from stalls. A massive success on the streets, the music did not make one mark on the mainstream. In the early seventies, there was only Israeli Broadcasting Authority (IBA) public service radio, one Army Radio station, and one IBA channel on TV. And they all blacklisted this music.

"One day I went to [the IBA radio station] Kol Israel," recalls Meir Reuveni, Asher's brother, from the record label's office in

---

*In a similarly prompted fusion, the "Yemeni step," a dance move associated with this community, is an integral part of the national folk dance, the hora.

Schunat HaTikva. "I said, 'Look, Elvis Presley, Tom Jones, and Frank Sinatra sell cassette music, does that make them low-quality? And who are you, anyway, to decide which music is quality and which music isn't? Are you a musicologist, did you learn in an academy?' " Still the music wasn't aired. The mostly Ashkenazi DJs and producers and presenters were sent countless songs, but the Mizrahi labels accuse them of using those records as Frisbees before binning them, unheard. There are stories of soldiers serving their three-year military duty as Army Radio DJs being threatened with kitchen shifts if they dared to air too much Mizrahi music, which was not on the playlists. Once, the producer kept to his word, sending the DJ down to the kitchen and bringing the chef into the studio. Regev and Seroussi, the Israeli pop music analysts, explain what was going on: "To the Western ear of dominant cultural producers in Israel, the sounds of Mizrahi music resembled those of Arab popular music; hence, this music was not a candidate for public presence. In other words, cultural power was the major determinant in the absence of Mizrahi music from radio broadcasting in Israel in its early years."[3]

Mizrahi music labels combined forces and protested, lobbying parliament until they secured a pledge to play a percentage of Mizrahi songs on IBA's music station. They couldn't do anything about commercial stations, of course. But by 1993, local radio stations had mushroomed and were championing the Mizrahi music cause. Still, as Army Radio's "Galgalaz" became the nation's favorite frequency, it remained almost entirely free of Oriental quarter-tones and guttural accents—the only time the station featured songs of this style was during its world music slots: the ethnic ghetto.

Nowadays the Mizrahi genre—also known as "music that makes you happy" or "Mediterranean music"—is ubiquitous at street markets, on cab-driver radios, at weddings and parties, on music TV. So accepted is the genre that contestants on *A Star Is Born*, the Israeli talent-spotting equivalent of *American Idol*, were required during one series' elimination round to sing a song in the Mizrahi style. Still, some of the genre's protagonists argue that the playing field remains hopelessly uneven, with essential compromises made to get this style accepted by the national palate.

One of the Mizrahi music industry's biggest beefs is over the categorizing of it as Mizrahi and not Israeli. The music is created locally, sung mostly in Hebrew, by native Israelis—so why the ethnic label? This is the point made by Avihu Medina, one of Mizrahi music's most prolific composers, who is of Yemeni origin. He is also a singer and the songwriter behind Mizrahi music's biggest breakthrough success, Zohar Argov. Dubbed the "king of Mizrahi music," Argov was the genre's hero, storming the music scene and achieving great commercial success despite not being played, initially, on mainstream radio. Argov died of a heroin overdose, aged thirty-two, in prison on rape charges in 1987. By that stage, a string of bands from the periphery—like Sfatayim, from Sderot—were bringing "ethnic pop" to center stage, a fusion of rock music with Oriental motifs. Medina, meanwhile, is still making music today, and does not consider his output Mizrahi. "My culture is not original Oriental; I am a mix," he says. "And that is the real Israeli culture, to be mixed. But they [Ashkenazis] want it to be pure European, Western."

The musician Yair Dalal is also battling the ethnic ghetto label. An oud player and violinist, Dalal is well known, having played at international music festivals such as WOMAD and having been nominated for a BBC Radio 3 world music prize in 2003. Of Iraqi descent, Dalal's sound draws on both Arabic and Jewish traditions of Middle Eastern music. In 1993, to mark the signing of the Oslo Peace Accords between Israeli and Palestine, Dalal was on stage in Norway to sing "Time for Peace," accompanied by a band comprising both Israeli and Palestinian musicians and a hundred choir-children from both nationalities. Behind them stood endless rows of Norwegian choral singers, fair, angelically white-robed, harmonic. Today, Dalal wants to know why his locally produced music is categorized "world" in Israel. "Irish music isn't called that in Ireland, is it?" he asks.

He studied with the old Jewish music masters from Iraq, who performed during the 1950s in the Arabic Orchestra of the Israeli Broadcasting Authority. This improbably named ensemble was featured on IBA's Arabic-language dial in once-a-week recorded performances. Dalal wanted to learn the Iraqi-Jewish musical traditions before it was too late, and is now passing this heritage on to students at his studio in Jaffa, the port city glued to the southern tail of Tel Aviv. "You teach a child of Mizrahi origin an Iraqi song, and suddenly something in their soul awakes," he says. "Afterwards, the child goes home and practices and comes back a week later and says, 'You know, my dad started to sing the song I was playing.' And that's the connection. That person is back on track."

Salim al-Nur, one of Yair Dalal's teachers, is an old friend of my father's—they studied together at Istanbul University, to which the Iraqi government regularly sent the nation's brightest students (although among them not my father or al-Nur). Al-Nur is in his eighties, living in Israel and still composing music. We meet one day at his central Tel Aviv flat, in a tiny room which he says is better for the music, because he can be intimate with it. We're surrounded by what look like thousands of cassettes, all neatly labeled, all in Arabic. Al-Nur, the experts say, represents the premier league of Arabic music composition, specializing in the Samai, a classical Oriental arrangement, the structure of which he taps out for me on the table.

His love for music was instilled in him by a family that would regularly invite distinguished musicians to play at their home in Baghdad. On several occasions, the Iraqi Jewish performers Salah and Daoud Kuwaiti played at the al-Nur residence. The Kuwaiti brothers, of Iraqi parentage, were born in the country of their surname and swiftly rose to fame in both nations. Their songs are still played today in the Gulf States. According to Salah's son, who lives in Israel, the Kuwaiti ruler Sheik Abdullah III al-Selim al-Sabah sent a limousine-delivered message to Baghdad airport in 1951, just as the musical brothers were boarding a plane to Israel. The ruler begged them not to emigrate, explaining that it would not only be a blow to Iraqi and Kuwaiti culture, but it would darken his own personal world too. But the brothers took the one-way ticket out of Iraq, never to return to that country or to experience such dizzying recognition for their talents.

These days, having been involved with the IBA's Arabic Orchestra, Salim al-Nur hosts weekly musical gatherings in a dilapidated trade-union building in a run-down suburb of Tel Aviv. It's a kind of all-Iraqi jam session, although they often focus on Egyptian classics. Sitting behind the musicians in the back row of a boxy room one day, I'm taken into the custody of a pair of smiling, sparkly-eyed women in their fifties. The women explain what's being sung and hand me morsels of food from the table: white cheese, long

cucumber slices, and pita bread in manicured fingers otherwise engaged in tapping out Oriental rhythms on tambourines and darbuka drums. Watching them, I immediately understand that my
mother, forever clapping a misfit, irregular beat over evenly synco-
pated Western tunes during my childhood, was simply marking out
a rhythm that I couldn't hear. The alien clapping is normal—
appreciated—in this room full of Iraqi Jews, in Israel.

These musicians are the vintage and quality of performers
that were cherished in their home country—whose music, ad-
mirers say, would move the audience to tears so copious that you
could water gardens with them. Here is Iman, considered a
queen of Arabic music, singing in Egyptian and Lebanese style,
frequently played on Arabic radio stations, she says. When she
was younger, in her musical prime, she enjoyed a Palestinian fan
base too. Here is Yacoub Alali, the man who was told to "Shhh!"
when he spoke Arabic during his early years in Israel. Alali,
seventy-four, is proud, straight-backed, masterfully in control of
his Arabic singing voice: sweet, strong, crystal-clear like his eyes.
Accompanying Iman and Alali is the musician Elias Shasha,
eighty years old and still debonair, his suit pressed sharp against
the scruffy walls behind him, wrinkled, spotted hands teasing
exquisite, meandering melodies out of the oud resting in his lap.

Yacoub Alali came to Israel in 1950, aged seventeen, but didn't
become a singer until the age of fifty, even though he'd wanted to
be one when he was much younger. Both he and Shasha were discovered by the Arabic Orchestra on IBA radio, performed live with
them for the half-hour weekly slot. Shasha traveled across the
globe with the Inbal troupe, an "ethnic" theater-dance company
set up by Sara Levi-Tanai, apparently when the national theater refused her on account of her Yemeni accent.

In early 2000, Alali played at a wedding in the Palestinian village of Salfit in the northern West Bank. The entire village was out on the street dancing to his song, Fatah men performing *debke** in long rows around him. Alali was initially afraid, he recalls, but they looked after him in Salfit and invited him to come again. He has composed and sent songs to the current Jordanian king, Abdullah, and his predecessor, King Hussein. He once performed in a club in Amman, where the crowd loved him and threw money at him. After he'd sung, a man from Saudi Arabia hugged him and the manager begged him to go onstage again. That was Alali's first time in Jordan—he had played to wild fans years before in Egypt—and he vowed that he would visit Amman every fortnight at least. Then the second intifada broke out and Alali didn't go to Jordan, or to Egypt, or to the Palestinian territories again.

In April 2007 I call Alali, and he is enthusing over an impending trip to Amman, breaking the five-year pause on travel to Jordan, where he hopes to perform in a club. It turns out that Alali and I will be in the country at the same time, and we start to coordinate. A few days later, Alali's voice is flat; the trip has been canceled. The Israeli Army has carried out a deadly attack in Gaza, and Alali's traveling companions worry that this would not be a good time to visit Jordan, home to thousands of Palestinian refugees. "I am not afraid," asserts Alali. "I sing to the enemy to bring them closer, to make them happy—so what?"

I often wonder if Alali, a naturally theatrical man, is exaggerating this brotherhood-of-Arabic aspect of his music. Then I

---

*Palestinian folk dancing.

meet a fan of his, in Ramallah. A friend of a friend, Nazim, tells me about the days prior to the second intifada when he worked for an Iraqi Jew in Ramat Gan, near Tel Aviv. They became friends, bonded in part by their love for Middle Eastern music, which they would go down to the beach together to play—the Iraqi sang like an angel. It has to be Yacoub Alali, and Nazim is delighted to discover that I know his Iraqi friend. Switching to fluent Hebrew, Nazim relates anecdotes of their times together, in each other's homes, at each other's family weddings, or just hanging out in Ramallah or in Tel Aviv.

For a few weeks after that, I become a messenger for the two, passing greetings between them ("Tell Nazim that we love him"; "Tell Yacoub and all his family that we love them, too, and wish them only health and happiness"). I wonder why they don't just talk to each other—if their politics are now too polarized, or if I am filtering out the frustration of their not being able to meet. Few Palestinians have the special permits that allow entry into Israeli areas. Meanwhile, Israelis are currently forbidden entry to most areas in the West Bank*—and, even if they weren't, would be afraid to go. The vast majority are similarly wary of visiting either Jordan or Egypt—which, along with Morocco and Tunisia, are the only Arab nations that allow visitors from the Jewish state. So for now, Alali and Shasha stick to performances within Israel. On one occasion that we meet, they are discussing a request from the Jordanian embassy in Tel Aviv

---

*Israelis are allowed into Jewish settlements of the Palestinian West Bank, but not into "Area A," nominally under Palestinian Authority control, or "Area B," where control over security is nominally shared by Israeli and Palestinian forces.

for a performance by Shasha, who wonders why the diplomats have chosen him. He remarks that there are plenty of excellent young Arab-Israeli musicians who might better fit the bill. "You know what they say about a Persian carpet," reasons Alali. "The older it is, the more valuable it becomes."

The Andalus Orchestra of Israel is also trying to develop a national audience. Founded in 1994, the orchestra comprises Western and Arabic ensembles seamed together: oud solos and heavy percussion; a stack of violins all playing the same tune; Oriental tones as staple. It sounds like Arabic classical music until the singing starts, in Hebrew, in its guttural pronunciation. In 2006, the orchestra won an Israeli prize for music, recognition of its presence on the national soundscape. It's a qualified success, say Asher Canafo and Motti Malka, then chairman and director general of the orchestra, respectively, when I meet them in Ashdod, on the southern Mediterranean coast, home of the Andalus orchestra. Both of Moroccan descent and steeped in cultures of both East and West, they speak a lush, poetic Hebrew with strong gutturals. The prize is great, says Canafo, but just the start. "We still have to work very hard so that we can get to the idea that things that come from the East are very good, just as things that come from the West are very good," he says. "We learned a lot from what the West brought to here—we learned almost only that—but I still don't see that the West learns from us what we know, what we have brought."

The orchestra's performances are based on *piyut*, prayers in song—dating back to the Gaonic period of around 690 C.E. and practiced in any part of the world where Jewish communities lived. These prayers are thought to have reached their highest level in Spain under Islamic rule, the Golden Age of Jewish religious and cultural development. Piyut traveled to North Africa in 1492—when Catholic monarchs expelled the Jews from Spain—and later moved with those migrants to Israel. Another strand of piyut, from the Babylonian era, was preserved in Israel thanks, in part, to Saddam Hussein. During the Scud missile attacks that Iraq fired into Israel in the first Gulf War, Menachem Cohen was a child seeking refuge in an air-raid shelter. His grandfather was down there too, not having a shelter of his own. Grandfather Cohen was one of the few people who knew a particular series of Iraqi piyut and recited them daily, in the small hours of the morning, in the family's Jerusalem shelter. The ten-year-old Menachem listened and learned and later became a *hazan*, a specialized Jewish liturgical singer. Only when his grandfather died did Menachem realize that he was one of the last people to know these prayers and ironically sent one to Saddam, who had unwittingly created the conditions for these precious liturgical songs to be passed on, ensuring their survival.

Jews and Muslims living in the same lands would often write different words of prayer over the same music. In another area of religious overlap, both faiths would also make pilgrimages to the same prophets, at burial sites in Morocco and Iraq. Menachem says that once, a friend in the States played him a prayer he'd heard on a documentary, from a Pakistani mosque. Menachem, already aware of the mutual melodies of Jewish and Muslim prayer, was stunned to realize that the Pakistanis were praying to the tune he knows as "Ya Ribon Alam," an Iraqi piyut* recited to bring in the Sabbath and which even an atheist might pronounce

---

*"Ya Ribon Alam" is thought to have originated in Iraq, although it has many versions all over the Jewish world.

a beautiful, spiritual song. "It was exactly the same, and they were singing 'O God the greatest' where we sing 'O God the creator of all,'" Menachem explains. "Four hundred years, and one doesn't know that the other is praying to the same tune!" Four centuries ago, the Jewish liturgical poet Rabbi Israel ben Moses Najara wrote the Aramaic lyrics for this prayer and set it to a popular Arabic tune of the time.

Once, I sit in on a singing group in Jerusalem, part of a revival movement with groups in several Israeli cities, that seeks to recover piyut in a secular setting—having realized that much Mizrahi culture is hiding in religious quarters. Listening to the singers learn a particular piyut, two lines taking two hours to perfect, it becomes obvious that the composition of these prayers is symphonic, defined: there are exact points where stretched consonants rise and fall to the complex melodies of the piyut. The Andalus Orchestra has taken these prayers out of the synagogue and displays them as classical music, precisely because that is what they are. Canafo and Malka, the orchestra's former heads, relate that it took eight years of performing until the orchestra received funding from the government culture department. They point out that there are over twenty publicly funded Western classical orchestras in Israel, but only one Mizrahi and one Arab-Israeli ensemble in Nazareth. Canafo adds that, much as they both love Western classical music, "With all due respect, these orchestras are not Israeli, are they? I mean, they play Mozart, Chopin, and Vivaldi. And many of the compositions are Christian creations." This, he emphasizes, is not intended as a criticism. It's just that the Andalus Orchestra, not venerated to the same degree as a Western ensemble in Israel, performs quintessentially Judaic arrangements.

"When we started the orchestra, we wrote that we hoped it would be used as a bridge of peace between Jews and Arabs," says Malka. "If I had to write that section again today, I'd write that the orchestra be used as a bridge between Jews and Jews—we need that, too." The orchestra has achieved this within its own ranks: many of its members are relatively recent immigrants from Russia. But the real measure of the orchestra's success, says Malka, will be when audiences of Ashkenazi origin start attending the performance in droves, as opposed to in a few instances. "I'm a Jew that came from the East and I have my heritage," he says. "My parents brought wonderful things with them . . . I want to save what was wonderful and to suggest it to all Israeli society, to say, 'Here, you enjoy it, too.'"

It's not just in the musical arena that Mizrahis feel underrepresented. During one meeting with the musicians Shasha and Alali, we are talking about the Israeli national poet, Haim Nachman Bialik. Widely considered a pioneer of modern Hebrew poetry, Bialik was born in the Ukraine and became a Zionist. His acclaimed poems provide a literary backbone to the Jewish homeland project. There's a statue of Bialik in Ramat Gan, a densely Iraqi suburb of Tel Aviv. "He is nothing to do with us, no, he does not belong to us," says Shasha of the national poet, who is rumored to have said: "I hate the Arabs because they remind me of the Sephardis." Alali observes, "He writes that he hates us and they put a statue of him here, amongst the Iraqis!" Elsewhere, Mizrahis profess admiration for the work of Bialik, but also a desire to learn as much about other poets. Some people express the sentiment that maybe there should be two national poets, one Mizrahi and one Ashkenazi, just as there exist in Israel two national rabbis, one from each community.

In other culture spheres, too, there are requests for more solid and sustaining platforms. The Moroccan-born actor Asher Cohen runs a Moroccan theater that puts on plays in the Jewish dialect of Moroccan Arabic, effectively an Oriental equivalent of Yiddish. The audience is necessarily narrowed by the theater's choice of language; there are an estimated eight hundred thousand Moroccan Jews in Israeli. But then so too are the audience figures for Israel's Yiddish and Russian theaters, both of which receive national funding—unlike Asher Cohen's company. When the director of the annual festival of Arabic dialects in Marrakesh, Morocco, saw Asher Cohen's theater perform once in Barcelona, he wanted the Jewish outfit to be featured in his festival. But on one condition: that the Israeli troupe describe itself as being from Palestine, not because it mattered to the director, he told Cohen, but so as not to prompt a boycott from Arab countries also performing at the festival. Not surprisingly, Cohen refused. A wide audience, one that would understand and appreciate the theater's work, was blocked off by a political checkpoint.

The Inbal dance theater, which the oud player Elias Shasha once toured with internationally, prides itself on performing a unique, Israeli fusion of East and West dance styles. "It's a new language," says the creative director of Inbal, Ilana Cohen. "The dancers are modern classic, the artistic understanding is Western, but our uniqueness is the material of movements and steps from the East." The theater, says Cohen, is standing still, treading water. With funds allocated partly on the basis of audience attendance, Inbal does not have the money for marketing, so nobody hears about them and the audiences stay small. This perennial problem of any small dance or theater company trying to make it bigger is viewed by Cohen through an ethnic filter. "I am certain it is cultural discrimination," she says. "I believe that if this [dance] language was developed somewhere else, it would have become a national theater by now, I have no doubt. The elite rules here, and they promote their own people and their own culture. They really want to be European, or American."

Disappointment at a lack of a significant Mizrahi cultural presence in Israel is sharpened by the knowledge that once, Judeo-Arabic creativity was in overdrive. While Jewish communities resided in Arab countries, they were enthusiastic contributors to a nascent secular culture. The founder of Egypt's first national theater in Cairo in 1870 was a Jewish-Egyptian nationalist dubbed the country's Moliere; the first Egyptian opera, in 1919, was written by a Jewish citizen, as, too, were dozens of films considered classics of Egyptian cinema. A member of the senate, one Egyptian rabbi was also one of the founders of the Arabic Language Academy. Legions of Jewish performers treaded the boardwalks in Cairo and Baghdad. Jewish musicians were adored, and not just in Iraq; in Egypt there was Layla Mourad, a singer and actress revered by the Arab world, chosen as the voice of the Egyptian revolution and later accused of spying for Israel. In Morocco, there was the legendary Zohara al-Fasiya, who sang for the king, and the master musician Rabbi David Buzaglo, whose son is the Mizrahi-accented philosopher now teaching at Jerusalem's Hebrew university. When Moroccan orchestra players had a technical query, it was to Rabbi Buzaglo that they turned for advice. Part of an intellectual elite, Oriental Jewish writers of the early twentieth century flourished, in Arabic. Authors such as the Iraqis Anwar Shaul, Shalom Darwish, and Samir Naqash had wide appeal until they left for Israel, where some of them continued to write in Arabic.

This gulf—between the prolific cultural output in Arab countries and a downplayed creativity in Israel—is understood to have one specific origin: that Israel's leadership was perennially paranoid about the possibility of the Jewish state sinking to a Levantine cultural level. There are myriad expressions of that, from the top. So, for instance, here is the England-educated Abba Eban, Israel's deputy prime minister in the 1960s: "The object should be to infuse the Sephardim with an Occidental spirit, rather than allow them to drag us into an unnatural Orientalism . . ." And also: "One of the great apprehensions which afflict us . . . is the danger lest the predominance of immigrants of Oriental origin force Israel to equalise its cultural level with that of the neighbouring world."[4]

There is nothing extraordinary about Eban's appraisal, and there are scores like it, from politicians and journalists at that time, all saying much the same thing: The Oriental spirit of the Mizrahi Jews, as manifested in their culture, was not welcome in the Jewish state. And while cultural doors have drastically opened in recent decades, the smell of this fundamental prejudice still lingers. Writing about the Russian migration to Israel of the 1990s, and welcoming it as a redress of the demographic balance between Jews from East and West, one journalist observed: "I still believe that given the choice between Paris and Baghdad, [Israel] will choose Paris. And I still believe that the more the distance there is between Baghdad and us, the better off we are."[5]

Today, the cultural battle continues, although perhaps less conspicuously. On the popular front, Mizrahi music has been widely successful; Israeli music journalists defined 1998 as the year of Mizrahi music. On the other hand, it is still patronized, considered common and low-quality. The accusations echo the description in George Orwell's *1984* of the manufactured, kitschy pop songs loved by the working classes. While this definition—insipid and mass-produced—could be applied to any commercial pop music from any nation, in Israel it seems to have stuck to Mizrahi songs.

Always, with this genre, there are dialogues over boundaries and inclusion—when is this music too Middle Eastern, too reminiscent of the enemy? When is it eligible for mainstream airing? In 2002, right in the middle of a series of Israeli military operations in the West Bank—curfews, arrests, killings—that preceded the reoccupation of Palestinian cities, a track by the Moroccan-Israeli singer Amir Benayun, a mainstream breakthrough artist, was played on a radio current affairs program. The track, "You're Gone," is sung in both Hebrew and Arabic. Tommy Lapid, then head of the liberal Shinui party and a guest on the program, responded to the airing: "I heard this song and I reached the conclusion that it was not us that conquered [the West Bank city of] Tulkarem, it was Tulkarem that conquered us." The comment sparked a furious debate on the connection Lapid had seemingly made between Moroccan Israelis and Palestinians. It brought that ever-present tension to the fore: what to do about these Israelis, essentially so close in culture to the Arab world?

Confusion over cultural capital swiftly segues into field battles, so that musicians such as Yair Dalal are still fighting for acceptance as Israeli artistes. In a film about his work, *Got No Jeep and My Camel Died*, Dalal is seen talking over the phone to the chief editor at the IBA's radio station, Reshet Gimmel, which has a policy of playing only Israeli music. This charter undoubtedly helped push Mizrahi music onto a national platform, but it has a fatal flaw: "It's very serious," says Dalal to the station's editor.

"Where did you get the policy that only Hebrew music is Israeli music? Who decided that the second official language in Israel, which is Arabic, will not be heard on Reshet Gimmel?" The countless Mizrahi tracks that feature Arabic are thus excluded from a public-service radio playlist. And that's not to mention the musical output of the 20 percent Arab population that, according to this station's remit, is not considered Israeli. In this context, Mizrahi culture creators who complain about underrepresentation have a lot in common with Arab-Israelis who describe experiencing something like a cultural genocide.

In the summer of 2007, Mizrahi artist Liran Tal released a single, "No End to Love," which became a hit on the local radio circuit. But the two mainstream stations, Reshet Gimmel and Galgalatz, with around 60 percent of the radio market share between them, rejected the song. Tal took his photo off the CD cover, changed the name of the track to "Always," changed his name to Sharon Keinan (an Ashkenazi surname) and credited the songwriting to a popular (Ashkenazi) singer, Arik Berman. The only thing that stayed the same was the song itself, which now instantly appeared on the playlists of the two stations. The story made the popular press, and the IBA, which runs Reshet Gimmel, issued a statement that it took the matter seriously and was looking into it. But for months after the event, almost every Mizrahi whom I interviewed about cultural discrimination pointed to this incident as proof that it is still very much in force.

Chapter 7

MADE TO FAIL

ONE OF THE striking things about the development towns with their majority Mizrahi populations is that there is, quite literally, nowhere to develop. Take Kiryat Shmona, where so many Moroccan-origin Israelis live on the Lebanese border in the north. It's a narrow, sausage-shaped town, hemmed in by a mountain range to the west and by kibbutz-managed land in every other direction. Kiryat Shmona, once the Palestinian village Khalsa, has twenty-five thousand inhabitants and fourteen thousand dunams of land. The surrounding areas belonging to the region's kibbutzes total 270,000 dunams. That's after the town petitioned for and was awarded two thousand dunams in 2000, released from the neighboring farms and marked for mostly residential development. Those fields are bogged down in lease terms and conditions that have prevented their use. Without land, the town can't build new houses or new businesses, the development of both being required to reverse the rate of residents leaving Kiryat Shmona. Sami Maloul, who works at the local council's planning department, says that land allocation isn't driven, but is influenced, by "ethnic issues." He explains: "It's all the historic legends of the early settlements and the fig leaf of agriculture that they ruled with, that gave them a stronghold on the land." Maloul uses "they" to refer to the people in control: the kibbutzes and European pioneers.

Relations with the "they" around them are a recurring theme in development towns. Historically, things have been a little frosty. Haim Uliel, the son of Raquel, one of the first residents of Sderot to arrive on the "boat to village" migration from Morocco, remembers this feature of his childhood: "When the kibbutzes had leftover apples, a surplus, they would dump them and pour petrol over them so that we wouldn't take them to eat or sell," he says. "They were just mean. To this day, if I have an apple, I can still smell the petrol." Uliel is the lead member of the popular Israeli "ethnic pop" band Sfatayim ("Lips"). A friend of his, also in Sderot, recalls that a nearby kibbutz would catch kids taking water from its land, pour the water away, and lock the children in a hut all day as punishment.

These assessments are a stark contrast to the idea of kibbutzes as Jewish socialist flagships, where the last thing you'd expect to see is acts of petty meanness. But in some Mizrahi circles, "kibbutznik," or someone from one of these collective farms, is shorthand for racist and hard-hearted. These farms never claimed to extend their socialism beyond the kibbutz. They had never argued that the entire country should work on collective principles, just their sections of it. But still, since Israel was supposed to be built as an integrated Jewish society, this doesn't exactly curb resentment from former hired hands, who relate how they were barred from kibbutz swimming pools, schools, and dining halls. Ex-employees don't believe these things happened because kibbutzes were trying to protect the ideology of the movement; they think that the drive was the ethnic superiority cultivated on those collective farms.

Kibbutzes, initially opposed to employing outside help of any sort, eventually found it necessary and hired workers from nearby development towns. The work was managed, if not always actually carried out, by the kibbutzes, so the farm movement took the glory for the toil, which generated a series of assumptions about who had "built the nation." A case in point is the draining of the Hula—one of the legendary achievements of the Jewish kibbutz/pioneer movement, famed for turning infested swamplands into productive farmlands. These days, much of the reclaimed Hula Valley is kibbutz-managed agricultural land. Prior to the 1950s, the area comprised peat-rich swamplands emitting all manner of noxious gases and breeding a virulent strain of malaria. Jewish settlers were not the first people to see the marshy lake and think "drainage," but they were the first to do it (with expertise and equipment supplied by an American contractor). At the time, the additional sixty thousand hectares reclaimed as a result was highly beneficial to the nation's development. Plus, it fulfilled objectives on two fronts: victory over pestilence, and land clearance. Two trophy-winners, these fit the double-edged Zionist narrative about Palestine, before Jewish settlement: not only was the land uninhabited, it was also uninhabitable.

Although the Hula drainage project did away with malaria and freed up great land, it wasn't an outright success. Around a third of the valley became the scene of a constant tussle between human and natural forces, which eventually led to the humans giving in and partially re-flooding Hula Lake in 1994. The dried land had proved too volatile; peaty lake beds fed a process of organic matter degradation in such a way that it would spontaneously combust in frequent underground fires, scorching the

land and turning the soil to dust. The phosphates and nitrates released from this temperamental valley seeped into the nearby
Lake Kinneret, a vital water source. Re-flooding to create the
artificial Hula Lake dealt with those problems and also spawned
a surprise outcome: migrating birds started treating the place as a
stopover on their travels between Europe and Africa. The project expanded accordingly, so that today it's a relaxed, eco-savvy
park, providing bed and board to around five hundred million
birds, a nature-lover's treat on the northern tourist trail.

Almost certainly the swamp-clearers had their own doubts
about the land at the time that it was drained. They were mostly
Moroccan and Tunisian workers from nearby development
towns. Lulu Nijar, in Kiryat Shmona, was one of them. "It was
just mud and water then, and malaria—and how!" says Nijar, in
a modest flat. "Of course it was dangerous, but that was our income," he relates. "Sometimes the land would open up and fire
would come out. Fire! About a third was okay, but the rest was
just rotten roots and mosquito eggs. If you stopped for one moment, the tractor would sink. We would drink milk every morning to clean the lungs—we didn't have masks then. It was
terrible work, but we had to do it." Nijar was twenty-nine when
he started this work in 1957, having migrated from Tunisia six
years earlier. Educated nearly to matriculation level, he "got
stuck" in early Israel, he says, because his Hebrew was poor. But
he did study in later years and now isn't bothered by the past:
"We received a low salary, but still we bought a house and raised
children," he says. "I am not one for grandiose things, I don't
need a villa. But I worked hard." The work he and others carried out cleared forty thousand dunams of arable land. According to David Sabah, head of the Hula Authority, which ran the

project until it closed—in debt—in 1973, the lands were distributed among the surrounding kibbutzes. Workers put up a four-
year fight to prevent the dismantling of the Hula Authority.
Kiryat Shmona and Hatzor HaGlilit, the towns from which
most of the Hula laborers came, campaigned to be allocated
some of that land. But the kibbutzes, it was argued, had a greater
need.

In Kiryat Shmona, Echiel Zafrani also remembers how things
were between the farms and the town. Careful to insist that relations today are better, much friendlier, Zafrani—who arrived
from Casablanca in 1959—describes an incident back in 1981,
when he was a bank clerk and also a local Likud party chief. As
part of the election campaign that year, the neighboring kibbutzes took out a full-page ad in the regional paper, in support
of the Labor party. "It was a cartoon of a donkey, covering the
whole page," recalls Zafrani, now in his sixties. "And Begin
[then leader of the Likud party] was riding the donkey, by
which they meant that he was riding us, the Mizrahis, taking advantage of us without our understanding." At that time, Begin's
election success was largely due to the Mizrahi vote. "Of course
the ad was racist!" says Zafrani. "Of course they meant the
Mizrahis, that Begin thinks we are donkeys, with no ideology,
nothing!"

Zafrani took out a full-page cartoon ad on behalf of the Likud
party, in retaliation. "I drew a big, strong gorilla and on its arms
and legs I wrote the names of the kibbutzes in the area . . . And
underneath I wrote, 'Kiryat Shmona, they are treading all over
you!' My response was worse than the donkey, I accept that." The
way Zafrani tells it, the local kibbutzes were phoning him the day
the ad appeared, at the bank where he worked, complaining. A

few months after the election the story reached national level, and Begin himself was asked to comment on the incident. He could have defused the situation. "He said the kibbutzes were hypocrites," Zafrani recounts. "Braggers that swim in their pools and have fun in tranquility while the Sephardis are suffering." The incensed kibbutzes threatened to remove their considerable accounts from the bank's town branch if that bank did not remove Zafrani from his position there, he says. So Zafrani resigned, took compensation, and set up his own insurance firm.

What exactly does he think the problem was between the development town and the kibbutzes surrounding it? "They don't like us," he says. "They don't sit with us, they don't live with us. They were not good neighbors. We are used to an open house. That's how we grew up in Morocco, with no closed doors. Arabs would come to our homes and eat and drink, and our lives were open." By contrast, he thinks that kibbutzniks preferred to close themselves off. "Everything stems," he adds, "from the fact that they didn't want us to succeed. They were afraid that we would win and then rule over them."

It's not hard to find voices to form a kibbutz-dislike choir. One man, who lived in Kiryat Shmona during the 1950s, continues the animal theme when he recalls employment on one of the neighborhood collectives: "They worked us like donkeys, really, they looked at us like we were really donkeys," he says. "And they would laugh at us and make us into nothing—of course, in the fifties we were a joke." But there is just as much talk of the kibbutzes as "wonderful, we worked with them, they were fine," in the words of one woman who came from Safi in Morocco. According to another Moroccan migrant who used to work as a laborer at kibbutz Kfar Blum, in the Upper Galilee, this place was "something extraordinary, beautiful, with lots of food which they told us to 'Eat! Eat!' "

But if resentment is rooted in personal experience, it also has a financial basis. Researchers have shown that kibbutzes and the veteran *moshavs* (farming cooperatives) received more and better land, centrally located and with more resources, than either the development towns or the later moshavs with Mizrahi majorities. Nowadays you hear Israelis explain that this happened because European Jewish settlers arrived first and had the best pick of land. But "I was here first!" is not the calling card of an integration-driven homeland project.* Both the size and the terms of land distribution created rifts that would continue to divide the country years later.

Laws passed in the early 1950s† placed 93 percent of Israeli land, much of which had "become available"‡—to use the neutral language of the time—after the 1948 war, under state management. The Israel Land Administration (ILA), formed in 1960, is in charge of all this public land, although control and ownership of some of it (mostly agricultural) is held by the Jewish National Fund (JNF), founded at the turn of the twentieth century to buy land for Jewish settlement. No land is ever sold—preserving state control keeps it both Jewish and collective. In 1997, Isaac al-Yashiv, director general of the JNF, told the Israeli mass circulation daily *Yediot Aharonot,* "We believe that ownership

---

*Although "We were here first!" *is* essentially the calling card of people who claim biblically decreed rights to land.

†Absentee property law, 1950; land acquisition law, 1953.

‡Much of this land had just been evacuated by Palestinians who intended to return.

of lands in Israel must remain in the hands of the state, and that the lands cannot be treated like other commodities, because otherwise they will eventually be purchased by petrodollars . . . rich Arabs offer a lot of dollars for the lands."[1] Land is leased with exact specifications over its use: farming, residential, retail, and so on. At first, Israel's priority was agriculture—because land redemption was an ethos, and food self-sufficiency was an objective. Even though, technically, nobody "owns" the land, kibbutzes and veteran moshavs were often awarded long-term leases and presumed de facto titleholders.

In the 1980s, the Israeli economy was beleagured by hyperinflation running at 400 percent, and the national ideology shifted to privatization along neoliberal lines. Previously protected markets were now exposed to foreign competition; meanwhile a government austerity program was introduced that hit all the people usually affected when state investment, benefits, and welfare systems are cut. Cushioned by government subsidies, the kibbutz movement had grown up in a shielded environment—which now collapsed. By the early 1990s, the state was bailing them out of million-dollar debts. Agriculture could no longer keep the kibbutz movement afloat, and by the end of the decade this dovetailed with a state drive to free up farmlands—more space was needed to cope with the influx of immigrants from the former Soviet bloc. In the early 1990s, a system change released and reclassified sections of agricultural land. Farms would be compensated for 50 percent of the commercial value of land that they had tended and which was rezoned for commercial use. This rezoning gave kibbutzes the ability to reinvent themselves as real-estate agents for industrial parks, business complexes, and large-scale shopping centers. It signaled a potential windfall for farms that sat on prime lands whose market value ran into the millions.

Land-rights campaigners, including the Mizrahi Democratic Rainbow (MDR), argued that the compensation was too high—the discussion was over state lands: public property, on lease, free of charge. "If the kibbutzes no longer farm much of their so-called land and now lease it for mega-profits to mega-companies who build shopping malls and gas stations, why shouldn't benefits be shared among the Israeli public,"[2] one campaigner asked. After appeals to the Supreme Court, and at the government's recommendation, compensation was cut to 20 percent of the land's commercial value. Israeli Professor Yossi Yonah and Ishak Saporta, both MDR members, documented all of this and reported that the kibbutz movement began a PR drive to reverse the reduction, proposing that the farms had built the state and should now be rewarded for it.

The kibbutz position was backed by media endorsements and by politicians of all shades, who invoked the image of the farms as national heroes. Shalom Simhon, a Labor party Knesset member (and then secretary of the Moshav movement), saw compensation as a historical opportunity "to grant the farmers the rights they deserve, not out of charity but out of justice, and to show these people who labor arduously and who protect the borders of the state, that the State of Israel knows how to repay them with gratitude."[3] The leader of the right-wing Likud party, Ariel Sharon, said: "Nothing would have existed if it were not for the farmers . . . I do not think for one second that anyone has the right to take this land from them, because they settled and cultivated it for sixty or seventy years."[4]

All this goodwill wasn't enough to persuade the court, which still held that high compensation rates were fundamentally unjust. If land allocation was an accident of timing, why should some sections of society profit from it? The entire policy was scrapped in 2002, but not before some kibbutzes had taken advantage of it as a windfall mechanism—and the revocation didn't apply to conversions already under way.

For development towns, the issue has another component: If agricultural land is de-zoned, why do kibbutzes still have a greater need for it? According to Sami Maloul at Kiryat Shmona's local council, kibbutzes in the area have built new housing units for non-members on newly defined residential land. These attract home-seekers from Kiryat Shmona who can't find property in town. Farmlands reclassified for retail use attract businesses that pay taxes to the leaseholders, kibbutz farms. Kiryat Shmona suffers because negative migration ensures that the town will never reach a population level—estimated to be around forty thousand—that precipitates external investment. Close to two hundred thousand people have left Kiryat Shmona since 1948, although Katyusha rocket attacks from neighboring Lebanon during both wars with that country might also account for the exodus.

Yonah and Saporta contrast the land rights incident with a campaign waged over public housing at around the same time. The Israeli government leases around 120,000 apartments to low-income tenants—often Mizrahi. In 1997, the government announced plans to outsource public housing to private management, at which point campaigners proposed that the occupants should be able to buy their homes at discount rates. Initially the campaign talked to the principles of housing rights for all. That didn't cut it, so the focus shifted, borrowing the rhetoric of the kibbutz movement. "Mizrahi immigrants who occupied the border neighbourhoods and towns were just as much pioneers and contributed just as much to the security of the state as the mythological Zionist farmer," one campaigner told the *Jerusalem Post*.[5] Mizrahi migrants were often settled along the Lebanese and Gazan borders, or in areas once populated by Palestinians—and thus they made a tangible defense contribution to the state. This nationalist pitch got more sympathy, and the Public Housing Act of 1998 introduced discount purchase rights to tenants. It hasn't been put into practice yet, since successive governments have suspended it through use of the law of arrangements.* But Yonah and Saporta argue that the dialogue surrounding this and the kibbutz campaign indicated a national practice of allocating benefits on the basis of a defined contribution to nation-building. Some land experts disagree with this analysis, describing it as "stretched" and pointing out that the public housing bill was pushed chiefly by the left-wing Meretz, not a party prone to using nationalistic rhetoric. Critics also hold that fewer kibbutzes benefited from the early compensation arrangements than is implied by this reading of events.

But in any case, there's an obvious problem with this campaign, based on a slogan of "The land is also mine!" Raef Zriek, an Arab-Israeli civil-rights activist, summarized it: "Mizrahis simply wish to join in the looting of Arab lands."[6] Or put another way by Nabil Bashir, then a member of the Mizrahi Democratic Rainbow: "I cannot transform myself, even for a moment, into a 'pioneer,' a 'settler' or a 'Zionist' . . . Equality

---

*In use since 1995, this law is effectively a bulk-bypass mechanism for the government to quash measures it doesn't like, or to introduce ones that the public won't.

should not be claimed on the grounds that 'I am also a Zionist,'
but on the grounds that I am also a human being, or at least on
the grounds that I am also a citizen or resident of the state."[7]
What began as a campaign for equal Jewish rights was inevitably
challenged by the thornier question of equal rights for everyone. Arab-Israelis, almost 20 percent of the population, own or
lease only around 4 percent of the land.

"Someone from Europe is a pioneer, while someone from the
East is a refugee and the country did him a favor that they even
allowed him to be here," says Aaron Madawal. "That's the way
the authorities understand it." Madawal is spokesman for the
land-rights campaign in Kfar Shalem, a southeastern satellite of
Tel Aviv, where he lives alongside other Jews with mostly Yemeni
roots, like his. "We will never be pioneers. Not unless some objective people come and rewrite the history books of this country." In early 2007, around four hundred families in Kfar Shalem
received eviction notices. The families have been leasing from
the state since 1948, when they were settled in the area recently
evacuated by its Palestinian occupants. The way Madawal heard it,
Kfar Shalem—then known as the Arab village Salama—had been
used as a base from which to attack the nearby Jewish neighborhood of Schunat HaTikva during the 1948 war. It hadn't been the
residents of Salama doing the attacking, he says, but it was they
who "fled" shortly thereafter. Madawal was told that the former
villagers had left because Arab countries had assured them a return
following a victory in the war against Israel. Or perhaps, he says,
"They heard about what happened at Deir Yassin* and became

---

*In April 1948, up to 120 Palestinians were killed at their village of Deir Yassin,
near Jerusalem, by the Zionist military group Irgun. Numerous Palestinian
and British reports describe the incident as bloody and brutal.

afraid." For Israel, a major concern after the war was that Palestinians didn't come back and reclaim residence.

There is still a mosque, intact and a bit mossy, on the outskirts of Kfar Shalem. It's prime real estate, this neighborhood, so close to Tel Aviv but village-like, quiet, perfect for property boomers looking for new land in the city outskirts. Which is why its residents have been dealt eviction notices. They, like other public-housing occupants, are on short-term government leases and as such have no rights against eviction. Those moral-occupancy rights that apply to kibbutz members apparently don't extend to the residents of Kfar Shalem.

Some of the neighborhood's protests against eviction were attended by Arab-Israelis from Jaffa, facing the same potential fate. From mid-2006, around five hundred eviction notices were sent to Arab families from neighborhoods of Jaffa, defined as a "mixed city," meaning that it is home to both Arabs and Jews. Regarding (Palestinian) Arab-Israelis demonstrating alongside Kfar Shalem's Jewish residents, who are resisting eviction from land once populated by Palestinians, Madawal says: "It shows that the personal identity that people deal with every day is a more decisive factor than national identity. Our connection with them is a lot stronger than our connection with Ashkenazis from north Tel Aviv.* There is the problem that they are trying to evict us both, now, in the present . . . We are definitely supporting their cause, definitely we relate to it." In December 2007, fifteen families were evicted from Kfar Shalem. A few months earlier, a Kfar Shalem resident of sixty years told *Haaretz*

---

*The connection between these two causes was mostly established by Ashkenazi activists, some of them from north Tel Aviv.

newspaper: "Those poor Ashkenazis. They suffered so much from anti-Semitism in Europe. Why are they taking it out on us?"[8] This lament, referring to Israelis as a whole, can be heard with predictable regularity in the Palestinian West Bank.

"The scariest thing actually, the moment they panicked, was when we did the alternative Holocaust ceremony," says Sami Shalom Chetrit, one of the founders of the Israeli independent high school Kedma. Based in Schunat HaTikva, near Tel Aviv, the school operated for four years until the government shut it down in 1995. Leading up to Holocaust Remembrance Day, which falls a week after the last day of Passover, schoolrooms in Israel are usually covered in displays, assembled in class, serving as commemoration and educational aids combined.

In 1995, Kedma decided to expand the standard Holocaust themes. "We talked about racism, Africans in America, the [American] Indians, Armenians, and then, even worse, we made this display," says Chetrit. "I called the Armenian church in the old city, in Jerusalem," says Chetrit. "I was speaking in Arabic, so when I explained that I was from a Jewish school, they were surprised. 'You want to teach this?' they asked and they sent us so much material, in a taxi." Between 1915 and 1918, one to one and a half million Armenians were killed under Ottoman rule. Most historians and many countries officially term this a genocide, although Turkey, America, Britain, and Israel do not. It has also been described as a holocaust, a massacre, or "the great calamity" by Armenians, many of whom escaped Ottoman rule and found refuge in other parts of the world. In Jerusalem's Old City, the Armenian Quarter is today lined with solemn bill posters narrating the story and directing further inquiries to the community's museum. Here, a worn, damp corner displays bleak documentation of the forgotten atrocity.

"We had a wall with the Jewish Holocaust and a wall with the Armenian Holocaust and pupils walking between them," remembers Chetrit, about the Kedma school display. "They could tell the difference because of the Star of David [on the Jewish side], but there were piles of bodies here and piles of bodies on the other side, too." The school wanted to study the essence of prejudice, asking: What is persecution? Since then, Yad Vashem, the Israeli Holocaust memorial and museum, has requested materials and video footage from Kedma's event, to use within its own workshops. By 2000, education minister Yossi Sarid attended Armenian Genocide Memorial Day in the Old City museum, breaking with the Israeli convention of not officially recognizing the term. By now, there have been a few alternative memorials that commemorate Holocaust Day and deviate in their own way from the traditional public ceremony. But in 1995, Kedma's alternative, with its universalist take on deadly persecution, was standing alone.

While schoolchildren all over the country were lighting six candles in memory of six million murdered Jews, one Holocaust survivor lit a seventh candle at Kedma's ceremony. "We have the tragic right to stand here, remember, and warn," pupils read. "There is no people, no culture, and no group of humans immune to hatred, racism, persecution, and extermination." The script stressed that the intention was not to belittle the "pain of our people's memory," nor was the purpose to compare holocausts. But the seventh candle honored other victims of persecution and extermination throughout human history. "We, born out of the greatest horror," the reading ended, "stand up tall today, in prayer for peace and fellowship between people, creeds, races, and cultures."

It didn't go down too well beyond the school walls. There is concern within Jewish society, both Israeli and Diasporic, about blurring the unique horror of the Holocaust by applying the term to any genocide. Knesset member Limor Livnat called for the Ministry of Education to close Kedma. A protest outside the school was joined by members of the Zionist youth movement, Betar. TV crews stormed the school and, denied access to it, hounded pupils on their way home. Chetrit recalls that one woman telephoned the school, screaming: "You Moroccans have already stolen everything from us, but this is it! Don't dare touch our Holocaust. You will not steal our Holocaust with your belly-dancing." That was the thing about Kedma: it was predominantly Mizrahis that attended it.

Kedma school in Schunat HaTikva closed soon after that. Officially the school, with its unconventional, parent-heavy leadership, had breached the rules of the local education authority. But the founders of this school, by then already accused of being an ethnic, separatist institution, say that closure had been a threat throughout its four-year existence. Chetrit believes that the extra Holocaust candle was just too much from an operation already deemed too radical. He narrates that the local mayor turned up at the school, flanked by a security official, and explained the decision to assembled parents. When they protested loudly, he responded: "You can yell and riot as much as you like, that is indeed your culture, a culture of screaming. It won't help you."[9] Today, the renovated school building is the headquarters of the Israeli Labor party.

Another Kedma school, in Jerusalem, survived, while a third, in the development town Kiryat Malachi, did not. A fourth is in the pipeline for the coastal city Netanya. The schools were set up by radical/progressive sociologists and educators, like Sami Shalom Chetrit and like Shlomo Swirski, whose systematic analysis of the formation of a Mizrahi working class in Israel cites schooling as one of the chief architects. Swirski's book *Israel the Oriental Majority* is titled *Not Failures but Made to Fail* in the original Hebrew. Catchier in the acrobatic-verbed native language, the title fits perfectly the Kedma analysis of Israel's education system. Despite all the talk of closing the ethnic "gaps" in school achievement, despite the programs put in place to do just that, Mizrahis are still at the wrong end of the performance tables. In some cases, third-generation Mizrahis have poorer levels of education than their grandparents, who were taught in Arab countries.

By the mid-fifties, it was clear that Mizrahis weren't doing well at school. A report in 1957 found that a quarter had to repeat first grade and only 7.8 percent made it through to twelfth grade. At that time Mizrahis comprised 55 percent of the total population of schoolchildren. In 1958, when Mizrahi pupils made up half of the total, 2.5 percent graduated from a liberal arts or sciences high school, while 42 percent attended vocational schools. At the Hebrew University the same year, 5 percent of all Jewish graduates were Mizrahi. The disparity dented a cornerstone of the melting-pot theory: equality. But it worried officials for other reasons too. One Israeli analyst identified a potential fallout: "Political leaders and the leaders of education [feared] that the cultural and social gaps between the Ashkenazi leadership and the Mizrahi public would bring the 'second Israel' [the Mizrahi community], who do not benefit from the services of academic high school education and of higher education to the same extent as the middle class, [to] reject the traditional leadership of the Zionist movement that originated in Europe."[10] In other words, officials were worried about an outbreak of protests over ethnic inequality. Taking over the ministry of education in 1961, Abba Eban announced that raising Mizrahi education levels was a top priority.

There are many theories about the causes of this wide, ethnically based gap in educational attainment. It could have been that Mizrahi communities didn't have equal access: "second Israel" contained mostly vocational schools and, during a nationwide teacher shortage, didn't attract the best. Aliza Loewenberg, a volunteer teacher in Kiryat Shmona, wrote: "The failure of our elementary schools is in fact a failure of the 'first Israel' [Ashkenazis], represented, sadly, by the teachers, who bring with them to the development towns concepts and notions that cause them, their work, and the children whose future they purport to guide, to fail."[11] Loewenberg describes "feelings of superiority" held by many teachers and the transference of those feelings "almost naturally to the children, who started to believe they are inferior from birth and that they have no chance of making it, that is, of becoming like the children of the veterans." The Israeli sociologist Sami Smooha documented that in studies carried out during the mid-1970s, schoolteachers who were asked to mark identical papers awarded much lower grades to those reportedly written by Orientally named students.

The education "gaps" might have been the product of an informally segregated system of teaching in mixed population areas. A volunteer teacher during the 1950s, Arnold Lewis observed that an established school changed in character after an influx of Mizrahi children. "For all practical purposes, the school was divided into two parts," he wrote. "One part was made up of small classes of veterans and new immigrant children from

Eastern Europe who progressed along the path toward academic high school. A second group of classes, which stressed reading, writing, and other basic skills, was opened and filled mostly by children of North African and Near Eastern immigrants."[12] The second group of children couldn't meet the admission standards of higher education. This sort of streaming, wrote Lewis, was still in place by the mid-1960s.

One education inspector posited another potential cause of the gap in 1958: curricula were based on European Jewish culture. "How can [Mizrahi pupils] relate to this culture, which, though Jewish, is particular to specific countries of the Diaspora, with which they were not connected?" he asked. "Our school books have almost nothing of the culture of the Mizrahi communities, not from their past nor from their present."[13]

The education minister of that time, Abba Eban, didn't seem to consider these factors. Interviewed by a London newspaper in September 1962, Eban explained the gap to be a result of "five centuries of Jewish history." The problem, he expanded, was that "One half of our population comes from communities which since the decline of Islamic culture have had no educational history or development. Their children, now in Israel, are the first generation for centuries to be educated at all."[14] The Iraqi-Israeli writer Nissim Rejwan wrote that Eban was manifesting "that mixture of historical fallacy and cultural agoraphobia which often sounds so painfully like built-in prejudice." Needless to say, Oriental Jews were not a homogenously uneducated mass. In places such as Iraq, Iran, Morocco, Algeria, Egypt, and Syria, sections of the Jewish middle and upper classes were well educated and at the forefront of cultural and intellectual developments. In most countries, state education wasn't even a privilege of the higher classes. And from 1860, a Western-style education was, quite often, provided by the French Alliance Israelite Universelle school system operational in the Middle East.

But by the time Minister Eban gave his analysis, it had already been sanctioned by Israeli experts, commissioned by a leading academic journal in the late 1950s to look into ways to assimilate the Mizrahi community. The rationale they came up with is frequently cited by Mizrahi campaigners as proof of the backbone premises of an education system stacked against the children of Oriental communities. The theorists were asked to explore why Israel's integration-driven social policies had thus far failed. Sociologist Carl Frankenstein, the most prominent among them, postulated that state policy had not taken into consideration "the primitive mentality of many of the immigrants from the backward countries."[15] The Israeli historian Tom Segev narrates that Frankenstein likened this mentality to "the primitive expression of children, the retarded, or the mentally disturbed."[16] The sociologist believed that, having spent so long in the Orient during its decline, the Mizrahi intellect had deteriorated, a process caused by "petrifaction or of a kind of collective forgetfulness."[17] Frankenstein is an Israeli prizewinner, often described as a social and educational architect. Similar theories were at the same time developed by another sociologist, Moshe Smilansky, head of the Hebrew University's government-established School of Education. "Members of that group [Mizrahis] have come to Israel, and have to acquire a position according to the values of the dominant society, which is already in an advanced stage of Western modernization, in the fields of science, technology, and society,"[18] he proposed. Sami Shalom Chetrit later pointed out that "Western modernization" is a relative concept. "Israeli soci-

ety may have appeared to be Western and modern to Eastern
European Jews, and to Oriental Jews from certain areas," he
wrote. "But many other Mizrahis who came . . . from such modern cities as Baghdad, Alexandria, Cairo, Algiers, Casablanca,
Tangier, Tehran, Constantinople, Damascus, and Beirut, report
being shocked to discover the technological and economic
backwardness of young Israel."[19] Another twist, adds Shlomo
Swirski, is that Mizrahis were the labor backbone during Israel's
period of industrial modernization.

Those development theories provided an explanation for
what had gone wrong with education policy: the Mizrahi communities were culturally disadvantaged and necessarily playing
catch-up. The gaps were the result of differing mentalities—not
genetically based, but caused by having lived in Arab countries;
disadvantageous environments. Moshe Smilansky, senior adviser
to the Ministry of Education by 1957, signaled a policy shift:
"The democratic concept of 'equal opportunity' " had to be interpreted as "the opportunity to enjoy a curriculum adapted to
the ability, needs, and goals of the individual, and in concordance
with his environment."[20] Since open access to education hadn't
leveled out the gaps, it would be much fairer to further develop
a streamed system. "It seems evident that any attempt to offer a
homogeneous curriculum to [two different achievement levels
of] children in the name of equality means not providing their
immediate needs, and in the long term—a blatant discrimination."[21] In other words, if Mizrahi kids were falling behind, why
put them on a high education track among smarter pupils with
whom they couldn't compete?

Education policy shifted its fulcrum from egalitarian, melting-
pot principles to one of compensation. Theorists had sanctioned

the separatist schooling system already in place in so many cases, with Mizrahis attending vocational schools while Ashkenazis were more often at academic schools. The government expanded investments on the vocational front: from 1965 to 1970, the number of children in vocational schools doubled, to 40 percent of all pupils. Those schools became typically Mizrahi schools, with a fourfold increase in attendance figures from this community.

Based on another theory, "Cultivation and Rehabilitation," a new policy was developed for disadvantaged children. They were tagged *teunei tipuach,* or "in need of special nurture," which was later reclassified to "underachievers." To be defined as such was dependent on such criteria as father's place of birth, father's education (the mother could be a doctor and it wouldn't matter), and the size of the family. This last qualifier was changed to place of residence, but it was testing for the same thing: If you come from a large family, the odds are that you're Mizrahi; if you live in a poor area, ditto.* By these criteria, a child of a large, low-income family from Morocco, where the father was schooled for less than ten years, is classed as a special-nurture case. The child's school grades were also a factor in assessment, but since it had already been noted that Mizrahi kids were failing in school, this didn't add much to the process except to rescue from "special nurture" schooling a few children who attained good grades against the odds. In the school year from 1974–75, 47 percent of schoolchildren were classed as teunei tipunach, and 95 percent of those were Oriental. Today, if that phrase is mentioned, it is still a Mizrahi face that people expect to see.

---

*Both criteria can readily apply to the Orthodox community too, but they attend separate, religious schools.

Special books and teaching colleges were set up to instruct on how to use rehabilitation methods in the classroom. It was developed as a form of affirmative action or positive discrimination. In 1963, a government-backed university research institute was established to work on teaching methods for special-nurture kids. One aim was to write a separate curriculum; but in the end, kids in the special-nurture category were taught from the same program, just much less of it.

Shlomo Swirski cites an education ministry memorandum from 1964 briefing primary school teachers on how to deal with special-nurture kids. "You know that for the most part they are the children of immigrants who come from a backward cultural environment."[22] Such children, the note explained, lacked maturity or the motivation to read; they couldn't cope with failure; they lacked basic educational habits and a basic vocabulary. The immaturity of these children was attributed to such factors as an "incomplete physiological development in the realms of motor function, hearing, and seeing"[23] and "lack of coordination between the eye and the page"[24] and a "mental age lower than chronological age."[25]

In 1968, the government rolled out a policy change labeled school "reform," later called "integration" (for Jewish pupils). It was planned as a reshuffle of schooling structure to create extra years on a post-elementary academic track. A vaunted practical consequence of this restructuring was that children of different backgrounds and ethnicities would now attend the same schools at a new intermediary level: junior high. This was a tacit admission that the education system was segregated along ethnic lines. Critics say that the kids didn't end up mixing so much after all—they continued to be taught in different classes, with Mizrahi children still stuck on vocational or underachiever tracks.

This reform did not apply to independent, ultra-Orthodox schools, both Mizrahi (Sephardi) and Ashkenazi variants of which do not have to comply with the state curriculum, much less the state's declared tenets of social integration. In a wider context, this opt-out capacity means that much of the discussion on Mizrahi education within the state system is irrelevant to the growing sections of the Mizrahi community in non-state religious schools. However, the state-education experience may be a factor in steering non-Orthodox Sephardi parents to ultra-Orthodox Sephardi schools.

Special-nurture programs had stopped receiving so much funding by 1994, but they still operate. Right across the country, Mizrahi parents talk of battling schools that have branded kids for life. That's a formidable prospect for a parent in a developing town, at such a disadvantage in dealing with school authority figures backed by an entire system of teaching that has, after all, been designed to help.

Israeli school streaming systems are based on Western models, like the U.S. program designed to equalize imbalances within an immigrant population. Vocational schools in Israel run much like English comprehensives, comprising academic and larger, nonacademic classes. Opinion about these schools in Israel is split. Some say they perpetuate education gaps, not least because they set students up to fail: teachers, parents, and the low-track children themselves all end up with lowered expectations which, in a self-fulfilling prophecy, are then met. Others counter that more children reach matriculation level—there might be a qualitative difference in the certificates gained, but more children get them. One academic and education campaigner denounces such a system as creating "retards with certificates."[26] Similar reservations

arise over the expansion of Israel's higher education network in
the 1990s. Degree-level colleges were built in development
towns, but some critics call them second-rate.

It's precisely these underachievers—disruptive, disadvantaged,
special-nurture pupils—that Kedma schools were founded to
teach. Clara Yona, former head teacher at Jerusalem's Kedma
school in the Mizrahi-dense, low-status Katamon district, used
to ask new pupils what they dreamed of becoming in adulthood.
They would reply things like "car mechanic" or "hairdresser,"
and she would tell them, "For that, you don't need to dream!"
Teachers at the school, like Yona, recall their own experiences of
being taught very well, but at a cost. Yona and her sister, deemed
bright pupils, were taken out of a local school and transferred to
a better one in another area. This was part of the "gifted disadvantaged" program operational at the time, which took high-
achieving Mizrahi kids out of their hometowns and put them in
boarding schools in better-off neighborhoods, so that they
might thrive in a more academically conducive setting. Since
predominantly children of European origin attended their new
school, the sisters stood out as "the blacks," relates Yona, adding
that the only way to surmount the stereotypes surrounding that
label was to hide their home culture and adapt to the dominant
one at school. "We wanted to leave many times," she says. "It
was a nightmare—I nearly was not at school. And why should
you have to pay this price, even? Why?" Those memories are a
powerful motivating force.

Kedma's teaching is inspired by the South American education theorist Paolo Friere, whose *Pedagogy of the Oppressed* argued, among other points, that education shouldn't be a system
of imparting the dominant culture. Parents might not share

Kedma's analysis, but send their children to the school anyway because the results speak for themselves. Yona says that local education-authority officials initially accused the school of being separatist and taking education policy back fifteen years, but they too must have been convinced by the school's achievements. Kedma, which doesn't screen entrants and is based in a community of school rejects, had 60 percent matriculation rates, with a further 20 percent a few points away from reaching certificate levels when its first pupils reached graduation.

Talking with some of the pupils at this school, it is obvious that they would have failed or dropped out of the schooling system altogether if they hadn't been caught by Kedma. "I was in school in Yavne, forty pupils in each class," says sixteen-year-old Linoy. "I was always trying to understand, but I never managed because there were too many children and so much noise. And the teachers didn't care." At that school, Linoy didn't think she'd sit matriculation exams because her grades weren't good enough. "I didn't succeed at anything there, and I tried. I really tried," she says. At Kedma, she is a top pupil, getting high grades and aiming for business studies at university. At the Yavne school, "They related only to the Ashkenazis, the ones with the long names; only they could succeed, so the teachers gave them more attention. It was so obvious, really obvious."

Reversing the fate of Mizrahi kids, Kedma also brings the Mizrahi back into history. In 2002, the artist Meir Gal was photographed holding up a few pages of an Israeli history book, for an artwork titled "Nine out of four hundred." That was the number of pages dealing with Mizrahi history. The book he held up wasn't exceptional. A survey of history books on the Israeli school curriculum in the 1990s found that none contained more than 4 percent content on Middle Eastern Jews. Also, just like the ads and the TV personalities and the media articles about Mizrahi characteristics, early schoolbooks were dealing in stereotypes. A study of textbooks from 1948 to 1967 found that Mizrahis were portrayed repeatedly as weak, dirty, poor, culturally deficient, and superstitious. Perhaps not surprisingly, given the lowly set of attributes associated with them, Mizrahis were also described as suffering an inferiority complex. The Education Ministry has since increased Mizrahi content in history books and pledged to increase it further, to 30 percent of the total. According to one official, things are on the verge of a large surge, since researchers are working on new books providing larger, wider, and more diverse coverage of Mizrahi history.

Moshe Shriki, head of the Kedma school in Jerusalem, is doing his own work while those new editions are in process. Pupils usually come to the school with hard-right, Arab-hating opinions, he says—views that are widely considered typical of Mizrahis. History books have Middle Eastern Jews in terrible crisis under Islamic rule and rescued from it by Israel. No doubt as a consequence, suggests Shriki, schoolkids assume that, in their manifest animosity for the Jewish state, Arab nations are continuing a tradition of hating Jews. "I tell them, go to your parents and your grandparents [who lived in Arab countries] and ask them what it was like," says Shriki, who teaches matriculation-level history. "They come back and say, 'We asked, and they said it wasn't bad' . . . And when we do this examination between Christianity and its history with the Jews and Islam and its history with the Jews, suddenly Islam is something that you can live with in peace. And then they start to ask different questions: 'Hang on, how did we get to the situation that we are in now? Why are they so against

us today?' And so you say, 'Okay, let's check that, too.' " The school
uses education ministry texts alongside the resources of the children themselves: their families, their heritage. Shriki says he does
not have a political agenda. "I don't believe in propaganda," he
explains. "I want the students to think critically, for themselves."

Meanwhile, another small revolution is taking place within a
different organization, also geared to raise education levels in deprived areas. Founded in 1987, HILA, the Israeli Committee for
Quality in Education, was the springboard for the Kedma schools
project. Just like Kedma, the Hila network only reaches a small
slice of the population. Its focus is at a grassroots level, within the
existing education system, providing parents with tools and information to fight for a better standard of schooling in development
towns and low-status city neighborhoods. HILA deals with parents
of any origin, although in practice that means Mizrahis, Soviets
from the former "stans," Ethiopians, and Arab-Israelis, since these
groups, and in that descending order, are at the bottom of the education ladder. This does not include Israel's Christian-Arab population, whose children tend to fare better at church schools.

HILA is a dynamic, action-based network that does a lot more
than hand out information packs. It has enabled hundreds of disadvantaged mothers to stand up to head teachers and psychologists
who have branded their kids "underachievers" and placed them in
education ghettos. Looking around HILA's 2007 annual seminar,
held in Tel Aviv, there are a few hundred Israelis present from all
over: Bedouin parents from the village of Rahat in the southern
Negev, Arab-Israeli parents from Umm al-Fahm in the center, and
Mizrahi parents from Tiberias in the north. But this mixed composition barely registers as an issue. In this forum focused on social
equality, it just seems obvious that this would be so.

Chapter 8

THE ETHNIC DEMON

IN JUNE 2007, I flick on the TV to find Channel 10's breakfast program, *Kol Boker* (Every Morning), asking: "Does the ethnic demon still exist?" "Demon" is how the Hebrew is more often translated—even though the thing referred to lives in a bottle and people keep releasing it, which seems more like genie behavior. Anyway, I'm in Sderot, where repeating the question that day to residents elicits a categorical response: "Of course it does! Where are you living?" The implication being: "On the dunce side of the moon," if I need to ask something so naïvely rhetorical.

The question arose when the morning TV people speculated about whether former president Moshe Katsav, accused of sexual harassment, and defense minister Amir Peretz, accused of blundering the Second Lebanon War and a bungled policy on Gaza, are being persecuted for ethnic reasons and not purely on the basis of their alleged misdeeds. They're both Mizrahi.

In truth, this demon is a bit of a pest—everyone wants it to shut up and go away; some people think it left the building long ago and others say it still holds center stage. Nobody knows who started using the term or when, but everybody knows what it means. It's as though every Israeli politician or public figure

carefully carries a glass bottle which sometimes unavoidably
cracks, releasing the demon and causing mayhem. When that
happens, the clumsy bottle-breaker is berated for "awakening
the demon." Some politicians, such as former right-wing prime
ministers Ariel Sharon and Binyamin Netanyahu, have in the
past proclaimed it time to "push the genie back into its bottle."
Others, like former Labor prime minister Ehud Barak, have
been accused of deliberately releasing it.

Yet this sneaky demon is visible only to certain people or at
certain junctures. Many Israelis hold that ethnicity is no longer a
determinant of success or failure, socially, politically, or in any
sphere. They don't see the demon—more often than not, they
label any Mizrahi who still complains about ethnic discrimination today a crybaby, an occupational whiner, incapable of embracing the ethnically blind social equality shining into the eyes
of anyone who chooses to see it. The subtext is that if the
Mizrahi stopped crying and started trying, he or she might actually succeed and then have nothing to mope over.* The crybaby
accusation is voiced by Mizrahis and Ashkenazis alike—and can
be heard in many contexts: in the media, on Internet forums,
and in the public space. It's the capitalist defense of meritocracy,
the cornerstone of the equal-opportunity American dream, re-
fashioned here to bat off ethnic grumbling.

Israeli's history contains myriad appearances of the demon,
in political and public life and popular protests. Recently, the

---

*In 2002, responding to accusations that his victory over Mizrahi Benyamin
Ben-Eliezer in the Labor leadership contest was secured against an "ethnic"
backdrop, Amram Mitzna said: "That's simply nonsense. Whoever tries to set
loose the 'ethnic genie' is generally someone who is worried about failure, or
for whom failure is already theirs." (From *Haaretz*, November 20, 2002.)

most spectacular political relationship with the demon is that experienced by Amir Peretz, who became leader of the Labor party in November 2005. Then, the Moroccan-born Peretz boldly claimed in his victory speech: "This is the moment we bury the ethnic demon in Israel."[1] The Israeli Labor party has traditionally been associated with Ashkenazi sectors of society and has almost blanket support among the kibbutzes. Peretz, who lives in the Moroccan-heavy development town of Sderot and whose father used to work as a hired hand on one of those kibbutzes, is the first Mizrahi leader of the Labor party. He's conspicuously Oriental: he wears the Middle Eastern facial accessory of a block moustache; he is frequently shown bearhugging and kissing people; he says that his dovish views are partly informed by having an Arab woman nurse him as a baby in Morocco. Formerly head of the Israeli trade union congress Histadrut, Peretz is politically in line with Labor voters. But for the party faithful actually to trust a Mizrahi as leader was—or so Peretz thought back then—indication of a great intercultural leap forward. It meant that to the majority Ashkenazi supporters of the Labor party, Peretz's Moroccan origins were not relevant.

Around two years later, Peretz was humiliatingly "kicked"* out of the defense ministry of Ehud Olmert's Kadima†-led coalition government. He was relieved of his position as Labor

---

*The word "kicked" was frequently featured in the Israeli press of the time as descriptive of what happened.

†Kadima is the center-right party established by Ariel Sharon in November 2005, breaking away from his former party, Likud. In early 2006, Sharon fell into a coma, leaving Olmert as acting prime minister. Olmert was then properly elected to this post in the January 2006 election.

party leader, too: as a result of internal elections in June 2007, the old-timer Ehud Barak took over.* Months later, Peretz publicly exhumed the demon, claiming that, sure, he'd made mistakes, but that he was also a victim of relentless racism. "It's a blow that shames you in front of all of those in the development towns that claimed that in Israeli society there are still undercurrents of ethnic, racial discrimination," he explained to a wide-circulation Israeli newspaper.[2] "I didn't agree with them, I fought against them and I said that we will bury the ethnic demon. In hindsight I was wrong. Maybe we tried to bury this demon, but on the other hand it carried on running around in the souls of the some of the best friends we have in the Labor party."

But digging up the demon elicited a bilious response in the *Haaretz* newspaper, for instance, where columnist Uzi Benziman wrote: "With utter cynicism and calculated restraint, Peretz pulls the pin from the fragmentation grenade of inter-ethnic animosity in order to use it to clear his way back to the forefront of the public stage."[3] There were other pronouncements similar to that one. But they did nothing to undermine the opinion in some quarters, such as Sderot, that Peretz was demeaned along ethnic lines from the start, set up for a crashing failure.

Back when he'd been elected head of the Labor party, newspapers, talk shows, and satire shows began to routinely present Peretz as stupid, inexperienced, and a bit of a buffoon. His

---

*Ehud Barak was head of the Labor party and prime minister from 1999 to 2001. Disgraced after the 2000 Camp David peace talks collapsed, Barak made a comeback in 2007, deposing Peretz as party leader and defense minister.

English-language skills became a huge problem and the object of more ridicule. Then Labor secured second place in the 2006 elections, winning nineteen seats and the right to join Ehud Olmert's coalition government. Running on the principle of proportional representation, Israel's electoral system frequently throws up hybrid governments comprising the soft left, the hard right, and everything in between. Politicians lunge from one end of the spectrum to the other to join coalitions. Amir Peretz wanted the position of finance minister, in order to make good the Labor party's electoral promises of a social policy charter. He was offered, and took, the defense ministry. This move left him open to negative media rumblings; he was said to be inexperienced and incapable. Critics say this lampooning was the hallmark work of the ethnic demon.

Amir Peretz failed as defense minister and was a crushing disappointment to everyone who believed his pre-election peace charter. In Gaza, he approved a series of "targeted" assassinations and later, following the kidnapping of an Israeli soldier, land invasions of the Strip. It was under his leadership that Israel bombed Gaza's electricity generator, leaving 1.4 million people without power during a Middle Eastern summer—outside Israel, such action was interpreted as an arrogant, cruel measure and a humanitarian disaster for Gazans. None of that stopped the Qassam attacks on southern Israel, on Peretz's home town of Sderot.

The deaths of 119 Israeli soldiers and 44 civilians in the 2006 Lebanon war, and the holding hostage of Israeli citizens in bunkers in the north for almost a month, caused thousands of protesters to call for the resignations of Israel's leaders. The deaths of five hundred Hezbollah fighters and an estimated 850 to 1191 Lebanese civilians in that war, and the devastating destruction of buildings and infrastructure, served as horrifying proof that Peretz was no peacenik.

It is not clear that Peretz failed in a manner more disastrous than any other defense minister. An investigative commission found that, in order to fight the better war* that the Israeli public clamored for, the Army should have been better organized, prepared, and equipped—historic failings, in other words, of defense-ministry predecessors. But the commission's report did hold the prime minster, the defense minister, and the Army chief of staff responsible. The latter two resigned; the prime minster hung on to his position. Then things escalated on the Gaza front again, and questions regarding the Lebanon border and that conflict were pushed aside.

On his way down and out of politics, Peretz suffered a chorus of reproach for his failings—as well he might, except that, again, some smelled the work of the demon around it. For instance, during the Labor party leadership elections in June 2007, some kibbutzes were running an anti-Peretz campaign which referred to him as a "man from the market"—carrying the implication of someone who is unprofessional or common. His development-town voters were described as "market stall traders" and "fishermen." One kibbutznik was quoted as telling Ayalon, a Labor party leadership contender who had allied with the failed former head, "Peretz's shadow covers you. The connection will only damage you. What have you come to do here, make the

---

*It was not "No War" but rather a kind of "Better War" that tens of thousands of protesters had gathered in Tel Aviv's Rabin Square to demand in May 2007.

unclean kosher?" These type of pronouncements are in Israeli code, and loaded. Every Israeli would doubtless understand the connotations and know that these comments would not be made in an Ashkenazi context; but at the same time, pointing out the negative, racially relevant associations of such language might swiftly be dismissed as an overreaction. Months later Benziman at *Haaretz* accused the former defense minister of using the wearisome comments of a just couple of kibbutzniks to incite sensitive Mizrahis.

While Peretz was pronounced a demon victim, too Oriental for Israel to handle, the former president Moshe Katsav was not. Katsav had never made being Mizrahi an issue, until he was accused of several counts of sexual assault. When he made a big turnaround speech about the demon presence, it smelled bad. Few believed him.

Amir Peretz is not the first figure to be stalked by the ethnic demon. Israel's political history is filled with characters accused of attempting to play an ethnic card, or ethnic organizing, or trying to form a separatist ethnic party. In this context, "ethnic" is always Mizrahi, something that the Sephardi Member of Knesset Elie Eliachar was the first to point out. This Mandate-era figure was a community leader and later president of the Sephardi Community Council. Once the first Israeli parliament formed, Eliachar appealed to Prime Minister Ben Gurion, as well as the other party leaders, to have Sephardi quotas on party lists so that this community would be politically represented. Party leaders declined. Eliachar says that the Sephardi Council was "forced" to stand for elections as a separate party. He wrote of that time: "Not one of the parties represented in the provisional Assembly could find a Sephardi to be included among its delegates."[5] Not even the Histadrut, the workers' union, let Sephardi representatives into decision-making echelons.

According to Eliachar, such political exclusion was having drastic consequences by the 1950s, at which point the majority of Israelis in transit camps were of Oriental origin. With European Jewry running the political show, the nation was divided into two distinct categories: "The givers—that is, the Ashkenazis, who controlled all the funds contributed by the Jewish people throughout the Diaspora for building the state—and the receivers," wrote Eliachar. "The latter had no true representation in order to claim what was rightfully theirs, and were totally dependent for their livelihood on what was doled out by the Ashkenazi establishment."[6] By his analysis, immigrants from the Oriental population were later turned into lackeys of the political system; representation was on the basis of political largesse. When the first government noted its entirely Ashkenazi composition, it was suggested that a Mizrahi be given a minor post, such as the Ministry of Police or the post office. Even that one position was disputed. A Mapai party member of the time said: "By allowing a Sephardi minister in the government, we would consolidate this ethnic gang for decades. We have no need of this."[7] The Ministry of Police and the Post Office Ministry were, right into the 1980s, associated with Mizrahi politicians. Eliachar points out that the Sephardi Council was frequently chastised for being ethnically divisive, but that no such accusations were ever hurled at the main political parties, which were then dominated by European Jewry.

During that first election campaign, after which the Sephardi list won four Knesset seats, a campaign leaflet was in circulation, attacking Eliachar: "He needs the Mizrahi communities in order to present them as poor, ignorant, and naked, to organize collections . . . Will you not rise up against the man who intentionally defames you, calculating to promote his own personal interests?"[8] The intention was clear: ethnic organizing goes not just against the nation-building enterprise, but against Mizrahi voters too. This double-edged rationale became a common refrain. Ironically, the exact opposite was true: it wasn't just the Oriental communities that suffered by not being on the political map, but also Israel as a whole. If there had been more representation of the Mizrahi community, which Eliachar defines as a "ready-made barometer of Arab sensibilities,"[9] the government might have been less paranoid about the country lowering its standards to those of the Arab neighborhood, more able to see the political advantages in not disparaging the East.

During the 1950s and the 1970s, there were two "ethnic protests" that burned themselves onto Israel's memory card to the extent that, even though they are now ancient history (for a sixty-year-old country, the 1970s are like the middle ages), they are still heavily referenced today. The miracle, some Israeli leaders of the 1950s said, was not that protests occurred, but that they did not occur more often. The umbrella explanation for this is that Mizrahis wanted to integrate, not agitate. There were rebellious patches throughout the 1950s, swelling out of the transit camps where people had simply had enough of poor conditions, no jobs, no control, and no way out. This daily reality was compounded by the added shock factor for the Mizrahis, that they were considered inferior. Wadi Salib, formerly a slum district of Haifa inhabited by Palestinians until the 1948 war, then became a slum district populated by mostly Moroccan- and Mizrahi-origin Jews after it. Frustration over social conditions sharpened against

the picture of a glaringly better life enjoyed by well-heeled Ashkenazi residents in the nearby neighborhood Hadar.

On July 9, 1959, Wadi Salib resident Yaakov Elkarif was getting too drunk in a local café and started a brawl. Police quelled
the mayhem by shooting Elkarif—a bullet to the leg. But rumors
spread that he had been killed, which set off angry protests at
the police station the next day. That soon got out of control as
crowds started looting and burned down establishment buildings
like the Labor party office. The demonstrators also specifically
targeted relatively well-heeled suburbs of Haifa, where roads
were blocked and cars burned. And protests also spread to other
parts of the country with dense Oriental populations. In Wadi
Salib, the violence was subdued by police force, but not before
dozens were injured or arrested. Nationwide, the protests had
ethnic unrest stamped all over them.

A commission set up to investigate the causes of the "Wadi
Salib events" heard countless testimonies that complained of individual and collective discrimination. Some commentators describe the media view of Wadi Salib as being within the frame
of a violent, Moroccan community out of control. The demon
was not given credit for its work.

Wadi Salib doubtless laid the socially aware foundations for
the next wave of rebellion, which this time struck on a far wider
scale. By the early 1970s, class divisions were de facto ethnic divisions; the promised smoothing out of initial inequalities hadn't
happened, as the majority of welfare-state dependents were still
Oriental in origin, while the majority of Israel's better-off had
European roots. During this period, it's fair to say that the ethnic
demon was running amok in public, as myriad voices gave vent
to a scope of fears all based on the same concern: that the

Oriental community was now a majority population in Israel and might in some way take over and trash everything.

That was in part voiced by fears that Israel would become Levantine and not European in culture, outlook, and levels of achievement. In 1964, *The Ashkenazi Revolution*, a book by Kalman Katznelson, argued that Mizrahis suffered some sort of genetic inferiority that endangered the quality of the Jewish state. Katznelson called for apartheid-style conditions between the ethnic groups and for the abolition of Mizrahi political rights. He also objected to mixed marriages and wanted Yiddish to be instituted as the national language, since Hebrew too closely resembled Arabic. The book was banned by a furious Ben Gurion, but by the time the ban had taken effect it had already become a bestseller. Eliachar, who appraised the book to be the work of a "Jewish Nazi," lamented that its content was a rabidly extreme version of a common current.

By the late 1960s, Mizrahis were represented in local and national politics, but still on low rungs. Attempts to form "ethnic parties" quickly fizzled out, according to Sami Shalom Chetrit, whose book *The Mizrahi Struggle* includes an exhaustive analysis of ethnic politics. For example, he reports, the Young Israel party formed in the early sixties with the intention of meeting the demand for social reform, as expressed by social protest, through party politics. Its leader was accused of spying for Egypt, in a trial kept secret for security reasons. That was the end of him and the end of that party, which until then was thought to have stood a chance of winning Knesset seats in its first attempt, the 1965 election.

Tarnishing Mizrahi candidates with the enemy brush began in 1955, says Chetrit, with an attack on Elie Eliachar. Knesset member

Shlomo Hillel, the Zionist underground operator who facilitated
the illegal exit of Iraqi Jews, told a party meeting that Eliachar's
chief supporter was Radio Damascus. The Syrian station had
called on Israel's Oriental community to vote for the Sephardi list
and not for Likud leader Menachem Begin. By the early 1960s,
two attempts to form Mizrahi parties had failed; they were, commentators say, routinely stigmatized and dissolved. Mizrahis were
still steered away from "ethnic organizing" on the grounds of national unity. Ben Gurion described it as "corruption and ca-
reerism of the lowest and most dangerous kind. Those whose
Jewish being does not defeat their pride in their foreign country
of birth are not worthy of being called Jewish and Israeli."[10]

Chetrit is not the only one to document this trend. Hanna
Herzog, a professor of sociology at Tel Aviv University, has written
widely on the issue of ethnicity in Israeli politics. She argues that
there has been a simultaneous delegitimization of ethnic politics
and an attempt to neutralize it through co-option. "The crux of
the struggle," she has observed, "resides in the attempts to thwart
organizations whose initiators are of Afro-Asian origin by con-
tending that such activity contradicts the idea of the integration
of the exiles. Such a political initiative is regarded in Israel as
charged with a separatist connotation and thereby as bearing a de-
structive potential that threatens the unity of the Jewish people."[11]
As a result, she argues, Mizrahis in the political field have often
played up the class struggle factor and played down the ethnic factor. She also notes that, in later years, the most successful Mizrahi
parties played up a religious component.

With nowhere else to go, ethnic discontent took to the streets
again in the 1970s. Musrara had been a barbed-wire border between East and West Jerusalem until 1967. After the "miracle

war" in which Israel took control of East Jerusalem from Jordan and united the city—a move not recognized under international law—the development of the surrounding area seemed to skip over Mizrahi-dense Musrara. Israel's preferences seemed clearly in evidence on TV as Russian immigrants of the early 1970s were enthusiastically greeted by Prime Minister Golda Meir. "Once again, real Jews are coming here," she reportedly said. "These are people of of a superior caste who will give us heroes."[12] Those new immigrants were offered benefits to ease them into Israeli life—and that contrasted sharply with the continued neglect in Mizrahi slums.

The Israeli Black Panthers began to organize, their name a conscious tribute to the American Black civil-rights movement, and a binding of the plight of African-Americans to that of the "blacks" in Israel. Following the announcement of a Jerusalem demonstration in March 1971, all seventeen identified members of the Israeli Black Panthers were rounded up and arrested—which had the converse effect of multiplying the crowds that did turn up to protest. Unlike the Wadi Salib protests, this one comprised Ashkenazi demonstrators too. And unlike those earlier Haifa protests, this one did not turn violent. In fact, the incident most worthy of note was Jerusalem mayor Teddy Kollek's remark to the demonstrators: "Get off the lawn, punks!"[13] He was on a drive to beautify the united city, and was evidently upset by the unsightly protests despoiling his efforts.

That was the start of a series of protests from the Israeli Black Panthers, which rapidly mobilized into a coherent movement with a support base of thousands. Just months after the Panthers had formed, its leaders demanded to see the prime minister and she agreed, only to later say that they were "Not very nice boys."[14] Golda Meir did not take their concerns seriously. Or, rather, she did, but she blamed the "social gap" on the fact that "immigrants from Islamic countries brought deprivation and discrimination with them."[15] Meir, as well as being in denial over Palestinians—having famously declared in 1969 that there were no such people—was also in denial about the ethnic demon.

Thousands of demonstrators gathered under a social-protest banner in May 1971 for what became known as "the night of the Panthers." It turned into a violent clash, as protesters met police batons and water jets with rocks and bottles. There were scores more demonstrations for months after, with the Black Panthers pulling no punches over its social agenda: Mizrahis did not just want an equal share in the national pie, they wanted to be involved in its distribution. The language was ethnically charged, talking of "Ashkenazi oppressors" and a "racist policy." A naked effigy of Golda Meir was burned at one demonstration, and some protesters carried placards reading, "Golda, teach us Yiddish!"

The Panthers urged the redress of inequalities "by any means necessary" and demonstrated against a World Zionist Congress meeting in Jerusalem with these words: "Abroad they promised us everything, just let us come to Israel. They promised us a good education and in fact have made us into criminals."[16] In 1970, 78 percent of all adult Jewish and 93 percent of all juvenile Jewish offenders were Mizrahi. This group has remained intransigently associated with blue-collar crime statistics. The Black Panthers organized Robin Hood–style actions, stealing milk from the doorsteps of middle-class neighborhoods of Jerusalem and redistributing it to the city's poor.

It constantly connected class with ethnicity and used a Marxist-style call to revolt. The Panthers were the first Israeli group to make contact with members of the PLO, recognizing the Palestinian right to self-determination and linking that to the Mizrahi cause. And it turned government attempts to crush the movement into a rallying cry—"Police state!"—that spoke to a wider public willing to support the Panthers. According to Sami Shalom Chetrit, who has documented the Panther story in both film and book format, there were more Mizrahi demonstrations in that two-year period than during Israel's entire history up to that point.

The Black Panthers as a protest group dissipated by the end of 1972. The violence and the media portrayal of it, if not the actual cause, turned the public against the movement; and many of the Panther leaders were by then pursuing parliamentary channels, which caused an internal split. Some commentators say that the protest movement proved incapable of transforming into a party political force. The Yom Kippur War of 1973 put a stop to the appearance of the Panthers on the public and the political-party radar, driving home something that the group had always tried to challenge: that security matters took precedence over social issues. "Moshe Dayan argued that you can't wave both flags of security and social affairs simultaneously," Black Panther leader Sa'adia Marciano had said. "But we strongly believed that a weak society could never be strong in its security."[17] This is similar in theme to the opinions of the first Sephardi Knesset member, Elie Eliachar, speaking in the fifties, and is still voiced by Mizrahi campaigners today. The core idea is that if Israeli Jewish society were more equal, more embracing of its own Oriental population, it might then have an entirely different take on relations with its Oriental neighbors, in the holy heart of the Middle East.

Even though the Black Panthers were not on the streets by the mid-1970s, the social message was by then on the public agenda. A commission investigating the causes of the Black Panther rebellion found the work of the ethnic demon in discriminatory practices that had severely disadvantaged the Mizrahi communities. The report acknowledged an almost total overlap between poverty and Mizrahi origins. Although the Panther protests were not recruited from the right wing—and, indeed, frequently clashed with the extreme right, Arab-hating Kahane movement that was active at the time—they did pave the ground for the Mizrahi electoral protest that put the right-wing Likud party in power. Likud leader Menachem Begin capitalized on the sense of alienation and hatred felt by Mizrahis toward the Labor party that dominated politics from 1948 until it was toppled in 1977. This election, consolidated in 1981, is often described as being characterized by "ethnic voting." It's a typically asymmetric assessment: throughout that period, Ashkenazis supported the Labor party to exactly the same degree that Mizrahis favored Likud—three out of every four voters. Yet support for Labor was not defined in ethnic terms.

But the voting habits that defined that period have created ethnic voter profiles. The right wing has a "greater Israel" concept of territory, believing that the Jewish state should encompass both the West Bank of the River Jordan and the Gaza Strip on the coast. The Israeli left wing is ostensibly more in line with world opinion, that Gaza and the West Bank are Palestinian lands occupied by Israel since it took possession of them after the 1967 war. In practice, it doesn't make much difference, since lands remain occupied under governments of both stripes. But according to these political definitions of intent, Ashkenazis are left-wing supporters, labelled as dovish, liberal, moderate, and secular; Mizrahis, meanwhile, fit a nationalistic, militaristic, and religious profile. They are not peace-seekers and they don't like Arabs. The picture does not take into account the historic hatred that many Mizrahis bear toward the Labor party, perceived as agents of oppression, a sentiment that is passed down from parent to child and continues to inform voting behavior today.

The religious component of the Mizrahi community profile is the frame from which the next period of "ethnic organizing" erupted. By the mid-eighties, Likud had failed to eradicate ethnic-class rifts, despite some antipoverty policies. Capitalist market adjustments were hitting poor sectors hard, and attempts to tackle inflation rates drove wages low, sent unemployment high, and stunted economic growth. The newly revitalized, ultra-orthodox religious party SHAS—a Hebrew acronym for Sephardi Torah Guardians—was where disillusioned, disadvantaged Mizrahis turned for a political solution. The party's rabbinical leaders accuse the Israeli establishment of bestowing economic hardships on the Mizrahi population and of disconnecting these Jews from their religious roots. SHAS won four seats for the first time in the 1984 election. The party, and in particular its Iraqi-born leader, Rabbi Ovadia Yosef, came into the media spotlight. Since then, the two main parties, Labor and Likud (and now also Kadima), solicit the support of SHAS to form coalition governments.

Like faith-propelled political movements around the world, SHAS consolidated its power by setting up alternate schools and social funding networks, and by making use of religion as a political rallying point. Initially holding a voter base of low-class, religious Mizrahis, the party later attracted secular and traditional Mizrahis because, despite the orthodox religious framework, it was seen as an agent of socioethnic justice. In this sense, SHAS capitalized on the social consciousness created by the Black Panthers. SHAS was also viewed as being less strict than the traditional, Ashkenazi ultra-Orthodox party, Agudat Israel (now operating in a coalition under the name United Torah Judaism), or the National Religious Party (NRP or Mafdal) which is hard line on both godly and territorial fronts and is the home of religious Zionism.

Rabbi Yosef is regarded as the spiritual leader not just of the SHAS party, but of the wider Sephardi community. He was the Sephardi chief rabbi from 1970 to 1983. He has pronounced that Israel's formation, contrary to the NRP's assessment, was not a religious event and should not be commemorated with a religious blessing. He decreed that Israel should relinquish control over the Occupied Territories, this being preferable to sacrificing Jewish lives in the fight over land. In the early 1990s, SHAS allied with Yitzhak Rabin's Labor coalition government, which began the Oslo peace process with the PLO as partners. It sliced through everyone's perceptions that the Mizrahi vote only favored a nationalist agenda. Yosef, however, later reneged on this sentiment, and the party has in recent years become increasingly territorial-expansionist, rightist, and racist.

SHAS is concerned more with religion than ethnicity or social justice—as shown by its use of the religious term "Sephardi" and not the sociopolitical appellation "Mizrahi." Its solutions were religious first and social as a byproduct if at all. But the party inevitably ended up being viewed through the prism of ethnicity, by its Mizrahi supporters and by Ashkenazi detractors who were accused of disguising racial hatred as antireligious sentiment.

The organization itself eventually talked to the ethnic agenda, a turnaround mostly precipitated by SHAS political leader Rabbi Arye Deri, who skillfully played up the Mizrahi factor for electoral gain. Rabbi Yosef saw a protégé in Deri, whose family arrived, comfortably middle class, from Morocco in 1968 but had a bumpy fall into the downbeat development town of Bet She'an. By 1988, under Deri's leadership, SHAS broke away from its ultra-Orthodox branding and started to canvass a wider Mizrahi base. Then the party garnered more seats and became a credible partner in coalition governments.

In the 1990s, corruption charges were filed against Deri. The investigation lasted ten years, and he was found guilty. Deri was imprisoned, to the outrage of SHAS voters who saw the trial and subsequent incarceration as racially motivated. The investigation served to strengthen support for SHAS, which, by 1996, had ten seats in parliament. At a large pro-Deri rally in Jerusalem in 1997, the son of Rabbi Ovadia Yosef said that the investigation was an attempt by "anti-religious elements to destroy Sephardic Jewry."[18] Deri's indicters took care to emphasize the opposite: "He and the defendants alone are blemished. This is not the crime of an ethnic group, nor is it the crime of a party, nor of a public,"[19] read the sentence. On the day of his imprisonment in September 2000, twenty thousand of Deri's supporters went to the jail compound to express solidarity with him and maintained a tent-based vigil thereafter. It turned into a sort of canvas yeshiva, with power and water supplies. A month later, in October, the camp fizzled out. The Palestinian al-Aqsa intifada broke out and, once again, interrelational problems in Israel took a back seat to defense, security, and the unequivocal need to form a united front against the common enemy.

But if SHAS played the ethnic card on a religious screen, there's a good reason for it. The God factor spoke to another Mizrahi complaint: that Ashkenazis have corrupted and disrespected Judaism in Israel. The broad brushstrokes of the story are that European Zionists saw in the religious tendencies of the Mizrahi community another hallmark of Middle Eastern backwardness and sought to redress it. Stories of European pioneers chopping the religious forelocks off Yemeni migrant children in the early transit camps are raised in this context: European officials said it was for reasons of hygiene; the Yemeni parents said it was an antireligious gesture. Today, pronouncements of religious elitism are corroborated by evidence of discrimination within Israeli ultra-Orthodox circles. Newspaper articles refer to racially motivated incidents in this sector: of Ashkenazis refusing to marry Mizrahis whom they consider inferior, and of Mizrahi kids being refused access to ultra-Orthodox, Ashkenazi-run schools. The schooling issue got so bad that in 2006 the Association for Civil Rights successfully petitioned the Jerusalem municipality education department to enforce antidiscrimination measures in ultra-Orthodox schools. The schools in question deny that any such practice takes place and explain that pupils are refused admission because they are "not suited." However, one Moroccan-origin woman, speaking anonymously to an Israeli newspaper in November 2007, said she had reasons to believe otherwise. The local ultra-Orthodox Beit Yaacov school, a prestigious, high-achieving school in Jerusalem, had refused to admit her six-year-old daughter. The school's secretary, upon hearing the Moroccan family name, told this mother that she should explore other options for the child. "I didn't understand why," the mother relates. "I came on the first day of registration; the list couldn't already have been full."[20] The mother was refused application forms despite numerous phone calls. She then started to receive visits from neighbors and strangers, suggesting that she might be better off sending her daughter to a Sephardi school.

There is a wider pan on this matter of religion. Some Mizrahi campaigners argue that if Israel was set to a European template, then so too was its Judaism. By neglecting the Sephardi— Middle Eastern—component of Judaism, Israel, they say, is presenting an incomplete form of Judaism lacking some of its foundations. The Sephardi tradition is viewed as more flexible and more accommodating than the Ashkenazi traditions. Some people consider this Sephardic trait of religious elasticity as an overlooked, potential salve to the ever-present tensions between religious and secular Jews in Israel. The Ashkenazi flavor of Judaism is manifest in the marking of religious festivals, which tend publicly at least—at official events—to follow European customs (although obviously people follow their own traditions in their own homes and communities). A glaring exception to that is the public, nationally recognized Moroccan *maimuna* celebrations marking the end of Passover. Around Jewish New Year in 2007, a friend related how she and her colleagues were discussing the tradition of eating gefilte fish at this time until they realized that, since none of the group was Ashkenazi, none of them would actually be putting this dish on the festive dinner table. So why discuss it at all, I ask her? "Because it's New Year! Everyone knows that's what you eat at New Year," she replies. Eli Bareket, head of the campaign group MiMizrah Shemesh ("From the Eastern Sun"), relates that as a child he failed a

school religious quiz because he'd given two answers that were
judged as wrong, because they followed interpretations in the
Sephardi religious tradition. "What did this make me think?" he
asks. "That I'm not good enough, that I don't know enough,
that my parents don't know enough, that their traditions are
loser traditions." Religion, being full of morals and parables, is
often used to teach nonreligious material. But if the system of
education is based on characters, stories, answers that are not
yours, suggests Bareket, then you soon lose interest in schooling. This is a variation of the argument stated by the government education inspector in the 1950s, who pointed out that the
overwhelmingly European cultural context of Israeli schooling
was excommunicating Mizrahi pupils. MiMizrah Shemesh seeks
to redress on the grassroots, socially—working with NGOs,
rabbis, and Mizrahi parents in deprived areas—the same issues
that the SHAS party declared as its intention to address politically (but arguably never did), as part of an Israeli government
coalition.

The nineties and onward were deemed to be the end of ethnic politics. No party runs on a specifically ethnic ticket, although
it is still clear that voting is partly predicated on ethnicity. The
prevalence of Mizrahi politicians is testament to a now-inclusive
political mainframe and makes ethnic separatism irrelevant. Some
analysts say that politics is now Israel's best example of social
integration—more so than the other usual measures: education
and income. Such reviews also question the Mizrahi voter profile, pointing out that second- and third-generation Mizrahis may
not have a particularly "Mizrahi consciousness." But critics argue
that the Oriental features of Israeli politicians mean nothing
more than that the system has endorsed Mizrahis precisely on the

condition that they don't mention their roots and don't highlight the specific and neglected needs of the Mizrahi community. Some political scientists disagree with the mainstream death knell for ethnic politics. They point out that the rise of SHAS and others such as the Russian immigrant party Yisrael B'Aliyah and the Ashkenazi-dominated Shinui party, which was rebranded as anti-clerical during the 1990s, indicate that ethnicity still holds sway in the political domain. As one example, commentators point to the SHAS election success of 1996, when the party pulled Mizrahi votes away from Likud by promising to renew and revitalize Sephardi Jewry. An underlying point to this strain of analysis is that the Oslo peace process of the 1990s allowed the Israeli focus to turn internal.

Oddly, a notorious demon comeback was staged by an Ashkenazi politician, the Labor party leader Ehud Barak. In a rare move in September 1997, Barak held a party convention in the southern development town of Netivot among its Mizrahi-dense, anti-Labor population. There, he apologized to the Oriental community, asking their "forgiveness" for what the "Labor party had done to them"[21] as immigrants during the 1950s. Barak explained that he had only realized, half a century later, the extent of the damage caused by his Labor predecessors, and his apology was intended as a first gesture in healing old scars.

His starter for reconciliation was phrased as collective and historical, on behalf of the Labor party. Of course, it was seen as a political tactic designed to earn Mizrahi votes in the forth-coming election—and Barak was accused of deliberately releasing the ethnic demon to this end. More telling was the reaction to the actual concept of an apology: The older generation of Labor stalwarts was outraged. Teddy Kollek, the Jerusalem mayor, put it bluntly: "I do not feel that I owe an apology to anyone. I did everything that I could to help the immigrants."[22] Others were similarly insulted by Barak's slur on Israel's revered pioneer years. "The period of mass immigration was a marvelous time in the history of Zionism, even if there were difficulties,"[23] pronounced one-time president Yitzhak Navon. And Shimon Peres had similar sentiments: "When I think of those days, my heart is filled with pride. Yes, mistakes were made, but I am proud of the accomplishments of the last fifty years."[24]

Half a century after the fact, an attempt by one national leader to apologize for a historical injustice prompted an avalanche of denial by other national heads. There was still, it seemed, a prevailing blindness to the scale of the damage caused by earlier discriminations and oblivion to the possibility that those disparities in opportunity and achievement, sharply drawn across ethnic lines, might still prevail. The demon was alive and well, but by now it had fully morphed into the elephant in the room.

If there is a set attitude to the Israeli-Palestinian conflict among Mizrahis, it is that the Ashkenazi elite is not capable of solving it. Time and again, Mizrahis insist that they could have done a better job, given the chance. Iraqi-Israeli Emmanuel Paamon thinks that European-origin Israelis fail in negotiations because "There is no understanding of relationships, of relating to people." By contrast, he is "able to speak with all the Arabs; I know how to talk in their language, with their honor." This take is not necessarily rooted in a liberal stance on the peace process; it comes more from a perceived understanding of the Middle Eastern mentality. Echiel Zafrani, the Moroccan-born former local Likud official in Kiryat Shmona, says: "We the Sephardis, if they had placed it in our hands to make peace with the Arabs, we would have done it, we would have succeeded better than the Ashkenazis because they don't have the mentality to speak with the Arabs. When I go to an Arab's house, immediately there will be a click between us . . . a natural, automatic click. But with the Ashkenazi there is no click. And we don't have the click with the Ashkenazi, either. That is the absurd truth."

Zafrani is right-wing: he could not be described by the standard political criteria as "pro-Arab." His assessment of Mizrahis doing a better job at the negotiating table is to do with culture; sensibility. It's a common perception, one that seems to view negotiations as constantly failing because of a lack of manners or mentality—a basic disrespect and a lack of instinctive understanding that crucially affects political relations.

This is not the perspective of Palestinians involved in the negotiation process, who see Israeli faces seated across the table and don't subcategorize beyond that. The nationally defined conflict has killed the click. Ask what went wrong in the past, and the most commonly cited cause is that Israeli negotiators expected their Palestinian counterparts to unilaterally compromise. As far as the Palestinian side is concerned, it has already agreed to cede most of historic Palestine—now Israel—and sees no reason why it should have to relinquish a right to any part of the remaining 22 percent of land that would form a future Palestinian state. There are other criticisms, too, such as the Israeli side using security concerns as a blanket veto, without further explanation, or not fulfilling its obligations as part of peace talks (by continuing to build and expand settlements and settlement infrastructure, for example, or by not removing checkpoints), or that Israel is chronically incapable of relinquishing control over Palestinian life, or that the entire process is too mired in mistrust to enable any sort of progress.

In all those considerations, it makes no difference whether the Israeli negotiating team comprises individuals of Iranian, Moroccan, or Polish origin—and the overarching point Palestinians make is that Mizrahis were not excluded or absent from such meetings. The decade of the Oslo peace process, culminating in the breakdown of negotiations at Camp David in 2000, was also the decade of the Mizrahi politician. Noticeably, these politicians had key positions in government—not prime minister, still not that—but the finance, foreign, and defense ministries. "I've seen Iraqi Jews sitting at the negotiating table. I've seen Yemeni Jews, Moroccans, Iranians, in the highest echelons of power and decision-making," says Saeb Erekat, chief negotiator for the Palestinian Authority. "Tell your Iraqi cousins and friends. Tell them that [I say], no, you *were* at the negotiating table, and you screwed."

There has been a specifically Mizrahi input to the negotiation process, over the issue of the Palestinian right of return. In 1976, the World Organization of Jews from Arab Countries (WOJAC) was founded, in France, with this purpose in mind: to state that Oriental Jews were expelled from Arab countries and hence should also be considered as refugees whose compensation rights were to be discussed and set off against any "debt" that Israel might pay out to Palestinian refugees. Since its creation, Israel has been asked to deal with this issue, of how to compensate the 711,000 Palestinian refugees who fled or were forced to leave the country in the 1948 war. Near the end of the war, the UN Security Council passed resolution 194—reaffirmed many times since—article II of which calls for the return of refugees and compensation for those not wishing to return. By the 1970s, with the formation of the Palestine Liberation Organization (PLO), the right of return and self-determination were being articulated internationally with greater force and eloquence. WOJAC was established as a counter; during the 1990s, one of its leaders, Dr. Jaques Barnes, defined the organization as "The Jewish answer to the PLO . . . to the right of return . . . that is why we exist."[25]

The organization still exists, primarily as a forum for collating the value of properties abandoned by Jews of Arab countries. There are others that operate with a similar remit. Justice for Jews from Arab Countries, for instance, is an advocacy group that claims it is concerned not so much with compensation as with public awareness and a redress of popular assumptions about who is the refugee in the Palestinian-Israeli conflict. Such arguments tend to gain media attention whenever there are peace talks between the two sides. So, by 2000, President Clinton agreed to a request from Israeli Prime Minister Ehud Barak to put the rights of Jewish refugees from Arab lands on the negotiating table at Camp David. This same issue resurfaced in world media articles around the time of the Annapolis revival of negotiations in October 2007, the first time that peace talks reconvened since their Camp David collapse. Various Internet sites and forums are dedicated to the "forgotten refugees"—Oriental Jews who feel that their fate has been glaringly overlooked in the Middle East discussion. The subject relates primarily to Iraqi, Syrian, and Egyptian Jews, all of whom were prevented from taking assets out of the countries that they left. To briefly summarize this position: Arab countries, having relentlessly persecuted

Jewish communities, made them depart penniless because of anti-Semitism and a desire to cripple the Israeli state. There are many recollections of forced, brutal, and impoverished fleeings from certain Arab countries at this time. However, addressing only timings and not the cruel details, one Arab counter to that might be "You started it," pointing to the Palestinian refugees created by the 1948 war and the consequent seizure of Palestinian property.

Unfortunately for WOJAC, which was for many years the prime body concerned with this debate, it became hopelessly entangled with the ethnic demon. That's an argument put forward by Yehouda Shenhav, professor of sociology and anthropology at Tel Aviv University, who has written extensively on the subject, based on archived, pristinely kept WOJAC minutes and records. He reports that, right from the start, the ethnicity factor was hovering in the wings, as the foreign minister, Yigal Alon, told one of WOJAC's founders, Mordechai Ben Porat (the Iraqi Zionist underground leader): "We know you and trust you, but what will happen if [the organization] falls into the hands of someone who exploits it for ethnic mobilization?"[26] Shenhav documents that this organization did not need to fall into anyone else's hands to evince the demon. Because, as it turned out, ethnicity was stamped all over WOJAC.

In 1949 a British plan, endorsed by the U.S., was proposed to Iraqi Prime Minister Nuri al-Said, that he "swap" Iraqi Jews for Palestinian refugees. Both Iraq and Israel refused the plan, but it was the first time that the lives of these two peoples were thrown together into one uniform fate. By 1951, when al-Said froze the properties of Iraqi Jews who were emigrating to Israel, the equation was cemented by the Jewish state's foreign minister. Speaking in a cabinet meeting in March that year, Moshe Sharett said: "An account already exists between us and the Arab world: the account of the compensation that accrues to the Arabs who left the territory of Israel and abandoned their property . . . The act that has now been perpetrated by the kingdom of Iraq . . . forces us to link the two accounts." Sharett proposed to take the value of Iraqi Jewish property into account "when calculating the compensation that we have undertaken to pay the Arabs who abandoned property in Israel."[27]

That account wasn't discussed much until the 1970s, when WOJAC, supported and funded by the Israeli Foreign Office, revived the argument. In fact, says Professor Shenhav, WOJAC's argument comprised three dimensions: that Jews from Arab countries have territorial claims to Israel based on their continued historic presence in the terrain of the Middle East; that the region had experienced a spontaneous exchange of refugees as Oriental Jews swapped homelands with Palestinian Arabs; and that the properties of both these population groups, Jews and Arabs, could be counterbalanced on any spreadsheet relating to refugee compensation.

There are all manner of objections to this proposition. First, there is no reason why the fate of Oriental Jews and Palestinian Arabs should be materially combined: such a proposition does little to promote good relations between Israel and its neighbors. Second, Shenhav proposes that this construction can be viewed as a form of "double-entry accounting." If Zionism engineered homelessness for both parties—removing Palestinians from Israel and Jews from Arab lands—the Israeli government would effectively reap the rewards twice over, following the proposed bookkeeping system. There is hostility, also, to a proposition that might compensate all Jews of Arab origin directly into an Israeli bank account, precluding the possibility of individual settlements for lost property. In this context, as in others, Jews living outside Israel do not always want to be represented by the Jewish state (and some Jews withing Israel have this same concern).

Another problem is WOJAC's core definition of Jews from Arab lands as "refugees"—because not everyone would define themselves as such. Back in 1975, Knesset speaker Yisrael Yeshayahu made his protestations known: "We did not want to call ourselves refugees," he said. "We came to this country before the establishment of the state, too . . . We had messianic aspirations."[28] The difficulty is that the expulsion theory of Jewish exodus from Arab countries infringes on the right of these migrants to define themselves as Zionists, or as anything other than refugees. There is a big difference between being forced to flee a land and purposefully leaving it out of love for Israel. Professor Shenhav documents that the Israeli foreign ministry quickly understood the implications of the refugee argument were it to fall into the wrong hands. Sure enough, in 1975, the PLO's political department sent a message to a WOJAC conference in Paris, urging that Oriental Jews return to Arab countries. In 1975, Libya's Muammar Ghadaffi invited former Jewish residents of that country to "return to the land of your birth!"[29] (He repeated the offer in 2004.) Then, in January 1979, Radio Baghdad broadcast, in Hebrew, an announcement that former Jewish citizens of Iraq were welcome back and would receive full rights in their birth country.

The dangerous subtext heard by Israelis in all these instances was: If these Jews return to their former Arab homelands, it will devalue the rationale for the Jewish state. In 2008, a U.S. Congress subcommittee passed a resolution to consider Jews from Arab lands refugees. The historian Tom Segev again highlighted the hidden meaning: "A spokesman for the Arab lobby in America might just welcome the decision," he wrote. "Terrific, he'll say; then all that's needed is for the Jews to return to their countries of origin and for the Palestinians to return to their homes [now in Israel] and everything will be fine."[30]

Throughout the 1980s and 1990s, WOJAC was still debating the refugee definition. In July 1987, Ran Cohen of the Meretz party told the Knesset: "I did not come to this country as a refugee. I stole across borders. I underwent a great deal of torment . . . I have no need for anyone to define the Jews of the East as refugee Jewry."[31] By 1998, Shlomo Hillel, who was not a member of WOJAC but had been a Zionist underground leader in Iraq, said: "I do not regard the exodus of Jews from Arab countries as refugees . . . The Jews in the Arab countries came because they wanted to come."[32] Both he and Cohen describe a narrative that holds sway in Israeli society, of a Jewish exodus fraught with difficulties but facilitated by a yearning for Zion and by the deft heroics of the Zionist underground in the face of persecution from hostile Islamic rulers. But refugee status complicates that story, collapsing a dichotomy and making room for all the gray in between: that Jews weren't always forced to leave Arab countries; that they didn't always want to leave; that they weren't en masse Zionists. No less significant is a fundamental difference between Palestinian and Oriental Jewish populations. For Palestinians, the idea is to return to the place from which they were exiled: the birth country, the motherland: "home." Jews migrating to Israel have already arrived "home" and therefore have no desire to return to their countries of birth.

But a more pertinent collapse is also charted by Professor Shenhav, who argues that the main factor in the decline of WO-JAC is the ethnic factor. The demon is in the details of WOJAC's first argument, that Middle Eastern Jews have land rights in Palestine, based on the unbroken presence of Jews in the region. WOJAC officials held that the twenty-five-hundred-year history of Middle Eastern Jews laid down foundations of legitimacy for the Jewish state. "We want to prove that we are part of the Middle East. We are not foreigners," said Mordechai Ben Porat. "We lived here before the arrival of the Arabs, before their conquests."[33] WOJAC, in this context, challenged the Arab argument that negates the Jewish state as a foreign presence in the region. Effectively, this Mizrahi-Jewish group says: Rubbish, we've been here forever. In other conversations, WOJAC suggested to Israeli officials that they might employ more "dark-skinned" representatives of the Jewish state on international platforms, so that the world might see the legitimate, Middle Eastern face of the Jewish state.

The trouble is: if Middle Eastern Jews have a territorial claim to Israel based on historic presence, what of their European brothers? By asserting Oriental Jewish rights, WOJAC seemed to have accidentally negated a European Jewish legitimacy to the land. By this stage, the Israeli government seemed to have had enough of WOJAC and stopped backing it. This group had been working as a representative of Israel, with the explicit purpose of providing a counter to the Palestinian refugee issue. Nobody could accuse WOJAC of being un-Israeli. But in the end, the loudest of the messages conveyed by this group was based on its ethnicity—the persistent, nagging voice of the demon.

Chapter 9

WE ARE NOT ARABS!

THREE WOMEN, ALL in their sixties perhaps, sitting along-side me on the long-haul, early-bird bus to Kiryat Shmona. Two sisters and a sister-in-law, talking nonstop in Iraqi-influenced Arabic, smooth and sparkly on this dreary coach rammed full of soldiers. They have a kind of middle-class, Iraqi-Jewish style about them: clothes a little on the glare side of bright, but cut smart and perfectly matched; good hairdressers; gold jewelry. "Oh, you understand us," they exclaim, as I break my own dawn curfew on small talk with strangers. They'd automatically pegged me as Polish.

The sister seated right next to me had left Baghdad at the age of ten, but left none of the Orient behind. She lives in central Tel Aviv and speaks Arabic constantly, listens to the music, adores the great singers like Fairuz and Farid al-Atrash. She has all the Arabic channels on TV and declares herself to be in love with the language. When I awake from a nap, she asks me if I slept well, in Arabic, and continues speaking in that language—which gives her the right of way. She relates that she is happy in Israel, of course, but that she was happy in Iraq too. She adores Arabic culture. But the Arabs themselves, they are killers. They like to die, she says; you see their mothers on TV, wishing for their son's death if it means they also kill some Jews.

There's nothing unusual about her views, which I've heard many times by now, layer upon damning layer of dehumanizing clichés—but this woman is conducting the tirade in her beloved language, her beautiful Arabic. It's too much. "Aren't you also an Arab?" I ask her. "I mean, you're Iraqi, right, so isn't that the same thing?" It's the conversational equivalent of slamming on the brakes and screeching into a dark alley. "Of course I'm not Arab!" she fires back. "I'm Jewish! Of course we are different!"

That the terms "Arab" and "Jew" might not be mutually exclusive is a desperately unpopular idea proposed in so-called "extreme" Israeli circles—those voices given a rare open-mike appearance in this book. Some "radical Mizrahi academics" define themselves as Arab Jews, deliberately reconnecting the identities that they argue Israel prized apart. Then it's dismissed as outlandish, provocative nonsense. But sometimes the theory gets an unexpected public airing, in unusual places and in a manner that eerily mimics real-life dialogue.

Love Hurts is a standard twenty-something sitcom, popular recently on peak-time Israeli TV. It's about a couple—Dana, of Ashkenazi origin, and Oren, a Mizrahi—who fight and break up and then make up. The first time that Dana meets Oren's family, for a Saturday lunch, the news on TV reports a suicide bomb explosion at a cinema. Oren's mum and brother are watching the screen, and the mum says, "They [Palestinians] don't care about the lives of others, they just don't care, what can we do?" And the brother says: "I'll kill them before they kill us, that's what." But that's no solution, the mother says: "They don't care if you kill them, that's what they like! They like to die! I lived with them, I was born there. I know what an Arab is." The family continue talking in this vein, with the additional tangent of how primitive "the Arabs" are.

The girlfriend character in *Love Hurts*, Dana, is from Tel Aviv, has Polish parents, and works in the media—all the classic Israeli markers of being left-wing. In fact, any of those labels— "Journalist," "Ashkenazi," or "Tel Aviv"—is practically code for being situated left of the political spectrum. "Left" and "right" may be informed by, but are not markers of, economic or social policy; the tags relate entirely to a stand on the conflict. So Dana the lefty challenges this Mizrahi family's views on the Palestinians and the reported bombing. "I don't know why you're so against the Arabs," she says. "You yourselves are Arabs. And if what you say is right, then *you* are primitives and *you* only understand force and *you* don't care about human life." The family stares at her, stone-silent. She carries on, asking if she's said something wrong. After all, surely this family knows that they are Arabs? More silent glaring, and then a short outburst from the father: "We are not Arabs!" Well, then, what are you, the girlfriend asks? "Jews!" they all shout in unison. The conversation carries on just long enough for the family to insist, first of all, that it is not possible to be both Jewish and Arab, and secondly, that Oren (whom the family address using a Mizrahi-sounding name), immediately removes his girlfriend from the family home.

This Dana character is a bit irritating, a kind of superficially in-vogue radical—and is given those lines as a means of lashing out, having suffered the presence of her boyfriend's childhood and perhaps current love at the Saturday lunch table. Also, her prescience is grating: wasn't it her forebears who condescended to the elders of the family she is now dining with, who taught them to bury their Arab traits? European Jews came to Israel voicing a Western superiority over the Levant, not the Oriental Jews, not this sitcom family who have internalized the prevailing view of Arab primitivism only to then have it thrown back in their faces by a smug TV character. If pioneer Zionists from Europe contributed to this present-day schism between Arab and Jew, then their children, privileged enough to be left-wing, are now shown lamenting it—a twisted development.

But the sitcom family's stance is the focus of a standard complaint among the Israeli left wing: that Mizrahis are rabid Arab-haters propelling an extreme nationalist ideology and stalling the peace process. In all the political polls, the Mizrahis are shown to be more prone to solutions that use force against Palestinians; more reluctant to let go of Jewish settlements in the West Bank. The Mizrahi sentiment that they might better handle negotiations with Arab neighbors is based on aspects of mindset and etiquette and not often upon an actual liberal Left position. Brutally anti-Arab views are manifest in Mizrahi-dense towns like Sderot and its neighbors, or Kiryat Shmona on the border with Lebanon, places under attack and in which you might argue that only the Dalai Lama could remain hate-free. There are countless exceptions to that statement, but the fierce animosity voiced by Mizrahis is visceral. A man in his thirties in Ofakim provides a typical view. "I say wipe out the Arabs. Yes, wipe them out, like people tried to wipe us out. Yes, I'm that extreme," he declares. "I was raised to believe that whoever hurt you, it doesn't matter, you just bring him to his knees. Don't give him a chance to breathe so he can return and do it again." This man puts his bully ethos into practice with a debating style based not so much on being right as on being relentless. His parents lived in Morocco and they've told him that there, the doors were always open to Arab neighbors, from which he can only conclude that these Arabs, the Palestinians, are not the same as the friendly Arabs in Morocco. That's another hypothesis among Israelis who originate in Middle Eastern countries, speaking volumes about a fundamental misconception over the causes of the conflict. The last thing this bully from Ofakim says, having wished a holocaust (his word) on the Palestinians, is that he is having an affair with an Arab-Israeli woman. "She would become a martyr for me," he jokes, of her devotion to him. Ok, as long as it's on your side.

Mostly, the Mizrahi hatred of Arabs is viewed as an indication of less-developed political sensibilities, a product of having come from Middle Eastern countries with no trace of liberalism or proper concepts of citizenship on the landscape. On top of which, Oriental Jews suffered dreadful persecution under Islam prior to their migration to Israel, so, actually, they have firsthand experience of how hateful the Arabs really are. This analysis is underpinned by the ambient appraisal of the relative morality of Arabs and Jews: "They kill; we don't." Such a verdict seems to be based on perceived intentions, rather than actual consequence: between September 2000, when the Second Intifada began, and October 2007, 1,027 Israelis and 4,345 Palestinians were killed because of the conflict between the two peoples. It's just as well that the moral difference is claimed to exist, because it would otherwise be more difficult for Mizrahis to prove that they are not Arabs. And prove it they must, since they can't be both. Arab and Jew are historic enemies, polar opposites. You can be a Moroccan Jew, or an Iraqi Jew—but an Arab Jew?

What do you call someone who lives in an Arab country, who prays and dreams in Arabic, who reads Arabic poetry and papers, whose mother and her mother cooked Arabic food, who loves Arabic film and music, and who lives by the customs of the Arab world? Why would you painstakingly persist on a definition that says the Jews lived like, but were not, Arabs? Would you also say that Jews who lived like Europeans were not European Jews? After several centuries of the actuality of "Arab Jews," in everyday life if not as a stated label, the Arab-Israeli conflict has in the space of a few decades not only eliminated such a classification, but claims that it never existed in the first place. No, Middle Eastern Jews are not Arabs, goes the floodwave of opinion; they just picked up some Arab characteristics while living under Muslim rule. The writer Ilan Halevi describes this analysis as employing "the fiction that the Jews had crossed a desert [upon migration to Israel] like drops of oil in water, without any interplay or metabolism."[1] The truth, he argues, using the banned hyphenated label, is that Arab-Jews were "engaged in a constant cultural and ideological exchange with their Muslim and Christian neighbors, an integral part of the Arabic-speaking mental world."[2]

When Zionist emissaries first encountered Oriental Jews, some had trouble discerning them amid the rest of the Arab population. One, reporting back from Libya, wrote of the Jewish community there: "They are handsome as far as their physique and outward appearance are concerned, but I found it difficult to tell them apart from the good quality Arab type."[3] Enzo Sereni, an envoy sent to Baghdad from the Jewish settlement in Palestine, wrote back to base: "The Jew lives like an Arab. His culture is Arab, he uses Arabic figures of speech, but nevertheless there is something that differentiates. A Jew knows that he is a Jew and that he is different from an Arab. To say what makes him different is difficult. Even in the social sense, there is no vast difference."[4] Sereni insisted on there being a distinction because there *was* one: religion. It wasn't as though the Jewish community of Baghdad had abandoned Judaism in a bid to assimilate—they were a part of Iraqi society without having to do so. There was no European renaissance here, of the style that pressured Jews to redefine identity, to decide the boundaries of faith and nation.

By the eighteenth century, Jewry in Central and Western Europe was almost entirely fused with the non-Jewish population. That same fusion happened far earlier in the Orient, so that there was just one discernible demographic difference—Jews were, as one nineteenth-century observer put it, "Arab in all but religion."[5] That's probably why external eyes couldn't spot the Jewish community amid the Iraqi population at large. When Zionism and Iraqi nationalism developed, in opposing directions, that forced Jewish citizens to choose: what are you, and to whom are you most loyal? Then, in Israel, the split became de facto law because, as Prime Minister David Ben Gurion insisted, "We do not want Israelis to become Arabs."[6] It wasn't just that the Middle Eastern Jews bore the manners of the enemy; it was the concern that these migrant manners might regress Israel.

If social membership, smooth assimilation, and a rise up the status ladder depend upon possessing certain characteristics and not others, people soon pick up which habits to drop. This is what scores of Mizrahi academics, campaigners, and individuals who are a long way from being defined as either now narrate: childhoods spent obscuring or morphing roots in order to belong. Professor Shenhav's real surname is "Shaharabani," a sure giveaway of a Mizrahi family tree. "I can remember encouraging my dad to change his name when I was twenty or twenty-one," he says now. "I pressured him to agree. I said it ruins my life, my career, that people have stereotypes over this name, that it doesn't associate with good standing, I said all that. Which was true, by the way: I felt stigma from the name." Initially, Shenhav's father refused, but the son was persistent. "One of the saddest things in my life now is to go to my father's grave and see the headstone, and see 'Shenhav' there rather than 'Shaharabani.'"

Name-changing is a known occurrence among Mizrahi Jews. At first, this practice applied to first names and was imposed by immigrant-absorption officials who would swap Arabic names for Hebrew-Israeli ones. Today it is carried out on surnames, voluntarily. Around the time that Shenhav was pestering his father for a name change, a common Israeli joke was "What does a Sephardi child want to be when he grows up? Ashkenazi!" Shenhav remembers that his mother was also a source of shame. "When I was still Sharhabani and a friend would ask me in the street after we bumped into my mother, 'Is this the maid?' I would say, 'Yes.' And you hear this story all over, this same old story." Moshe Karif, another Mizrahi campaigner, says: "My grandmother looked like a Palestinian, so I asked her not to come to school to pick me up."[7]

Henriette Dahan-Kalev, professor of political science at Ben Gurion University, invented an entire personality for herself after being told so often as a child, "You're so pretty, you don't look Moroccan." Her family's move from one city to another provided the ten-year-old Dahan-Kalev with a perfect opportunity for an exhaustive character overhaul. "I told my new Jerusalem friends that I was born in France," she says. "In order to be convincing, I

consciously eliminated my distinctive Arab accent and trained myself to adopt the typical Ashkenazi accent. Obviously, I did not invite any of my friends home . . . I was afraid that they would hear
my mother speak to me in Arabic. I forbade her absolutely to
speak Arabic when outside the house. Soon I began to believe my
own deceptive tales as, little by little, I constructed a desirable
identity for myself . . . to which I added additional biographical
details that were meant to ensure my acceptance amongst the children in my class." All this, Professor Dahan-Kalev says, was based
on information she had absorbed from a social environment of
contempt for Arab culture. "All that is Mizrahi is retarded, degen-
erate, and primitive, and therefore I had to choose the Ashkenazi
alternative," she says. "For me this meant . . . destroying, down to
the roots, the identity that my parents gave me . . . rejecting
everything: their past, their language, their values, their loves, their
hates, their pains, and their joys."[8]

What Dahan-Kalev and others describe was the de facto end
goal of a philosophy of assimilation developed in Israel. Mizrahi
campaigners often refer to the work of Professor Noel Shmuel
Eisenstadt, the grandfather of Israeli sociology. One of his theories, "Absorption Through Modernization," developed during
the 1950s, argued a process of social integration by which, to
paraphrase, backward peoples ditch their lowly customs and get
with the modern Western program. That, he held, was the way
to close the social and cultural gap between Ashkenazi and
Mizrahi Jews in Israel. If not, there would be trouble: "The potential spread of a formless culture of the masses, and the possibility of a revival of what is known as Levantinization and
Provincialism, can weaken the trend for cultural and social horizons and commitments, and finally sweep away their foundations

and institutional nuclei.'"[9] There it was again, that fear: if the Mizrahis didn't come up to Western speed, Israel would be sunk.

Years after Mizrahi kids had faked white identities, one Labor Knesset member argued that this approach had been a mistake. "We, the Ashkenazis, were carried away by a wave of condescension toward the Arab world," says Arie Lova Eliav. "We made Arabic and Arab culture into something somewhat inferior." Eliav, who served in five Knessets during a political career spanning three decades, explains that when he made that point in the 1960s, it went very much against the consensus. He thinks that Israel is far more inclusive of Oriental culture these days, but still has a long way to go before achieving cultural equality.

It's not just Mizrahi academics and activists who have experienced a sort of "awakening" over an anti-Arab–fueled oppression. Sasson, an Iraqi former teacher in Sderot, is discussing politics with me when, unprompted, he changes the subject. "I don't have a cultural identity; the nation stripped the culture of my parents," he says. "I would always switch channels when my dad was listening to [Arabic music and news], because I didn't like it, because at school they would say, you need to be a new Israeli, you can't stay with your parents' culture, so they tried to wipe it out, you understand?" Sasson would hear Israeli songs at school and in clubs, but it didn't resonate. "My heart is in the East and my culture is Western culture, Ashkenazi culture," he says. "They dressed me up in a culture that isn't mine." Now he wonders about his children. "What culture will [they] have?" he asks. "Their culture has gone. It has all been wiped out, you understand?"

Sometimes self-erasure isn't enough to curb social stigmas. Scores of young Mizrahis talk about not being able to get into certain city nightclubs because of the color of their skin. The

Israeli papers frequently carry reports of this. Bouncers respond that they are not specifically screening out Oriental Jews, but are screening for potential troublemakers—but Mizrahis are so deeply associated with disorder and violence that it is practically the same thing. A few years ago, one Mizrahi politician, debating the issue on a TV panel, brought the argument right back to its core, exasperated: "What can I do," he asked, "if I look like the enemy?"[10]

Mizrahis often describe being stopped by police in the street, especially if they happen to be walking the streets of mixed cities. "It's a kind of Jerusalem experience to be considered Arab," says the half-Mizrahi prizewinning writer Almog Behar, a teacher at the city's Kedma school. "It happens to me lots of times, like I'm standing in the bus station and military police stop me to ask me for an ID card and so on." Behar says that during a bearded period of his life, his looks made a woman get off a bus they'd both been traveling on. "She was so frightened," he says. "I was thinking of assuring her in some way but decided not to, and she left the bus." One young woman from Sderot recalls driving one night to Ashkelon with her boyfriend and a Yemeni friend who "looks Bedouin." She wasn't the only one to have that thought: "A police detective stopped us, shone a torch in his face, got us out of the car, and turned everything inside it upside down." In this sort of environment, donning conspicuous symbols of Judaism—a Star of David or *Chai** necklace, a skullcap on the head—might not always be an act of faith so much as an act of proving membership to it.

---

*Chai, in Hebrew letters and meaning "living," is a common symbol of Judaism.

Looking at Zfania, you'd have to admit that he would not stand out in a crowd in Ramallah—although he disagrees: "They would identify me as an Israeli straight away," he says. "You can tell, from far away." He might have a point; in a region that is hypersensitive to national-religious identity, Israelis and Palestinians are sometimes so good at telling each other apart that you wonder if they're using ESP. But Zfania's looks were enough to raise suspicion within Israel when he was returning home from military duty on the Lebanese border in 1998. "I get on a bus in Haifa, fall asleep, and wake up at Tel Aviv station," he says. At the capital's central bus station (and others), a security official boards and inspects every incoming bus before it can proceed to the parking bay, where passengers get off. "I'm not in uniform and have a weapon on me, so the security man's suspicious," says Zfania. "He goes to the end of bus and then he comes back to me, and I already have my ID card ready. He puts one hand on me and his other hand is on his weapon, and he says, 'Have you got a military ID card?' and I say [he puts on an Arabic accent]: 'Walla, you don't need to be scared, I won't speak with an accent at all.'" Zfania is still furious about this incident. "What a disgrace! He should be ashamed of himself." That wasn't the end of it, since Zfania then had to go through the passenger check before entering the main building, the only way out of the bus-station complex. "I get off the bus and go to enter the station, and hell, it is the same check," he says. "They turn my bags inside out and check me like I don't know what, and then a white boy passes, also a soldier with the same bags, like me not in uniform, but he is passed without a check!" Zfania thinks that the security officials should have been more professional, better trained to spot potential trouble using more reliable clues. He sounds like any male, Middle

Eastern–looking resident of the post-9/11 West, subjected to searches and scrutiny on that basis alone.

Neither Zfania nor Sasson would self-define as Arab Jews— few Mizrahis would—and in their perspectives on the conflict, both are on the right. Some Mizrahi activists argue this to be the product of a Marxist-style false consciousness. Just as capitalist social forces blind workers to their true motivations, so Zionist social forces nurture a similar effect in Mizrahis. After so many years of learning to hate their own rejected Arab features and having to hide them, the Mizrahis simply projected all that revulsion onto the neighboring Arab community—because self-loathing is hard to maintain and because there, in the enemy, was the perfect outlet for it.

Another tangent is that the Mizrahi population needed to prove an allegiance to the nation. They had not invented Zionism, nor "pioneered" the state, nor (in most cases) suffered the Holocaust that gave it urgent legitimacy. Hating the national enemy with a passion is a way of securing admission to the club. Those who argue such points talk from personal experience, having gone through a process of rejecting previously held beliefs predicated on those foundations. But false consciousness is a component of a vanguard theory by which the masses, following the calls of an intellectual elite, wake up, break out, and rise up.

The Mizrahi elite is unlikely to precipitate a large-scale revolt in the middle of the Oriental Jewish population because it—like all vanguard movements—remains far removed, politically, socially, and mentally, from this community. Crucially, polled Mizrahis put a high value on inter-Jewish integration and have nothing to gain by going against it. Also, false-consciousness theories of any flavor employ a baseline assumption of denial: the "self-hating Jew" label, stuck on to anyone who is both a critic of Israel and a member of the tribe, is essentially founded on the same thing.

The Mizrahi experience is in one sense a kind of universal integration experience: every immigrant, struggling to fit into any new country, might start adopting the norms of the dominant culture. There are basic flaws in the premise of why the dominant culture of a Middle Eastern country should have been set by its European minority. But also, in Israel, it cuts deeper than that: Mizrahis who don't embrace the normative aren't just on the outside, they're out there with the enemy. If you've got an entry pass called "Jewish," why jeopardize it by casting your lot with the socioeconomically inferior and adversary squad? Worse still, it's an alliance with the side that is branded as violent, uncivilized, and primitive. If the Israeli-Arab conflict has conflated the words "Jewish" and "Zionist," then the supposed modern-day battle between East and West has tried to make synonyms of "Arab" and "violent Muslim extremist." The Arab world has been given appalling PR.

In the post-9/11 world, Israel cannily hitched a ride on the War on Terror wagon, rebranding the narrative: it is not fighting a national insurrectionary movement on its borders, but a local branch of the worldwide fundamentalist-killer network. Serving to cement the partnership, Western experts have argued that, for the Islamic resistance movement Hamas, the Israeli occupation is causal and not ideologically integral to its agenda—in other words, that Hamas is cannily hitching a ride on the Palestinian liberation wagon to mainline a deeply reactionary, violent religious charter.

Within Israel, the narrative redesign simply consolidated one already set by the Second Intifada of 2000. This was the period of the suicide-bomb attacks, which blew to pieces any sympathy felt within Israeli borders for the Palestinian nationalist struggle. Bitterly felt on both sides, the Second Intifada had a disastrous effect on the Arab-Jew debate, making Mizrahis even less tolerant of any ambivalence over identity. Casual friendships between Israelis and Palestinians disintegrated. And these relations, because of the commonality of language and culture, had previously been a regular occurrence among the Mizrahi population. Sasson in Sderot recounts frequent trips to nearby Gaza, dinner and wedding invitations, overnight stays, all reciprocated. Staunchly nationalistic, he says to me: "You might be more left-wing, but I bet you that I have more friends in Gaza." Today, it has been years since Sasson and his Gazan friend last spoke, much less actually met. Everything about this hopelessly reductive discourse tells the Oriental Jews to absolutely bind their fate with the winning team, Israel, the Western country, the bulwark of modern values in the scarily, violently Islamified Middle East. Drop everything that might allude to a commonality with the Arab world or invite the label "Arab Jew." Drop the term itself.

All of which might go some way toward explaining why the hyphenated term precipitates both angry rejection and some contorted linguistic acrobatics today. Yacoub Alali and Elias Shasha, the two Iraqi-Jewish musicians who would not look out of place performing in the nightclubs of neighboring Arab nations, are discussing the label one day, at my suggestion. "Arab Jews?" asks Alali. "Yes, that's what they call us. We say we are Iraqi Jews. No, we don't say we are Arabs." Shasha the oud player disagrees: "But the truth is that we are Arabs!" he says. "We were born Arabs, but we are Jews," suggests Alali. "Jewish is just religion. I'm Arab, but Jewish." To which Shasha responds with this formula: "We were born Arabs in Iraq, and 'Jewish' is our religion."

The Arab Jew label might be an awkward fit on actual immigrants from Arab countries, but Professor Shenhav argues that the hyphenated label was never intended to be descriptive of their Israeli-born progeny, or the entire Mizrahi community. "Once upon a time there were Arab Jews, and this category was erased or vanished from discourse," he says. "What does it do to re-present a category, against the grain? It doesn't mean that it characterizes a group of people sociologically, but it means that you use this category to challenge a discourse." Shenhav says that not using a term doesn't mean that the term does not exist; when there was no word for "homosexual," it still existed as a fact of life. The sociologist argues that outside of Israel, away from the territorial battle between Jews and Arabs, Oriental Jews more readily define themselves using the taboo appellation.

On the flip side of the debate, the Tunisian-Israeli writer Albert Memmi says that he would happily adopt the label, if the Arab world had ever allowed him to do so. He pronounces the Arab-Jew appellation "lovely words," but deems the idea of Jews ever having lived in harmony with Arab co-nationalists to be fantasy, pushed for propaganda purposes and surviving only because of a left-wing blind spot. "Yes, indeed, we were Arab Jews—in our habits, our culture, our music, our menu," he wrote. "But must one remain an Arab Jew if, in return, one has to tremble for one's life and the future of one's children and always be denied a normal existence?" He concludes: "We would have liked to be Arab Jews. If we abandoned the idea, it is because over the centuries the Moslem Arabs systematically prevented its realization by their contempt and cruelty."[11] Many Jews who are

fine with being culturally Arab would draw the line at the same
point and for similar reasons. Texts appearing on the Web sites
of organizations that comprise and focus on the fate of the
"forgotten refugees," Jews from Arab countries, take a similar
approach.

It's a linguistic tug-of-war. Proponents of one position use
the discussion to dwell on the horrors of past lives and the irrec-
oncilable differences between the two. Pulling the other side of
the rope are those who focus on harmonious experiences between citizens of the Middle East, Muslim and Jewish, now
wrenched apart. The latter category locates the Arab Jew in the
position of a bridge, a way back, an embodiment of how two
seemingly contrary identities can coexist in the same body, the
same space. It's from this position that hands have sometimes
stretched across the national-political divide. It happened with
the Black Panthers' first attempts to connect the Mizrahi struggle with the Palestinian struggle as they established a dialogue
with the PLO—absolutely taboo at that time in the early 1970s,
years before Israel would even recognize the Palestinian organization, years before the ice-breaker peace treaty with Egypt in
1979. It happened again when Mizrahi and Palestinian politicians, writers, and academics held a joint conference in Toledo,
Spain, in 1989, years before Israel and Palestine were officially
talking. Among the Mizrahis present in Spain were the Moroccan-
born poet Erez Bitton, Professor Ella Shohat, and the Iraqi actor
Yoseph Shiloah, who was initially refused roles in Israeli theaters
because of his guttural-accented Hebrew. Among those repre-
senting the Palestinian side were the de facto national poet Mahmoud Darwish and Palestinian president Mahmoud Abbas,
who spoke of the connection between these two groups: "It is

important to negotiate with Mizrahis, who represent the majority in Israel," he said. "They are an organic part of our culture,
of our Arab Muslim society, a part of our history and our memory. We must renew our memory and use our common culture
in order to overcome our present and plan our future."[12]

Like the Panthers before them, these Mizrahi activists at
Toledo suffered an overwhelming assault within an Israeli society that rejects outright those two core premises: that Oriental
Jews were in any way victims of the Jewish state, or that this
might be linked to any victimhood suffered by the Palestinians.
Attempts by Mizrahi activists to act as political bridges between
Israelis and Palestinians collapse under the weight of improba-
bility, vilified on all sides, occupying a narrow strip of dialogue
in the middle of two polar-opposite faces that squeeze it off the
spectrum. Once the Second Intifada broke out in 2000, all this
talk seemed irrelevant, and even some of those who had once
been bridge activists abandoned the idea.

Other bridges, forged in a sister factory, haven't fared much
better. Based on a cultural-linguistic understanding of "Arab
Jew," these argue a peace charter from that terrain. Sasson
Somekh, the Iraqi-origin professor of Arabic literature at Tel
Aviv University, is definitively a culture bridge. The professor
enjoyed a lifelong friendship with the revered Egyptian writer
Naguib Mahfouz on precisely that basis. He is not so enamored
with the political usage of the term "Arab Jew," preferring to
keep it as a real-time descriptive of former residents of Arab
countries. "Arab Jew means someone who is immersed, or grew
up, in Arab culture, lived in Arab culture, with Arabs, and knows
the way of the life," he says. "In my case, it so happened I was a
lucky person. I stayed in Iraq until I was seventeen, I graduated

from high school in Baghdad, and I was a perfect Arab." Although framed in a cultural context, Professor Somekh suc-
cinctly defines what this hybrid might mean in political terms:
"When I heard what was happening in [Hitler's] Europe, my reaction was as a Jew, definitely I was thinking of my kith and
kin," he says in one sentence. And then shortly after, describing
school years in Baghdad: "I studied Arab history and Iraqi history as an Arab. When I heard that the Arabs were winning over
the Persians and the Byzantines, I would be on their side . . . And
when I saw films about [the Muslim ruler] Salah al Din liberating
Jerusalem [from the Crusaders], I was very happy, as an Iraqi—as
an Arab."

Professor Somekh views his work, translating Arabic writers
into Hebrew, maintaining a dialogue with Arab writers including Palestinians such as Mahmoud Darwish, as an effort to
bridge the two worlds: Europe-facing Israel on one side, and the
Arab neighborhood on the other. It makes sense because the
professor is so obviously of both worlds, engaged in both cultures and a link between them. He has no illusions: "I am aware
that my efforts did not produce any important results," he says.
"But I am not going to stop it." Perfectly equipped to do so,
Professor Somekh's endeavors to introduce Israel to the literary
feats of the Middle East don't get far in an overarching climate
of mistrust and disinterest.

But locating Arab Jew in linguistic turf has a broader application. Zvi Yehezkeli, head of the Arab affairs desk on Israeli
Channel 10 TV, also self-defines in the hyphen term—and not
because of his Iraqi-Kurdish family tree. "I'm an Arab," he says,
explaining the concept of the Arab nation as being predicated
on tongue, not faith. "My language is Arabic, I'm a Jew, but I'm

Arabic." Yehezkeli's regular TV slots deliver news gleaned from
a constant gaze on the Middle East—he's either physically in it
or watching its media. Showcasing topics, from the Arab take on
AIDS to the Arab perspective on Israel's definition as a Jewish
state, Yehezkeli's reports often come over as an exercise in getting to know the neighbors. His approach implies that Arab Jew
isn't dependent on geography or genealogy—it's a mindset that
tilts the Israeli fulcrum from Europe to the Middle East, in language, in culture, in a linkup with the tastes of the territory.
From the early European pioneers who learned Arabic, wore local dress, and spoke Hebrew with gutturals, to the present-day
European-origin Israelis who learn Arabic, switch on to Middle
Eastern media, and visit Jordan or Egypt, this definition has always had real-life manifestations. With so much Jewish rooted in
the Arab Middle East, Israeli society might grow more gen-
uinely, autonomously robust if it at least partially adopts this version of Arab-Jewish. There's only so long you can blame the
neighbors for not feeling at home.

Friends in Tel Aviv, liberal and a bit new age-y, suggest that
my frequent minor illnesses after trips to the Israeli periphery
are the result of having "absorbed so much toxicity" in the form
of Arab-hatred. If there is a symbiotic relationship between
body and spirit, it's more likely that the colds are a consequence
of a crashed pet theory: the Mizrahi bridge hypothesis. Spending time in those towns, it's obvious that Mizrahis are no bridges
of peace, even though I meet many who do bear exactly that
potential. Among the older generation, who easily relate the past
synergy between Arab and Jewish in their descriptions of lives
once intimately shared, there exist hard-wired cultural affinities
to the Arab world, preserved against the odds. But these do not

inform most Mizrahis' political analysis of the Israeli-Palestinian conflict; instead, they hold tight to the national script. Bridges don't build a way out of a territorial war—they might only evolve after that war is over, and that's assuming it ends fairly. So this theory's pathologically detached from reality, a type of falsely cheery wallpaper that refuses to stick to walls too wet with blood.

Regional events are making the likelihood of it sticking seem even more absurd. Gaza has turned into "the world's largest open-air prison," entirely dependent on foreign aid and a grudgingly temperamental Israeli supply line; it's a refugee camp in all but name, and one that's still under fire. As of the spring of 2008, rockets from Gaza keep falling on Sderot, prompting more and more Israeli attacks on the Strip, which often kill innocent bystanders and send the whole deadly cycle into another fast spin. There are daily reports from the West Bank, of raids by the Israeli Army, or "targeted" assassinations, or house demolitions, or injuries, or arrests that add to a swelling population of Palestinians inside Israeli prisons, hundreds of them underage or detained without charge. Visits to the West Bank confirm that it is choked by the Israeli separation barrier and internal blocks and barriers, and by a series of Israeli military rules that make travel, trade, normal life impossible. Israel holds that all this, while regrettable, is required to prevent terror attacks on the Jewish state. By Israel's analysis, it is the Palestinians who write the terms of their own occupation.

Daily e-mails warn of hatred brewing on all Israeli borders, of agitators propagating more viciously anti-Semitic narratives and calling for the obliteration of the Jewish state. Other corners of the Internet seethe with increasingly outlandish conspiracy theories casting Israel as a resident evil, a mutant entity. Daily Web sites glare with a different kind of hatred, circulated by Israelis trapped in a victimhood that only blames others, a perpetual rage against eternal enemies painted as increasingly inhuman. Daily e-mails fume over Israeli academics using national funds to push an anti-Israel agenda from within the Jewish state's best educational establishments. Among the names are several featured in this book, whose desire of a just solution for both sides is obvious within five minutes of talking with them. There's deadly, renewable-source loathing everywhere; a corrosive, entrenched polarity everywhere; and that jarringly cheerful wallpaper seems at best an irrelevance, at worst trivial and misleading. If you want a logical conclusion, you'd have to go with that one.

Hagar is sixteen when I meet her, with her family in Sderot. She broke down at school once, following a rocket attack that struck frighteningly close to it. Hagar, half Moroccan, a quarter Iraqi, a quarter Polish, 100 percent Israeli, holds the sort of anti-Arab views that are common in this unhappy town. But she is talking about a recent trip, to Tel Aviv, which changed all that. In May 2007, a period of increased Qassam attacks, she and four hundred others were taken away from Sderot, courtesy of an Israeli billionaire businessman, Arcadi Gaydamak, who bused them into a specially created "tent city" in Tel Aviv for a weekend break. There, she and some friends caught a cab arranged by the Russian-Israeli donor, and it turned out that the driver was an Arab Israeli. "We decided to go out clubbing," she says, somewhat incongruously. "But then the nightclub agreed to let everyone in except the driver, so we went to Jaffa to an Arabic restaurant." They loved it, Hagar and her Sderot friends and the Arab Israeli driver and his friends in Jaffa. "They treated me in a way that no one has ever treated me," she says of the restaurant staff. "There was food fit for a king, nargile, everything was done in nicest possible way . . . and then we went on to a party, the [Arab] restaurant workers came with us." She starts to laugh, and says: "So it was exactly when I was escaping the Qassams, that suddenly I discovered a different side to the Arabs."

Something about this story doesn't quite jell, so I ask her: What made you decide to spend the evening with the cab driver in the first place? "It was the music," Hagar replies. "He was playing Umm Kalsoum and things like that. Music that we love, that we listen to. You know, in the home."

ACKNOWLEDGMENTS

Thanks to my agent, Ben Mason, and publisher, George Gibson, for their vision and enthusiasm, for believing in this book when it was just an outline—they literally drove me to it, in the best way. I'm also enormously grateful to Jacqueline Johnson for her talented editing—an inspiring combination of skill, sensitivity, and grace. Thanks also to Greg Villepique, Liz Peters, and other editors at Walker & Company, who carefully and adroitly managed this book's production.

I will always be grateful and indebted to the hundreds of people who agreed to be interviewed for this book—it is their time, thoughts, research, efforts and experiences that made it possible: thank you.

For being patiently available as phone directories, info lines, or expert resources, thanks to Ktzia Alon, Almog Bahar, Anat Balint, Dr. Gaby Birenboim, Yosef Dahoh Halevi, Eli Hamo, Professor Ephraim Hazan, Avraham Pinto, Rafi Shubeli, Ruvik Rosental, Professor Yosef Tobi, Yael Ben Yefet, Professor Yossi Yonah, Ofra Yeshua-Lyth, and so many others who generously responded to what were quite often pesky or oblique requests. Thanks also to staff at the British Library and Tel Aviv University.

For reading and commenting on sections of the manuscript, I am extremely grateful to Professor Michel Abitbol, Dr. Yossi Dahan, Professor Eran Feitelson, Professor Lev Grinberg, Dr. Bat-Zion Eraqi Klorman, Professor Hubert Law-Yone, Dr. Gal Levy, Professor Yehuda Nini, Dr. Esther Meir-Glitzenstein, Yossi Ohana, Professor Eran Razin, Professor Sami Smooha, Professor Sasson Somekh, Yael Tzadok, and Professor Alex Weingrod.

For their friendship and sustaining support in multiple guises, thanks to Firas al-Atraqchi, Tony Barrell, Mel Bradman, Jordi Blanchard, Eyal Eithcowich, Ersoy Emin, Frank Jordans, Dafna Kaplan, Carine Libermann, Chris McGreal, Mauro Minella, Arthur Neslen, Rachel Puttick, Linda Rogers, Majid Sattar, Aboodi Shabi, Shiri Sopher, Paola Tedeschi, Gali Tibbon, Picona Vilalta, and Katharine Viner.

Thanks to my relatives "in the Diaspora," for always being there to read, direct, or offer personal insights. Thanks also to my relations in Israel, whose doors were hospitably held open throughout our frequent political disagreements.

Finally, eternal thanks and love to my sister, Anat, and parents, Joseph and Maureen, whose tolerance, generosity, and kindness far exceed mine, who helped in every possible way, and whom I have the extreme good fortune to call family.

NOTES

Chapter 1: VEILING ITS FACE

1. David Kaufman. "Seaside Revelation in Tel Aviv." *Time* magazine (online), September 12, 2007.
2. Jonathan M. Hess. "Johann David Michaelis and the Colonial Imaginary: Orientalism and the Emergence of Racial Anti-Semitism in Eighteenth-Century Germany." *Jewish Social Studies,* January 2000, Vol. 6, No. 2, p. 87.
3. Michael Selzer. *The Aryanization of the Jewish State.* New York: Black Star Publishing, 1967, p. 48.
4. Ibid.
5. Ibid., p. 35.
6. Theodor Herzl. *The Jewish State.* New York: Dover Publications, 1988 (reprint of 1896 ed.), p. 96.
7. Aziza Khazzoom. "The Great Chain of Orientalism." *American Sociological Review,* Vol. 68, August 2003, p. 500.
8. Sami Shalom Chetrit. *The Mizrahi Struggle.* Tel Aviv: Am Oved, 2004 (Hebrew), p. 49.
9. Tom Segev. *The First Israelis.* New York: Owl Books, 1998, p. 157.
10. Chetrit, *Mizrahi Struggle,* p. 50.

Chapter 2: MEET THE FAMILY

1. *Journey through the First Settlements*. Israeli Ministry of Education, Department of Teaching Programs, Jerusalem, 2002 (Hebrew), p. 135.
2. Ibid., p. 136.
3. Arye Gelblum, *Haaretz*, April 22, 1949.
4. Ella Shohat. *Israeli Cinema: East/West and the Politics of Representation*. Austin: University of Texas Press, 1989, p. 116.
5. Esther Meir-Glitzenstein. *Zionism in an Arab Country: Jews in Iraq in the Early 1940s*. London: Routledge, 2004, p. 70.
6. Sami Shalom Chetrit. The Mizrahi Struggle. Tel Aviv, Am Oved, 2004 (Hebrew), p. 53.
7. Elie Eliachar. *Living with Jews*. London: Weidenfeld & Nicholson, 1983, p. 207.
8. Ibid., p. 41.
9. Ibid., p. 41.
10. Ibid., p. 216.
11. Sammy Smooha. *Israel: Pluralism and Conflict*. Berkeley: University of California Press, 1978, p. 88.
12. Eliachar, *Living with Jews*, p. 132.
13. Ella Shohat. "Sephardim in Israel: Zionism from the Standpoint of its Jewish Victims." *Dangerous Liaisons: Gender, Nation, and Postcolonial Perspectives*, Anne McClintock, Aamir Mufti, and Ella Shohat, editors. Minneapolis: University of Minnesota Press, 1997, p. 50. First published in *Social Text*, vol. 19/20, Fall 1988, p. 135.
14. Chetrit, *Mizrahi Struggle*, p. 54.

15. Reuben Ahroni. *Yemenite Jewry: Origins, Culture, and Literature.* Bloomington: Indiana University Press, 1986, p. 165.
16. Smooha, *Pluralism and Conflict*, p. 55.
17. Bat-Zion Eraqi Klorman. *The Jews of Yemen in the Nineteenth Century: A Portrait of a Messianic Community.* Leiden, New York, Koln: Brill, 1993, p. 183.
18. Ibid. p. 182.
19. Smooha, *Pluralism and Conflict*, p. 55.
20. Gershon Shafir and Yoav Peled. *Being Israeli: The Dynamics of Multiple Citizenship.* Cambridge, New York: Cambridge University Press, 2002, p. 76.
21. Tom Segev. *1949: The First Israelis.* New York: Henry Holt, 1998, p. 186.
22. Ahroni, *Yemeni Jewry*, p. 2.
23. Segev, *First Israelis*, p. 182.
24. Ibid., p. 176.
25. Chetrit, *Mizrahi Struggle*, p. 81.
26. Ibid, p. 147.
27. Raphael Patai. *Israel between East and West.* (Second Edition). Westport, CT: Greenwood Publishing, 1970, p. 314.
28. Amnon Dankner. "I Have No Sister." *Haaretz*, February 18, 1983.

Chapter 3: DEVELOPMENT TOWNS

1. Shmulik Hadad. "Peres: Enough with Qassam Hysteria." *Ynet,* June 20, 2006, http://www.ynetnews.com/articles/0,7340,L-3264980,00.html.
2. Documentary film, *The Pioneers*, Sigal Vanunu Gadish productions, Sderot, Tel Aviv, 2007.

3. Robert Satloff. *Among the Righteous: Lost Stories from the Holocaust's Long Reach into Arab Lands*. New York: Public Affairs, 2006, p. 111.

4. Ella Shohat. "Rupture and Return: Zionist Discourse and the Study of Arab-Jews." *Social Text*, Vol. 21, No. 2, Summer 2003, pp. 47–94.

5. Ella Shohat. "Sephardim in Israel: Zionism from the Standpoint of its Jewish Victims." *Dangerous Liaisons: Gender, Nation, and Postcolonial Perspectives*, Anne McClintock, Aamir Mufti, and Ella Shohat, editors. Minneapolis: University of Minnesota Press, 1997. First published in *Social Text*, vol 19/20, Fall 1988, p. 135.

6. Aziza Khazzoom. "Did the Israeli State Engineer Segregation? On the Placement of Jewish Immigrants in Development Towns in the 1950s." *Social Forces*, Vol. 84, No. 1, September 2005, p. 116.

7. Hanna Herzog, *Contest of Symbols—the Sociology of Election Campaigns through Israeli Ephemera*. Cambridge, MA: Harvard University Press, 1987, p. 117.

8. Menachem Begin. "*Chah Chahim* Speech." June 1981. http://www.betar.org.il/ideology/chachahim.htm (Hebrew).

9. Herzog, *Contest of Symbols*, 33.

Chapter 4: BABYLON CALLING

1. *The Holy Bible*, New International Version, Jeremiah 27; 5–7.

2. Nissim Rejwan. *The Last Jews in Baghdad: Remembering a Lost Homeland*. Austin: University of Texas Press, 2004, p. 215.

3. Esther Meir-Glitzenstein. *Zionism in an Arab Country: Jews in Iraq in the Early 1940s*. London: Routledge, 2004, p. 7.

4. Moshe Gat. *The Jewish Exodus from Iraq, 1948–1951*. London: Frank Cass, 1997, p. 7.

5. Abbas Shiblak. *Iraqi Jews: A History of Mass Exodus*. London: Saqi Books, 2005 (first published as *The Lure of Zion*, London, 1986), p. 75.

6. Meir-Glitzenstein, *Zionism*, p. 53.

7. Ibid. p. 52.

8. Shlomo Hillel. *Operation Babylon*. London: Collins, 1988, p. 278.

9. David Hirst. *The Gun and the Olive Branch: The Roots of Violence in the Middle East*. London: Faber, 1977.

10. Shiblak, *Iraqi Jews*, p. 153.

11. Ibid., p. 154.

12. Marion Woolfson. *Prophets in Babylon: Jews in the Arab World*. London: Faber, 1980, p. 199.

13. Norman A. Stillman. *Jews of Arab Lands in Modern Times*. Philadelphia: The Jewish Publication Society, 1991, p. 331.

14. Shiblak, *Iraqi Jews*, p. 78.

15. Meir-Glitzenstein, *Zionism*, p. 147.

16. Shiblak, *Iraqi Jews*, p. 82, quoting Y. Atlas, *The Jewish Underground Movement in Iraq* (Hebrew) (Tel Aviv: Ma'arakot, 1969).

17. Ibid., p. 83.

18. Ibid.

19. Chetrit, *Mizrahi Struggle*, p. 61.

20. Rejwan, *Last Jews*, p. 107.

21. Meir-Glitzenstein, *Zionism*, p. 143.

22. Ibid., p. 138.

23. Ibid.

24. Nissim Rejwan. *Outsider in the Promised Land*. Austin: Texas University Press, 2006, p. 89, quoting from Shimon Ballas, *The Transit Camp* (Hebrew).

25. Shimon Ballas. "Iya." In *Keys to the Garden*, edited by Ammiel Alcalay. San Francisco: City Lights Books, 1996, p. 98.

Chapter 5: TALK THIS WAY

1. Shohat, *Israeli Cinema* p. 55.
2. Ibid. p. 125.
3. Ibid.
4. Ella Shohat, "Sephardim in Israel."
5. Shimon Ballas, *The Transit Camps* (Hebrew) quoted in Nissim Rejwan, *Outsider in the Promised Land*, Austin: Texas University Press, 2006, p. 89.

Chapter 6: EVERYONE DESERVES MUSIC

1. Motti Regev and Edwin Seroussi. *Popular Music and National Culture in Israel.* Berkeley: University of California Press, 2004, p. 5.
2. Lily Galili. "Shadow Government." *Haaretz*, August 1, 2003.
3. Regev and Seroussi, *Popular Music*, p. 205.
4. Shohat, *Israeli Cinema* p. 116 (but from Smooha).
5. Yehouda Shenhav. *The Arab Jews: A Postcolonial Reading of Nationalism, Religion, and Ethnicity.* Stanford: Stanford University Press, 2006, p. 192.

Chapter 7: MADE TO FAIL

1. Yossi Yonah and Ishak Saporta. "The Politics of Lands and Housing in Israel." *Social Identities*, Vol. 8, No. 1, 2002, p. 92.

2. Oren Yiftachel. "'Ethnocracy' and its discontents; minorities, protest and the Israeli polity." *Critical Inquiry*, Vol. 27, Summer 2000, p. 725.

3. Yonah and Saporta, "Politics of Lands," p. 100.

4. Ibid., p. 101.

5. Ibid., p. 102.

6. Yiftachel, "Ethnocracy," p. 726.

7. Yonah and Saporta, "Politics of Lands," p. 102.

8. Ibid., p. 103.

9. Chetrit, *Mizrahi Struggle*, p. 286.

10. Shlomo Swirski. *Politics and Education in Israel: Comparisons with the United States.* New York, London: Falmer, 1999, p. 174.

11. Ibid., p. 11.

12. Ibid., p. 169.

13. Ibid., p. 168.

14. Nissim Rejwan. *Outsider in the Promised Land.* Austin: Texas University Press, 2006, p. 126.

15. Segev, *First Israelis*, p. 157.

16. Ibid.

17. Chetrit, *Mizrahi Struggle*, p. 43.

18. Ibid., p. 46.

19. Ibid.

20. Swirski, *Israeli Education*, p. 176.

21. Chetrit, *Mizrahi Struggle*, p. 76.

22. Swirski, *Israeli Education*, p. 183.

23. Ibid., p. 184.

24. Ibid.

25. Ibid.

Chapter 8: THE ETHNIC DEMON

1. Greg Myre. "Major Blow to Israeli Coalition." *International Herald Tribune*, 11 November 2005.

2. Amir Shoan and Amira Lom "They Betrayed Me," *Yediot Aharonot*, August 31, 2000.

3. Uzi Benziman. "Peretz's Denons." *Haaretz*, September 5, 2007.

4. Yuval Karni "Kibbutzniks to Ayalon: 'why did you go with peretz? He's a man of the market.'" *Yediot Aharonot* June 7, 2007.

5. Eliachar, *Living with Jews*, p. 132.

6. Ibid., p. 145.

7. Chetrit, *Mizrahi Struggle*, p. 88.

8. Ibid., p. 87.

9. Eliachar, *Living with Jews*, p. 200.

10. Chetrit, *Mizrahi Struggle*, p. 124.

11. Hanna Herzog. "Midway Between Political and Cultural Ethnicity: An Analysis of the 'Ethnic Lists' in the 1984 Elections." In *Israel's Odd Couple: The 1984 Elections and National Unity Government*, edited by Daniel J. Elazar and Shmuel Sandler. Detroit: Wayne State University Press, 1990, p. 115.

12. Marion Woolfson. *Prophets in Babylon: Jews in the Arab World*. London: Faber, 1980, p. 267.

13. Chetrit, *Mizrahi Struggle*, p. 144.

14. Eliacher, Living with Jews, p. 183.

15. Nissim Rejwan. *Israel's Place in the Middle East*. p. 144.

16. Chetrit, *Mizrahi Struggle*, p. 155.

17. Ibid., p. 181.

18. Joel Greenberg. "Sephardic Jews see Israeli Indictment as More Bias." *New York Times,* April 28, 1997.

19. Chetrit, *Mizrahi Struggle,* p. 115.

20. Kamouna Shamouny. "Out of School." *The Jerusalem Report,* November 14, 2007.

21. Alex Weingrod. "Ehud Barak's Apology: Letters From the Israeli Press." *Israel Studies,* Vol. 3, No. 2, Fall 1998, p. 238.

22. Ibid., p. 240.

23. Ibid.

24. Ibid.

25. Yehouda Shenhav. "Jews from Arab Countries and the Palestinian Right of Return." *British Journal of Middle Eastern Studies,* 29(1): 27–56, 2002.

26. Ibid.

27. Shenhav, *The Arab Jews* p. 127.

28. Shenhav, "Jews from Arab Countries."

29. Albert Memmi. "Who Is an Arab Jew?" February 1975, Jews Indigenous to the Middle East and North Africa, http://www.jimena.org/Memmi.htm.

30. Tom Segev. "Selective Memories." *Haaretz,* March 13, 2008.

31. Yehouda Shenhav. "Hitching a Ride on the Magic Carpet." *Haaretz,* August 15, 2003.

32. Ibid.

33. Shenhav, "Jews from Arab Countries."

Chapter 9: WE ARE NOT ARABS!

1. Ilan Halevi. *A History of the Jews.* London, New Jersey: Zed Books, 1987, p. 219.

2. Ibid.

3. Ammiel Alcalay. *After Jews and Arabs*. Minneapolis: University of Minnesota Press, 1993, p. 222.

4. Shenhav, *The Arab Jews*, p. 61.

5. Raphael Patai. *Israel between East and West*. Westport, Conn: Greenwood, 1970, p. 18.

6. Smooha, *Pluralism and Conflict*, p. 88.

7. "A Nation of Tribes: Rough guide to a fractions society," *Economist*, April 23, 1998.

8. Henriette Dahan-Kalev. "You're so pretty, you don't look Moroccan." *Israel Studies*, Vol. 6, No. 1, pp. 1–14, 2001.

9. Noah Eisenstadt, p. 197.

10. Eli Ben Menachem, 'Politika', Israeli Channel 1, June 29, 2004.

11 Memmi, "Who Is an Arab Jew?"

12. Chetrit, *Mizrahi Struggle*, p. 274.

INDEX

Abbas, Mahmoud, 233–34
Abd-Wahab, Mohammed, 137
Abdul, Ilah, Prince of Iraq, 86–87
Abraham (biblical), 20n, 30, 79
absentee property law (1950), 163n
Absorption through Modernization,
    225–26
Academy of the Hebrew Language, 132
Adas, Shafiq, 90
Agudat Israel, 202
al-Aqsa intifada, 146–47, 203, 221, 230–31,
    234
al-Atrash, Farid, 137
al-Fasiya, Zohara, 153
al-Kabir, Ibrahim, 84, 98
al-Kabir, Yusuf, 95, 98
al-Nur, Salim, 143–44, 144–45
al-Sabah, Sheik Abdullah III al-Selim, 144
al-Said, Nuri, 86, 99, 212
al-Usbua (AZL newspaper), 96
al-Yashiv, Isaac, 163–64
Alali, Yacoub, 126–27, 145–47, 231
Alfi, Yossi, 115, 121–22
Algeria, 62–63
Algobi, Dorit, 122–23
Ali al-Gailani, Rashid, 86
aliyah (ascent to Israel), 7, 30, 64. *See also*
    migration
Alleg, Henri, 62
Alliance Israelite Universelle, 58, 83, 176
Alon, Yigal, 212

Altneuland (Herzl), 22–23
"Always" (Tal, as Sharon Keinan), 156
American Joint Distribution Committee, 58
Amman, Jordan, 146
Amnesty International, 52, 53
Andalus Orchestra of Israel, 148, 150–51
anti-Semitism
    Christian invention of, 82–83
    in Europe, 23, 24
    in Iraq, 86–88, 89–90
    lack of, in Middle East, 23–24, 60–62,
        183
    in Tunisia and Algeria, 62, 63
Anti-Zionist League (AZL), 96–97
Arabic
    distaste for, 125–26, 127
    usage in Hebrew, 131–32
    common roots of Hebrew and, 32,
        130–31
    in Israeli prison population, 133
    Labor politician with skills in, 129
    Marrakesh festival of dialects, 152
    in Moroccan Jewish theater, 152
    as official second language, but . . . ,
        126–27, 128–30
    Palestinian, 131–32
    Russian language vs., 133–34
    See also Arab-Israelis; Mizrahi Jews
Arabic Language Academy, 153
Arab-Israeli War (1948), 9n, 11–12, 55,
    94–95, 163, 168–69, 210

Arab-Israeli War (1967), 69, 71–75,
    94, 200
Arab-Israelis
    failure to play music of, 156
    discrimination against, 238
    and Israeli theater, 114–15
    terrorist violence by, 54
    See also Arabic
Arab Jews
    denial of Arab ancestors, 217–18
    as mind-set, 236
    hope for, 238–39
    as oxymoron, 218, 221–23, 227–29,
        231–33
    working definition, 234–35
    See also Mizrahi Jews
Arabs, during European rule, 4, 22
Argov, Zohar, 142
Ariel, Occupied Territories, 72
Armenian Genocide memorial day, 171
Armenian Quarter of Jerusalem,
    170–72
Army Radio's "Galgalaz," 141
Artzi, Hed, 122–23
Ashkelon, Israel, 54, 63–64
Ashkenazi Jews
    and absence of Mizrahi from national
        definitive, 17–19
    and belief that Mizrahi are uneducated,
        27, 68, 100, 175–77
    and Bialik statue in Ramat Gan,
        151
    and Bourekas films, 117–19
    casting as Mizrahi in theater, 115
    control of historical memory, 34,
        120–21, 175, 182, 221
    and cutting off forelocks of Yemeni
        Jews, 204
    derogatory stereotypes of, 23, 49
    as dominant and definitive in Israel,
        11–12, 16–17, 68–69, 191–94
    early relationship with Palestinian Jews,
        31–33
    Elinor on damage caused by, 47–50
    failure in Israeli-Palestinian conflict,
        208–9

fear of sinking to Levantine cultural
    level, 27, 33–34, 68, 154, 223, 225–26
joining Black Panther protest, 197
and kibbutzes, 157–62
and melting pot theory, 5–6, 139, 173,
    178–80
and Mizrahi as refugees, 168, 212–16
New Settlement, 28–29, 32–33, 36–38, 48
and officials' denigration of Mizrahi,
    172, 175
percentage of population, 12, 21
and schoolteachers' "feelings of
    superiority," 174
alleged stealing from Yemeni migrants,
    40–41, 43–46
Western influence, 3–4, 150
and Yemenis as labor supply, 36–37
The Ashkenazi Revolution (Katznelson), 195
assimilation, philosophy of, 225–26
Avoda Ivrit (Hebrew Labor), 36–37
Aznar, José Maria, 129

Babylonian Jewry Heritage Center
    (Or Yehuda, Israel), 77, 78, 87–88,
    95, 99–105, 105
Babylonian Jews. See Iraqi Jews; Mizrahi
    Jews
Babylonian music, 142–45, 148–49
Babylonian Talmud, 81
Baghdad, Iraq, 83–84, 86, 91–95, 99–105
    Iraqi Jewish music performances in, 144
Balfour Declaration, 95
Ballas, Shimon, 103–4, 128
Barak, Ehud, 186, 188, 207, 211
    from kibbutz movement, 39
Bareket, Eli, 205–6
Barnes, Jaques, 211
Baron, Salo, 61
Bashir, Nabil, 167–68
Basri, Me'ir, 95
BBC Radio 3 world music prize, 143
Begin, Menachem, 69–71, 161–62, 200
Behar, Almog, 227
Ben-Eliezer, Benyamin (Fuad), 72
Ben-Eliezer, Benyamin Mizrahi, 186n
Ben Gurion, David

banning Katznelson's book on controlling Mizrahis, 195
declaring independence for Israel, 11n
disdain for Mizrahi Jews, 27, 33–34, 68, 223
on ethnic organizing, 196
on Jewish people as European Jews, 24
Million Person plan, 88–95, 223
on TV and the Beatles, 120–21
Ben Israel, David, 39
Ben Porat, Mordechai, 212, 216
Ben Yehuda, Eliezer, 111–12, 116
Benayun, Amir, 155
Benziman, Uzi, 188
Berlusconi, Silvio, 129
Bet She'an (development town), 55
Bialik, Haim Nachman, 151
Biluists (Russian Jewish idealists), 34
Bitton, Erez, 233–34
Black and White Minstrel Show (BBC TV), 117n
Black Panthers, 197–200, 233, 234
Bourekas genre of films, 116–19
British Mandate in Palestine
British prefer Ashkenazi, 31, 33n
controlling migration in 1940s, 46n
demographics at time of, 11–12
and English-speaking Israelis, 111
and Jewish Agency, 24, 31, 128
Mizrahi accent chosen during, 111–12
UN termination of (1948), 11n, 97
British presence in Iraq, 1–2, 83–87
Buzaglo, Meir, 130–31
Buzaglo, Rabbi David, 153

Cameri repertory theater (Tel Aviv), 114
Camp Redemption (Aden), 42–44
camps for migrants, 46–48, 64, 65, 118–19
Canafo, Asher, 148
Casablan (musical comedy), 119
Chai (symbol of Judaism), 227
Charlie and a Half (film), 119
Chetrit, Sami Shalom, 170–73, 176–77, 195–96, 199
Christianity, 82–83
Cohen, Aharale, 55–56, 128

Cohen, Asher, 139, 152
Cohen, Haim, 84
Cohen, Ilana, 152–53
Cohen, Menachem, 149
Cohen, Ran, 215
Cohen, Smadar, 40–41
colonialism, 1–2, 4–5, 57, 59, 62, 83–87.
See also British Mandate
Committee for Language, 111–12
communal farms, 18, 37, 39, 65, 163
communism, 62, 89, 96–97, 99
Communist party in Algeria, 62
Community theater, 115
Crusaders, 30
"Cultivation and Rehabilitation" theory of education, 178–80
cultural bridges, 234–36
culture. *See* Ashkenazi Jews; Israeli culture; Mizrahi Jews
Cyprus, 46
Cyrus, king of Persia, 80

Dahan-Kalev, Henriette, 224–25
Dalal, Yair, 142–44, 155–56
Damari, Shoshana, 140
Daniel, Menahem Saleh, 95
Dankner, Amnon, 49–50
Darwish, Mahmoud, 233–34
Davidson, Boaz, 117
Dayan, Dorit, 124
Dayan, Moshe, 39, 199
Deir Yassin (Palestine), 168–69
Deri, Rabbi Arye, 203
development towns
Bet She'an, 55
and communal farms, 18, 65
conflict with kibbutzes, 18–19, 157–62, 163
demographics of residents, 64–65
economic growth or lack of, 66–67
Kiryat Gat, 72
Kiryat Shmona, 55, 157–62, 166
labor-intensive, low-skill, industry in, 65–66, 72
Ofakim, Israel, 55, 67–68
official policy for settling, 56

development towns (*continued*)
  optimism in 1950s, 64, 65
  Sderot, 51, 52–56, 127, 188, 237–38
  settlement towns vs., 71–73
  See also Or Yehuda, Israel
dhimmi status, 81–83
Diaspora
  character of Jews from, 14–15, 36–37
  as longing for holy land, 7, 78–79
  and melting pot theory, 139
  New Settlement's contempt for, 48
  discrimination. *See* ethnic inequality
Dobkin, Eliyahu, 88
Doha, Qatar, 128–29
Draft Law in Iraq, 90–91
drug culture, language of, 132–33
Dzigan and Schumacher comedy duo,
  116n

Eastern European Jews, 23
Eban, Abba, 154, 174
Edlman, Amiram, 41
education
  in Arabic, 126
  Ashkenazi belief that Mizrahi had
    none, 27, 68, 100, 175–77
  "Cultivation and Rehabilitation"
    theory of, 178–80
  ethnic gaps in, 19, 31, 173–80
  hierarchy of ethnicities, 183–84
  Kedma schools, 170–73, 179–83
  "The Little Yemeni" form of, 25–27, 28
  of Middle Eastern Jews pre-Israel, 58,
    90, 100–101, 175–76
  of Mizrahi with Ashkenazi, 180–82
  segregation in schools, 174–75
  ultra-Orthodox schools, 204–5
  vocational, for Mizrahi, 66, 172–74,
    177–78, 180
  Western school streaming, 179
Egypt, 93, 103, 153
Eisenstadt, Noel Shmuel, 225–26
Eliachar, Elie, 31–34, 191–93, 195–96, 199
Elias, Arye, 114–15
Eliav, Arie Lova, 226
Elinor, Dvora, 47

Elkarif, Yaakov, 194
England, Iraqi Jews in, 1–3. *See also*
  British Mandate
English language, 126–27, 129, 133, 189
Erekat, Saeb, 210
Eretz Nehederet (TV program), 120
Eretz Yisrael, 78
ethnic demon, 185–86, 191
ethnic inequality
  of Arab-Israelis, 12
  Ashkenazi leave camps faster than
    others, 47
  author's intent to expose, 21–22
  Begin's promise to end, 70
  in early power dynamics, 11–12, 34
  in employment, 18, 38–39, 50
  gaps in school achievement, 19, 31,
    173–80
  government report on, 199–200
  integration of society vs., 12–13
  in land distribution, 39–41, 64–69,
    157–58, 163
  low priority of, 20–21, 74–75
  in music, 137–38, 139–43, 156
  in state support for the arts, 150–53
  in wealth distribution, 163–70
  See also development towns; education;
    inter-Jewish discrimination
ethnic subgroups, 16
ethnic voter profiles, 200–201
Europe, 223. *See also specific European
  countries*
European Jews, 22–23, 112–13, 216. *See
  also* Ashkenazi Jews
Eurovision song contest, 15
Eveland, Wilbur Grane, 93
Every Morning (TV program), 185
eviction of Mizrahi and Arab-Israelis, 168,
  169–70
Ezekiel, the prophet, 80
Ezra, the prophet, 91n

Faisal, King of Syria, 85
Farah, Jafar, 134
Farhud (pogrom) in Iraq, 86–88
Fiddler on the Roof (film), 4

"Fire" (Peretz), 135, 136–37
Frankenstein, Carl, 176
French Alliance Israelite Universelle, 58, 83, 176
French rule in the Middle East, 57
Friere, Paolo, 181

Gal, Meir, 182
Galgalatz, 156
Galilee area, 30, 39–41, 112, 162–63
Gat, Moshe, 92
Gaydamak, Arcadi, 238
Gaza Strip, 51, 52, 53, 189, 190, 237
Gelblum, Arye, 27, 58
German Jews. See Ashkenazi Jews
German language, 133
Ghadaffi, Muammar, 214
Golden Age poetry, 130
Got No Jeep and My Camel Died (film), 155–56
grad missiles, 54
Great Synagogue (Baghdad, Iraq), 105
greater Israel concept of territory, 200

Haaretz (Israeli daily newspaper), 169–70, 186n, 188
Habima theater company (Tel Aviv), 114
Hadar, Israel, 194
Hadash (Jewish-Arab party), 72
Haddad, Ezra, 98
Hadrian, emperor of Rome, 81
Haifa, 56, 134, 194
Hakham Bashi, 31, 83
Halevi, Ilan, 222
Hamas, 52, 74, 230
hamsas (hand-shaped charms), 13–14
Ha'olam Hazeh (magazine), 92
Hasan II, Sultan of Morocco, 57
hazan (Jewish liturgical singer), 149
Hebrew
    accent of TV personalities, 119–20
    and Arabic, from common roots, 32, 130–31
    as Ashkenazi "discovery," 108–9, 113
    foreign words integrated into, 131–33
    with Israeli Hebrew accent, 107–8

as language of belonging, 9–10, 127–28, 223–24
    with Mizrahi accent, 106–8, 110–12, 114, 121–25, 130
    and Mizrahi label, 16
    preservation of some aspects of original, 113
    in theater, 114–15
Hebrew University, 62, 73, 130–31
Hebron, Palestine, 29–30, 71
Herzl, Theodor, 22–23
Hever, Amnon, 44
Hillel, Shlomo, 92, 196, 215
Hitman, Uzi, 139n
Holocaust, 68, 170–72
Holocaust survivors, 46, 48
Hula drainage project, 159–61
Human Rights Watch, 52
Hungarian Jews. See Ashkenazi Jews

Imam (musician), 145
Inbal dance theater, 152–53
industries, 65–66, 72–73
Inta Omri (Kalsoum), 13
inter-Jewish discrimination
    Ashkenazi music as Israeli, Mizrahi music as "world," 142
    and Hebrew accent, 110–16, 120–21
    on radio stations, 156
    special nurture schooling, 178–80
    in TV ads, 124–25
    in ultra-Orthodox schools, 204–5
    See also ethnic inequality; stereotypes
inter-Jewish integration
    of Hebrew, 131–33
    melting pot theory, 5–6, 139, 173, 178–80
    of Mizrahi elite, 229–30
    philosophy of assimilation, 225–26
intifada, 146–47, 203, 221, 230–31, 234
Iran, 2
Iranian Jews, 13. See also Mizrahi Jews
Iraq
    British presence in, 1–2, 83–87
    Communist party in, 96–97, 99
    Draft Law, 90–91

Iraq (*continued*)
    prosecution of Nazi agitators, 87
    Scud missile attacks on Israel, 149
    Zionism in, 85, 88–93, 95
Iraq Times, 95
Iraqi Criminal Investigation Department, 93
Iraqi Jews in Iraq, 3, 79–83, 88–95,
        100–101, 223
Iraqi Jews in Israel
    and Arab aspect of themselves, 217–18
    as authors, in Arabic, 153
    Ballas, Shimon, 103–4
    Elias, Arye 114–15
    as Levantine-Arabs, 29
    migration to Israel, 1–2, 3, 46–47, 78–79
    music of, 142–45, 148–49
    plan to swap for Palestinian refugees,
        212–14
    pride in homeland, 1, 77, 104–5
    Somekh, Sasson, 102–3
    See also Mizrahi Jews; Or Yehuda, Israel
Iraqi Jews in United Kingdom, 1–3, 78
Islam. *See* Muslims
Israel Broadcasting Authority (IBA)
    Arabic Orchestra, 143, 144, 145
    discrimination against Mizrahi
        performers, 140–41
    exclusion of Mizrahi tracks with
        Arabic, 156
    Israeli Mizrahi chooses Mizrahi accent,
        106–7, 108
    in Mandate times, 112
    See also television
Israel Cinema (Shohat), 118n
Israel Land Administration (ILA), 163
Israel the Oriental Majority (Swirski), 173
Israeli Black Panthers, 197–200, 233, 234
Israeli Committee for Quality in
    Education (HILA), 184
Israeli culture
    folk songs, 138
    as presented globally, 14–15, 21
    as work in progress, 17–18, 21–22
Israeli government
    arts, state support for, 150–53
    austerity program in 1980s, 164

concern about Mizrahi protests, 173–74
    on ethnic inequality, 199–200
    Lavon affair, 93
    priority after Six-Day War, 69, 71–75
    support for settlement towns vs.
        development towns, 71–73
Israeli Holocaust Museum, 171
Israeli military, 53–54, 69, 126, 155, 190
Israeli Ministry for Education and
    Culture, 25–27, 28
Israeli-Palestinian conflict
    Gaza Strip, 51, 52, 53, 189, 190, 237
    Mizrahi view of, 208–10
    polarizing Zionist and pan-Arab
        nationalism, 59
    as priority over internal social justice,
        20–21
    and WOJAC, 210, 211–16
    See also West Bank
"Iya" (Ballas), 103–4

Jabotinsky, Valdimir, 113
Jaffa, Israel, 169
Jeremiah, the prophet, 80
Jerusalem, 28, 29–30, 170–72, 196–97
Jerusalem Post, 167
Jewish Agency, 24, 31, 128
Jewish-Arab Hadash party, 72
Jewish Chronicle, 97
Jewish demographics in Israel, 3–4
Jewish National Fund (JNF), 118n,
        163–64
Jewish Responsa age, 82
Jewish settler movement, 28n
Jews
    and Abraham, 20n, 30, 79
    Levantine-Arab, 29, 33–34, 154, 195, 220
    music for prayer shared with Muslims,
        149–50
    and Muslims, in Iraq, 100–102, 103–5
    and Muslims, in Morocco, 57
    and Muslims, in Ottoman Empire, 15–16
    and Muslims, in Spain, 15
    and Muslims, in Tunisia, 60, 61
    Muslims and, 20n, 60–62, 183, 222–23,
        233–35

Jordan, 146, 147–48
Jospin, Lionel, 129
Justice for Jews from Arab Countries, 211

Kadima party, 187–88
Kahane movement, 200
Kalsoum, Umm, 13, 137
Karif, Moshe, 224
Katsav, Moshe, 185, 191
Katznelson, Kalman, 195
Kedma analysis of Israeli educational
    system, 173
Kedma (Israeli independent high school),
    170–73, 179–83
Kfar Blum kibbutz (Upper Galilee), 162–63
Kfar Shalem, Israel, 168–70
Khattan, Haim, 102
Khazzoom, Aziza, 64
Khedouri, Rabbi Sassoon, 97, 99
kibbutzes
    anti-Peretz campaign, 190–91
    and development towns, 18, 65, 158,
        159, 160
    in Kinneret, 40–41
    and Mizrahi, 39–42, 162
    overview, 39
    preferential treatment of, 40–41,
        157–58, 163–65
    Yemenis as cheap labor supply, 37
kibbutzniks, 158, 162, 191
Kinneret region (Galilee), 39–41
Kiryat Gat (development town), 72
Kiryat Shmona (development town), 55,
    157–62, 166
Kishon, Efrayim, 118
Klorman, Bat-Zion Eraqi, 38
Kollek, Teddy, 197, 207
Kook, Rabbi Avraham, 28n
Kurdish Jews, 55–56
Kuwaiti, Daoud, 144
Kuwaiti, Salah, 144

Labor party, 69–71, 161, 187–88, 201, 207
Ladino spoken in Sephardi areas, 111, 128
language in Israel
    and Bourekas films, 117–19

of drug culture, 132–33
    Ladino in Sephardi areas, 111
    philosophy professor advocates Mizrahi
        accent, 130–31
    Russian influence, 133–34
    Yiddish, 111, 116, 127–28, 131, 152, 197
    See also Arabic; Hebrew
Lapid, Tommy, 155
Law of Return (1950), 11
League of Arab Nations, 11n
Lebanon war (2006), 189–90
Levant, 29, 33–34, 220. See also Israel
Levantine-Arab Jews, 29, 33–34, 154, 195,
    220
Levi-Tanai, Sara, 145–46
Levine, Tzila, 45
Levy, Ezra, 94
Lewis, Arnold, 174–75
Libyan Jews, 56
Likud party, 69–71, 121, 161–62, 200
"The Little Yemeni" (Israeli Ministry for
    Education and Culture), 25–27, 28
Livnat, Limor, 172
Loewenberg, Aliza, 174
London, Yaron, 120, 124
Love Hurts (TV sitcom), 218–20

Ma'ariv (mid-market newspaper), 50
Madawal, Aaron, 168, 169
Mahfouz, Naguib, 103, 234
Mahmud II, Ottoman emperor, 83
maimuna celebrations, 205
Malka, Motti, 148, 150–51
Maloul, Sami, 157–58, 166
Marciano, Sa'adia, 199
Mayne Yidishe Mame (film), 116
media
    BBC Radio 3 world music prize, 143
    Radio Baghdad, 214
    Radio Damascus, 196
    Radio Israel, 97
    Russian language influence, 133–34
    See also Israel Broadcasting Authority;
        television
Medina, Avihu, 142
Meir, Golda, 118n, 127–28, 197–98

Meir-Glitzenstein, Esther, 92
melting pot theory, 5–6, 139, 173, 178–80
Memmi, Albert, 232
Meretz party, 167, 215
Middle East. *See specific Middle Eastern countries*
Middle Eastern Jews
  compromising of, 88–93
  creativity and cultural contributions, 153
  education opportunities for, 58, 83–84, 100, 175–76
  land rights in Palestine, 215–16
  See also Mizrahi Jews
Middle Eastern music in Israel, 135–37, 142–45, 148–49, 154–55
migrants
  and absorption officials, 224
  disinfectant spray for, 56
  Holocaust survivors, 48
  as "human material," 48–49
  native Jews vs., 28, 29–32, 36–37, 42
  schools for, 106–7, 109
  transit camps for, 46–48, 64, 65, 118–19
  See also development towns; Or Yehuda
migration
  British control in 1940s, 46n
  deluge from 1948–1951, 46
  of European Jews, 11–12, 23–24
  of Iraqi Jews, 1–2, 3, 46–47, 78–79
  of Middle Eastern Jews, 3–4, 113
  of Moroccan Jews, 56, 58, 60–61
  of Russian Biluist Jews, 34
  of Soviet Jews, 12, 29, 65
  of Yemeni Jews, 34–35, 40–46
migration department of Jewish Agency, 24
Million Person plan, 88–95, 223
Mitzna, Amram, 186n
Mizrahi Democratic Rainbow (MDR), 17, 165
Mizrahi Jews (the Eastern ethnicities)
  adapting label in Israel, 16–17
  as Arab-haters, 217–21, 229, 236–37
  and Bourekas films, 116–19
  culture and origin of, 4, 13–14

derogatory stereotypes, 15, 25–27, 49, 123–25, 182, 198, 225, 230
derogatory terms, 5–6, 70, 111, 117
education system tailored to Ashkenazi, 175
effect of European colonization of Middle East, 4–5
equal opportunity concept as applied to, 177
living in "the second Israel," 18–19
music of, 14, 135–37, 142–45, 154–55
name and identity changes to avoid stereotypes, 223–25
organizing protests, 20–21, 26, 68, 193–95, 197–99
and Palestinian friends, 231
Palestinian Jews as, 28, 29–32, 42
percentage of Israel's population, 12, 21, 182
police harassment of, 227–28
as political bridges between Palestinians and Israelis, 233–37
refugee status vs. Zionist aspirations, 212–16
  See also Arab Jews
The Mizrahi Struggle (Chetrit), 195–96
Mohammad V, Sultan of Morocco, 57
Mohammad VI, Sultan of Morocco, 57
Moroccan Jews
  discrimination against, in Israel, 64–65, 67–68
  in Kiryat Shmona, 55, 157–62, 166
  maimuna celebrations, 205
  migration to Israel, 56, 58, 60–61
  in Morocco, 58–59, 60, 63–64
  music by, 155
  Peretz, Amir, 129, 185, 186–91
  Revah, Ze'ev, 119
  in Sderot, Israel, 54–55
  speaking Arabic, 127
  theater for, 152
  Zafrain, Echiel, 161–62
Morocco, treatment of Jews living in, 58–59, 60, 63–64
moshavot (Jewish farming co-ops), 18, 37, 39, 65, 163. *See also* kibbutzes

Mossawa advocacy center for Arab-Israeli citizens, 134
Mourad, Layla, 153
music
    Andalus Orchestra of Israel, 148, 150–51
    Arabic Orchestra, 143, 144, 145
    and arts, state support for, 150–53
    collaboration of Ashkenazi with Yemeni Jews, 140
    ethnic inequality of IBA, 137–38, 139–41, 156
    ethnic pop, 142
    of European composers, 150
    folk songs, 138
    Iraqi Jews performing in Baghdad, 144
    Mizrahi music in Israel, 14, 135–37, 142–45, 154–55
    Russian influence, 139
    Spanish music in Israel, 148–49
    Yemeni Jews collaborating with Ashkenazi composers, 140
    See also Israel Broadcasting Authority
Muslims
    and Abraham, 20n, 30, 79
    expelled from Spain, 15
    and Jews, in Iraq, 100–102, 103–5
    and Jews, in Morocco, 57
    and Jews, in Ottoman Empire, 15–16
    and Jews, in Spain, 15
    and Jews, in Tunisia, 60, 61
    Jews and, 20n, 60–62, 183, 222–23, 233–35
    music for prayer shared with Jews, 149–50
    and "People of the Book," 81–82
    Saladin (Salah al-Din), 30
    and Yemen Jews, 35–36
Musrara, Jerusalem, 196–97
My Jewish Mother (film), 116

Najara, Rabbi Israel ben Moses, 150
name changes of Mizrahi, 223–24
National Religious Party (NRP or Mafdal), 71, 202

national theater of Israel, 114–15
National Unity government, 72
Navon, Yitzhak, 208
Nazi influence, 62, 85–86, 88–89
Nebuchadnezzar II, King, 79
Negev desert, 51
Nehemiah, the prophet, 91n
New Historians, 11n
New Settlement, 28–29, 32–33, 36–38, 48
Nijar, Lulu, 160
1984 (Orwell), 155
Nini, Yehuda, 40–41
"No End to Love" (Tal), 156
"Nobody Runs Away" (Spielberg Jewish Film Archive), 62–63
"Noladeti La Shalom" (Hitman), 139n
North African Jews, 57. See also Mizrahi Jews
Nostalgia for the Primus Stoves (Yosef), 77

occupied territories, 53, 69, 74, 202. See also Israeli-Palestinian conflict; West Bank
Ofakim (development town), 55, 67–68
Office of the Land of Israel, 37–38, 37n, 40–41
Ohalim (tents) movement, 72
Old Settlement, 28, 29–32, 36–37, 42
Olmert, Ehud, 187–88, 189
Omessi, Margalit, 45
Operation "From the Boat to the Town," 55
Or Yehuda, Israel "Little Iraq" (development town)
    Babylonian Jewry Heritage Center, 77, 78, 87–88, 95, 99–105, 105
    belief in Zionist bombing in Iraq, 93–94
    Iraqi-born Jews in, 100–103
    overview, 76
Oriental gestures, 14
Oriental Jews, 3–4, 16, 222–23. See also Mizrahi Jews
Orwell, George, 155
Oslo peace process, 202, 207, 210

Ottoman Empire
  Babylonian Jews under, 82, 83
  equal treatment for Jews in Palestine,
    30–31
  genocide of Armenians, 170–72
  as "Golden Age," 15–16
  Turkish as official language, 111
  and Yemeni Jews, 36

Paamon, Emmanuel, 100–101, 208
Palestine
  early history of, 79–81
  Jerusalem, 28, 29–30, 170–72, 196–97
  Jews and Muslims as "cousins," 20n
  pre-Israel, 11, 26–34
  UN 1948 partition plan, 11n
Palestine Bureau, 39–41
Palestine Liberation Organization (PLO),
    199, 202, 211, 214, 233
Palestine Office of WZO, 37–38, 37n,
    40–41
Palestinian Arabic, 131–32
Palestinian Arabs
  al-Aqsa intifada, 203
  deaths of, 52
  and Israeli friends, 231
  Mizrahi as replacement labor for, 36–37
  music not played on IBA, 156
  paying taxes to Israel, 71
  relationship with Jews pre–British
    Mandate, 31–33
  and *sabra*, 116n
  second intifada, 146–47, 203, 221,
    230–31, 234
  See also Arab-Israelis; Arab Jews; Israeli-
    Palestinian conflict
Palestinian Authority (PA), 52, 210
Palestinian Broadcasting Authority,
    112
Palestinian Jews
  and Babylon, 79, 80–81
  Old Settlement, 28, 29–32, 36–37, 42
  See also Arab Jews; Yemeni Jews
Palestinian territories, 53, 69, 74, 202. *See
    also* Israeli-Palestinian conflict; West
    Bank

pan-Arab nationalism, 59n, 85
Patai, Raphael, 49
peace bridges, 236–37
Pedagogy of the Oppressed (Friere),
    181
Peled, Yoav, 42
People of the Book, 30, 81, 83. *See also*
    Jews; Muslims
Peres, Shimon, 53, 129, 208
Peres Peace Center, 128
Peretz, Amir, 129, 185, 186–91
Peretz, Moshe, 135, 136–37
piyut (prayers in song), 148–50
Polish Jews, 47, 64. *See also* Ashkenazi Jews
political bridges between Palestinians and
    Israelis, 233–37
political Zionism, 28, 41, 98–99
politics
  anti-Peretz campaign, 190–91
  Ashkenazi inability to work with
    Mizrahi, 11–12, 191–94
  Communist party, 62, 96–97, 99
  ethnic voter profiles, 200–201,
    206–7
  Hadash party, 72
  Kadima party, 187–88
  Labor party, 69–71, 161, 187–88, 201,
    207
  leaders' denial of problems, 198, 208
  Likud party, 69–71, 121, 161–62, 200
  manipulation of, 195–96
  Meretz party, 214–15
  National Religious Party, 71, 202
  Young Israel party, 195–96
Popular Music and National Culture in Israel
    (Regev and Seroussi), 138, 141
post–9/11 world, 230
prejudice. *See* ethnic inequality; inter-
    Jewish discrimination
prison population, 133
protests of Mizrahi Jews, 20–21, 26, 68,
    193–95, 197–99
Public Housing Act (1998), 167

Qasim, Abd al-Karim, 94
Qassam attacks on Sderot, 51, 53

racism, 170–72, 188, 204. *See also* ethnic inequality
Radio Baghdad, 214
Radio Damascus, 196
Radio Israel, 97
Ramat Aviv, Tel Aviv, 54
Refael, Itzhak, 47
Regev, Motti, 138, 141
rehabilitation methods for Mizrahi children, 178–80
Rehovot, Israel, 40–41
Rejwan, Nissim, 83–84, 85, 102, 175
Religious Nationalist Party, 28n
religious Zionism, 28, 202
Reshet Aleph (IBA radio station), 106
Reshet Gimmel, 156
Reuveni, Asher, 140
Reuveni, Meir, 140–41
Reuveni Brothers music label, 140
Revah, Ze'ev, 119
revisionist Zionism, 113
Rocca, Tony, 87
Romans in Palestine, 81
Rosenthal, Rubik, 131–33
Rothschild, Baron, 36
Ruppin, Arthur, 37–38
Russian Jews, 151, 152, 197. *See also* Ashkenazi Jews
Russian language, 133–34

Sabah, David, 160
Sabra (film), 116
Safed, Israel, 30
Saladin (Salah al-Din), 30, 235
Salah Shabbati (film), 118
Salama, Palestine, 168
Salfit, West Bank, 146
Saporta, Ishak, 165, 166–67
Sarid, Yossi, 171
Sarkozy, Nicholas, 129
Schumacher and Dzigan comedy duo, 116n
Schunat HaTikva, Israel, 140–41, 170
Schunat Hayim (TV program for children), 121–22
Sderot (development town), 51, 52–56, 127, 188, 237–38

second intifada, 146–47, 203, 221, 230–31, 234
"the second Israel," 18–19
Segev, Tom, 44, 48, 214
segregation in schools, 174–75
Sephardi Council, 193
Sephardi Jews
  Ashkenazi ignoring rather than learning from, 32–34, 205
  Hebrew of, 106–8, 110, 111–12, 114
  Incorrect use of term, 16
  Muslim-Jewish coexistence pre-Israel, 61–62
  origin of, 15
  Palestinian Jews as, 28, 29–34, 42
  spiritual leader of, 202
  See also Mizrahi Jews
Sephardi Torah Guardians (SHAS), 201–4
Sephardim Tehorim (Palestinian Jews), 28, 29–34, 42
Sereni, Enzo, 29, 33, 96
Seroussi, Edwin, 138, 141
settlement towns, 71–73. *See also* development towns
Sfatayim, 142, 158
Shafir, Gershon, 42
Sharett, Moshe, 213
Sharon, Ariel, 72, 131n, 187n
Shasha, Elias, 145–46, 148, 152, 231
Shemesh, MiMizrah, 206
Shenhav, Yehouda, 212–16, 223–24, 232
Shiloah, Yoseph, 233–34
Shina, Salman, 84
Shohat, Ella, 116, 117, 118–19, 128, 233–34
Shriki, Moshe, 183–84
Shubeli, Rafi, 16–17
Shuki (Yemeni Israeli), 34–35
Simhon, Shalom, 165
Six-Day War (1967), 69, 71–75, 200
Smilansky, Moshe, 176, 177
Smooha, Sami, 64–65, 174
social indoctrination, 122–25, 180–81, 222–26
socialism at kibbutzes, 39
Solomon, King, 35

Somekh, Sasson, 102–3, 235
Soviet Jews, 12, 29, 65, 114, 133–34
Spain, 15, 30, 148–49, 233–34
special nurture schooling, 178–80
A Star Is Born (talent show), 142
stereotypes
    in Bourekas films, 116–19
    burying Arab history to get rid of,
        223–25
    Herzl's intent to do away with, 23
    The Little Yemeni, 25–27, 28
    of Mizrahi, 49, 119, 121
    in *Schunat Hayim,* 122
    social indoctrination with, 122–25,
        180–81, 222–26
suicide-bomb attacks, 231
superiority in Western cultures, 22
Swirski, Shlomo, 65–66, 71, 173, 177, 179

Tal, Liran, 156
Tel Aviv, Israel, 9, 125–26, 135, 238–39
Tel Aviv University, 71
television
    advertisements, 124–25
    Ben Gurion on the Beatles and, 120–21
    Black and White Minstrel Show (BBC
        TV), 117n
    Eretz Nehederet, 120
    Every Morning, 185
    Hebrew accent on, 119–20
    Israeli, 119–24
    Israeli Arab Jew on news from the
        Middle East, 235–36
    Love Hurts sitcom, 218–20
    Russian, 133–34
    Schunat Hayim, 121–22
    A Star Is Born, 142
    Tuvia Tzafir, 122–23
    Who Wants to Be a Millionaire? (Arabic
        TV), 101
teunei tipuach (underachievers), 178–80
theater of Israel, 114–15
Tiberias (Sea of Galilee), 30, 39–41, 112,
    162–63
"Time for Peace" (Dalal), 143
Time magazine, 9

Toledo, Spain, 233–34
Topaz, Dudu, 70
The Transit Camp (Balas), 103, 128
transit camps for migrants, 46–48, 64, 65,
    118–19. *See also* development towns
Triki, Yitzhak, 56
Tunisia, 59
Tunisian Jews, 59–60, 160
Tuvia Tzafir (TV series and videos), 122–23
Tzadok, Yael, 106–8, 110, 112, 114

UEFA cup, 15
Uliel, Haim, 158
Uliel, Raquel, 63
ulpan (schools for migrants), 106–7, 109
ultra-Orthodox schools, 204–5
United Nations, 11n, 53
United Nations Security Council, 210
urban regeneration program, 71
U.S. Congress resolution on Mizrahi, 214
Ussishkin, Menahem, 32

vocational schools, 66, 172–74, 177–78, 180

Wadi Salib, 193–94
Wailing Wall (Jerusalem), 29–30
Warburg, Otto, 37
West Bank
    Iraqi Jew performing in, 146
    Israeli acquisition of, 69
    Israeli military in, 155, 237
    Israelis forbidden entry to, 147
    settlement of, as priority, 71–72
Who Wants to Be a Millionaire? (Arabic
    TV), 101
Woolfson, Marion, 91
World Organization of Jews from Arab
    Countries (WOJAC), 210, 211–16
World Zionist Congress, 198
World Zionist Organization (WZO), 33,
    37–38, 37n, 40–41

Ya Ribon Alam (Iraqi *piyut*), 149–50
Yad Vashem, 171
Yavnieli (Samuel Warshavsky disguised as
    a rabbi), 37–38

Yehezkel, Sasson, 84
Yehezkeli, Zvi, 235–36
Yehuda, Ben, 130
Yemeni Jews
    Ashkenazi prejudice against, 40–41
    Ashkenazi theft from, 43–46
    collaboration with Ashkenazi
        composers, 140
    in Kfar Shalem, 168
    and King Solomon, 35
    in Kinneret region, 39–41
    and "The Little Yemeni" story, 25–27, 28
    and MDR, 17
    Medina, Avihu, 142
    migration to Palestine, 34–35, 40–46
    and New Settlement Jews, 28, 36–38
    and Ottoman Empire, 36
    See also Mizrahi Jews
Yeshayahu, Yisrael, 214
Yiddish, 111, 116, 127–28, 131, 152, 197
Yom Kippur war (1973), 199
Yona, Clara, 181–82
Yonah, Yossi, 165, 166–67

Yosef, David, 76, 77
Yosef, Rabbi Ovadia, 201, 202–3
Young Israel party, 195–96
"You're Gone" (Benayun), 155

Zafrani, Echiel, 161–62, 208
Zionism
    Babylonian Jewry Heritage Center on,
        78–79
    birth of, 23–24
    fusion of socialism and, 39
    Herzl on, 22–23
    Iraqi Jews in favor of, 87, 96, 101
    Iraqi Jews' opposition to, 79, 94–95,
        96–99
    political Zionism, 28, 41, 98–99
    religious Zionism, 28, 202
    revisionist Zionism, 113
    See also Jewish Agency
Zionist military group (Irgun), 168–69
Zionist youth movement, 172
Zionists, 91–95, 222–23
Zriek, Raef, 167

A NOTE ON THE AUTHOR

RACHEL SHABI was born in Israel to Iraqi parents and grew up in England. A journalist, she has been published in a variety of national and international newspapers, including the *Guardian*, the London *Sunday Times*, the *Independent*, and the *Daily Express*. She also has been published on the English Aljazeera online and Salon.com. While researching this book, she relocated to Israel; she is currently based in Tel Aviv, where she reports on the Middle East conflict.